BEGINNER'S
GREEK

HIPPOCRENE BEGINNER'S SERIES

Arabic
Armenian
Assyrian
Basque
Bulgarian
Chinese
Czech
Dutch
French
Gaelic
Greek
Hungarian
Irish
Italian
Japanese
Lithuanian
Maori
Persian
Polish
Romanian
Russian
Serbo-Croatian
Shona
Sicilian
Slovak
Spanish (Latin American)
Swedish
Turkish
Ukrainian
Vietnamese
Welsh

BEGINNER'S
GREEK

ELIZABETH G. UHLIG

Hippocrene Books, Inc.
New York

Book design and composition by Susan A. Ahlquist, East Hampton, New York.

For more information, address:
HIPPOCRENE BOOKS, INC.
171 Madison Avenue
New York, NY 10016

ISBN 0-7818-1001-9

Cataloging-in-Publication Data available from the Library of Congress.

Printed in the United States of America.

This book is dedicated
to
my Greek teacher, Trifon Tsifas.

TABLE OF CONTENTS

TABLE OF ABBREVIATIONS

adj.	adjective
art.	article
def.	definite
fam.	familiar
fem.	feminine
indef.	indefinite
intrans.	intransitive verb (does not take a direct object)
masc.	masculine
neut.	neuter
per.	person
pol.	polite
pl.	plural
trans.	transitive verb (takes a direct object)

INTRODUCTION

Why Learn Greek?

To learn Greek is to bring home to ourselves the sweetness and sensual plea-sures of a journey through a varied and colorful landscape. Through the language, we navigate intricate layers of culture that have been seasoned by a perpetually changing population within the constancy of a rugged, ancient terrain.

We do not need to take on the untenable task of delving into eons of Greek history to enjoy the gentle, succinct flow of the Greek language. When we speak Greek, the essence of the culture reveals itself through the sound of the words and the elision between the words. It is a means by which we can experience the contrasts of smoothness and roughness that are inherent in Greek life.

Greece is a small country that encompasses a wide spectrum of elements. It is not characterized by just one color palette or one climate. It offers the traveler the opportunity to experience awe and wonder upon gazing at ancient, ruined monuments; yet, with a turn of the head, that same traveler finds himself in the dappled sunlight and leaf-shaped shadows of a sidewalk taverna. He may hear the metallic echo of the bouzouki and the silky timbre of a singer's voice. Yet he may also hear the music of the wind as it whistles through now-vacant temples, or the chanting of pilgrims on a nighttime, candlelit procession.

The bygone days of classical Greece blend seamlessly with the latter centuries in a pleasant jumble of white marble, cobblestone, glossy, blue paint and wildflowers. Friendly, affectionate countrymen invite you to share their food, their wine, their lush vegetation and seemingly endless Aegean.

Diminutive grandmothers with pearl-white hair, kind-faced gentlemen whose smiles provoke the deep lines of their swarthy skin, children accustomed to the casual and easily-flowing affection of their families, all beckon you into their community.

And all of the senses are captured in this language, so that when we learn to speak Greek, we can experience the beauty and tonality of Greek culture. Learning Greek can be an evolutionary step for you; you will be expanded and uplifted by the language's depth of color and sound.

Learning a language is about applying principles. Once you learn a grammatical structure, you can apply its principles to more and more sophisticated concepts. This gives you a sense of mastery over the language. In this book, each chapter is designed to build upon the knowledge you have gained in the previous one. You will arrive at the end with enough Greek to feel satisfaction and confidence when you speak. I invite you to start now, at the most basic level, to delight in the process of integrating Greek into your life.

THE GREEK ALPHABET

There are 24 letters in the Greek alphabet, and many of them are the same as the letters we use in English.

UPPER CASE	LOWER CASE	NAME OF LETTER	SOUND OF LETTER
A	α	alpha	as in dr*a*ma
B	β	veeta	as in *v*ain
Γ	γ	ghamma	between *g* and *y*
Δ	δ	thelta	as in *th*en
E	ε	epsilon	as in s*e*t
Z	ζ	zeeta	as in *z*ero
H	η	eeta	as in mar*i*ne
Θ	θ	theta	as in *th*ick
I	ι*	yota	as in mar*i*ne
K	κ	kappa	as in *k*ing
Λ	λ	lamtha	as in *l*ong
M	μ	mee	as in *m*e
N	ν	nee	as in *n*o
Ξ	ξ	ksee	as in e*x*act
O	ο	omicron	as in *o*wn
Π	π	pee	as in *p*ool
P	ρ	rho	as in *r*eal
Σ	σ/ς**	sigma	as in *s*end
T	τ	taf	as in *t*ea
Y	υ	ipsilon	as in mar*i*ne

*The letter **yota** is not dotted, as is the English letter "i."
The letter **sigma in the second form shown is used only at the end of a word.

Φ	φ	phee	as in *f*ine
X	χ	chee	as in *h*umor
Ψ	ψ	psee	as in li*ps*
Ω	ω	omega	as in *o*wn

Try writing these words in lower case letters:

ΠΩΣ   PE

ΤΗΝ   ΤΩΝ

ΠΡΟΣ   ΩΣ

ΔΡΥΣ   ΔΕΝ

ΘΑ   ΖΩ

(Did you remember to use ς for your final "s"?)

Now do your best to pronounce the words above, according to the pronunciation guide.

LESSON 1

Placement of Accents

Where do we put the stress in words of more than one syllable?

In Greek it is easy to know exactly which syllable is emphasized. Every word of more than one syllable has an accent mark over the syllable that is stressed.

Try saying these short words, noting the pronunciation as well as the emphasis:

Practice writing each word a few times here:

γάλα (milk)

μέσα (inside)

από (from)

πίσω (behind)

δίπλα (beside)

ανήκω (to belong to)

πατώ (to step on)

γεμάτος (full)

σοβαρός (serious)

φτάνω (to arrive)

κοστίζω (to cost)

τυχερός (lucky)

Sometimes two words are spelled the same way, but their accents fall in different places. For example:

γερός (strong, healthy)   νόμος (the law)

γέρος (an elderly man)   νομός (prefecture)

There are no accent marks on capital vowels, except for those that:

1. begin a sentence *or*

2. are the *first* letters of proper nouns.

In such cases, the accent is placed just to the left of the letter, like this:

᾽Α ᾽Ε ᾽Η ᾽Ι ᾽Ο ᾽Υ ᾽Ω

For example, if a sentence began with the word "No," it would look like this: ῎Οχι.

Here are two proper nouns that begin with vowels:

῎Ελληνας (Greek man)

῎Αγγλος (Englishman)

(<u>Note</u>: In Lesson 2 you will learn some extra rules about accents.)

Some Vowel Combinations and How to Pronounce Them

Many Greek words contain combinations of vowels. These have their own rules for pronunciation.

1. αι sounds similar to ε. Try pronouncing these words: και, παίρνω, αίμα

2. ει and οι sound the same as ι, η and υ. This means that there are five ways to make this sound in Greek!

   Pronounce the following words, noting the vowel sounds that are the same: εκεί, αρνί, ρήμα, άκρη, δύση, ίσως, επίσης, νύφη, άλλοι

3. ου sounds like the English "oo" as in "boot." Try these: που, κουτί, σούπα

4. αυ is pronounced either "av" or "af," depending on the letter that follows it. As you speak, the right pronunciation will become apparent; your mouth will follow the most natural flow of the letters.

   For example, when you say the word θαύμα, it is easier to pronounce the υ as a "v," rather than as an "f." Try pronouncing θαύμα now.

   In the word αυτός, the υ becomes more of an "f."

   Now try to pronounce μαύρος. Which way feels more comfortable?

5. ευ, similarly, is pronounced either "ev" and "ef." Pronounce these words: εύκολο, ρεύμα, λιγοστεύω.
   Try to see which is the more natural choice as you pronounce each word.

Consonant Combinations and How to Pronounce Them

There are some consonant combinations and double consonants that make specific sounds:

1. γγ sounds like the English "ng" as in these words: επάγγελμα, Αγγλία, ᾽Αγγλος

2. γκ sounds like a hard English "g" as in "go." Some examples are: αγκώνας and γκάζι

3. μπ can sound like an English "b" as in the word μπαίνω. It can also sound like "mb" as in the word γαμπρός. You will learn the difference as you progress.

4. ντ can sound like an English "d" as in ντρέπομαι. It can also sound like "nd" as in the words εξήντα and σύντομος.

ο Διάλογος:

The following is a simple dialogue between two high school students in Athens, Anna and Nikos. Nikos is Greek and is studying English. He hopes to go to New York to study theater. Anna has come to Athens from New York and is studying the Greek language and art.

(Note: In Greek, a question mark looks like an English semicolon.)

Νίκος: Γειά σας! Με λένε Νίκο. Εσάς, πώς σας λένε;

Άννα: Με λένε Άννα. Είστε μαθητής εδώ;

Νίκος: Ναι, είμαι. Μαθαίνω αγγλικά.

Άννα: Είμαι κι' εγώ μαθήτρια. Είμαι από την Νέα Υόρκη και μαθαίνω ελληνικά.

Νίκος: Σας αρέσει η Αθήνα;

Άννα: Μάλιστα! Είναι πολύ διαφορετική από την Νέα Υόρκη. Γιατί μαθαίνετε αγγλικά;

Νίκος: Θέλω να σπουδάσω στις Ηνωμένες Πολιτείες. Αλλά η Αγγλική γλώσσα είναι δύσκολη!

Άννα: Καταλαβαίνω, αλλά σιγά-σιγά θα την μάθετε.

Dialogue:

Nikos: Hello! My name is Nikos. What is your name? (literally: Hello! They call me Nikos. How do they call you?)

Anna: My name is Anna. Are you a student here?

Nikos: Yes, I am. I am studying English.

Anna: I am also a student. I come from New York and I am studying Greek. ·

Nikos: Do you like Athens? (literally: Does Athens please you?)

Anna: Of course! It's very different from New York. Why are you studying English?

Nikos: I want to study in the United States. But the English language is difficult!

Anna: I understand, but little by little you'll learn it.

VOCABULARY

Note: Some of the words in the vocabulary lists in this book appear in a form that is slightly different from that which you see in the dialogue. This is because of rules of grammar that you will learn later.

τα αγγλικά	English (language)
αλλά	but
από	from (there are also other meanings)
αρέσω	to please, to be pleasing
γιατί	why
η γλώσσα	language
διαφορετικός	different
δύσκολος	difficult
εδώ	here
είμαι	to be
τα ελληνικά	Greek (language)
θα	{particle used with a verb to create the future and other tenses}
θέλω	to want
και	and
καταλαβαίνω	to understand
μαθαίνω	to learn, to study
ο μαθητής	student (masc. form)
η μαθήτρια	student (fem. form)
να	{particle used with a verb to create the infinitive and other tenses}
ναι	yes
η Νέα Υόρκη	New York
οι Ηνωμένες Πολιτείες	United States
πολύ	very
πως	how
σπουδάζω	to study

USEFUL EXPRESSIONS AND COMPOUND WORDS

Γειά σας!	Hello! (There are many other meanings)
Μάλιστα!	Of course! Certainly!
με λένε ...	my name is ...
Πώς σας λένε;	What is your name?
σιγά-σιγά	little by little; slowly

GRAMMATICAL NOTES

Formal and Informal Speech:

When Nikos says "Γειά σας!" to Anna, he is addressing her with the formal "you." This is because they have just met. Later on, when they become friends, they will address each other with the familiar form of "you" and they will greet each other as friends do: "Γειά σου!"

Similarly, in this dialogue, the verb "to be" is used with the formal "you": είστε. In later dialogues, Nikos and Anna will use this and all other verbs in the familiar form. (Conjugation of verbs starts in Lesson 2.)

Gender:

You will notice that Nikos says he is a μαθητής and Anna is a μαθήτρια, yet they are both *students*. These two forms of the word for "student" demonstrate the concept of gender in Greek.

Every noun has a gender: masculine, feminine or neuter. Some nouns exist in more than one gender form, as in the case of the word "student." In Lesson 2, we will learn how a noun's gender dictates what its corresponding definite and indefinite articles will be. For now, though, let's talk a little about the Greek manner of meeting and greeting people.

CULTURAL TIP

Greek Expressions of Greeting

When we observe Greeks meeting one another or foreigners, be they friends, family or business associates, one thing is apparent: Greeks enjoy human contact and interaction. They greet the next person with warmth and an evident readiness to engage in conversation.

The Greek language offers a wide repertoire of expressions for meeting and greeting, for all times of day and for all levels of relationship. The most casual meeting of friends on the street or the most sophisticated professional situation both have appropriate greetings. In Greek, there is a charm and politeness, an affection and gentility that accompany all human contact.

Should a newcomer, for example, enter a group situation where Greeks are already engaged in conversation—say, when several people are seated around a restaurant table—what usually ensues is a lot of smiling, handshaking, sometimes, double-cheek kissing, embracing and exchanging of any number of sincerely articulated expressions of greeting.

Therefore, as a speaker of Greek, you will want to equip yourself with the vocabulary for these situations. For as you interact with Greek culture, you will be drawn from the outer circle into the inner circle, and you will make good use of the many ways to connect with others in conversation.

As you progress through this book, the dialogues will provide you with many useful expressions for meeting and greeting!

LESSON 2

ο Διάλογος:

Anna and Nikos meet on campus and begin to chat about life at school:

'Αννα: Καλημέρα, Νίκο! Τι κάνετε;

Νίκος: Καλημέρα, 'Αννα. Είμαι καλά, ευχαριστώ, κι' εσείς; Σε ποια τάξη είστε;

'Αννα: Σπουδάζω τέχνη. Είμαστε μια μικρή τάξη. Ο κύριος Τζούμας είναι ο δάσκαλός μας.

Νίκος: Ω! Η αδελφή μου είναι στην τάξη σας. Την λένε Δάφνη. Την ξέρετε;

'Αννα: Μάλιστα! Η Δάφνη είναι στην τάξη μας. Την ξέρω καλά. Κι' εσείς, τι σπουδάζετε εδώ;

Νίκος: Σπουδάζω δράμα, δηλαδή, θεατρικά έργα. Οι δασκαλές μας είναι από τις Ηνωμένες Πολιτείες. Γι' αυτό θέλω να μάθω αγγλικά.

'Αννα: Αλλά τα καλύτερα θεατρικά έργα είναι από την Ελλάδα!

Νίκος: Νομίζετε; 'Ισως, αλλά θέλω να ξέρω κι' άλλα.

Dialogue:

Anna: Good morning, Nikos! How are you?

Nikos: Good morning, Anna. I'm well, thank you, and you? Which class are you in?

Anna: I am studying art. We are a small class. Mr. Tjoumas is our teacher.

Nikos: Oh! My sister is in your class. Her name is Daphne. Do you know her?

Anna: Of course! Daphne is in our class. I know her well. And what are you studying here?

Nikos: I am studying drama, that is, theatrical works. Our teachers come from the United States. That's why I want to learn English.

Anna: But the best theatrical works come from Greece!

Nikos: Do you think so? Perhaps, but I want to know more of them.

Two Grammatical Points

1. Why are there two accents on **δάσκαλός**? It has to do with the word "our" (**μας**) coming after a 3-syllable word in which the accent falls on the first syllable. This rule will be explained in the chapter on possessives.

2. Why does Anna call Nikos "Niko?" This is an example of the grammatical concept of *direct speech*. When a name ends in an "s," that "s" drops off when that person is being addressed directly. This is also true of masculine words that end in **ας**, for example, **πατέρας** (father). If one were to address one's father directly, he/she would say "**Πατέρα!**"

Masculine words that end in **ος** drop that ending and take an **ε** instead. For example, with the word **γιατρός** (doctor), in direct speech, one would say "**Γιατρέ!**"

Other examples of words that behave this way are **φίλος** (friend) and **κύριος** (Mr., sir).

VOCABULARY

η δασκάλα	teacher (fem. form)
ο δάσκαλος	teacher (masc. form)
δηλαδή	that is to say
το δράμα	drama
το έργο	work
θεατρικός	theatrical
ίσως	maybe, perhaps
ο κύριος, κύριος, κ.	gentleman, Sir, Mr.
μας	our
μικρή	small (fem. form)
μου	my
νομίζω	to think
ξέρω	to know
η τάξη	class
η τέχνη	art

SMALL BUT IMPORTANT WORDS FOR SENTENCE BUILDING

In each chapter, we will isolate these small words from the rest of the dialogue's vocabulary. These words should be thought of as a special lexicon that will enrich your ability to form sentences.

αλλά	but
καλά	well
ποια	what, which (fem. form)
σε	in, at, on, to (in the dialogue above, it means "in")

USEFUL EXPRESSIONS AND COMPOUND WORDS

είμαι καλά	I am fine
Ευχαριστώ	Thank you
γι'αυτό	that's why (literally: "for that")
Καλημέρα	Good morning!
κι'άλλα	others, the rest
ο καλύτερος	the best
τι κάνετε;	How are you?
Ω!	Oh!

GRAMMATICAL NOTES AND EXERCISES

Gender, Definite and Indefinite Articles:

As is the case with many other European languages, every Greek noun has one of three genders: masculine, feminine or neuter. The gender of a noun does not necessarily have anything to do with that noun's quality. For example, "father" is masculine, but so is "garden." "Woman" is feminine, but one of the words for "girl" is neuter. In this chapter, you will learn how to recognize the genders of most words by their spelling.

There is a corresponding definite article ("the") and indefinite article ("a" or "an") for each gender.

What you are about to learn about definite and indefinite articles applies when the noun is in the **nominative case**. This means that these articles are used when the noun (or pronoun) is the **subject** of a sentence.

Within each gender group there are categories of nouns; they are characterized by different endings.

We are going to start with **masculine nouns**. Their endings fall into three major categories (and some minor ones). There will also be some masculine nouns that are exceptions and they have to be learned as you go along.

Major Categories of Endings: ας, ος, ης

ας as in πατέρας	(father)
άνδρας	(man or husband)
ταμίας	(cashier)

ος as in **κήπος**	(garden)
δάσκαλος	(male teacher)
φίλος	(male friend)

ης as in **μαθητής**	(male student)
πελάτης	(customer)
καθρέφτης	(mirror)

The **definite article** used with singular, masculine nouns is **o**. Write each of the nouns from the above list with its definite article, next to its English equivalent.

EXAMPLE: **o πατέρας** — the father

the man   ο άνδρας
the garden ο κήπος
the teacher ο δάσκαλος
the cashier ο ταμίας
the friend
the student
the customer
the mirror

The **indefinite article** for **masculine nouns** is **ένας**. Now write the same nouns with their indefinite articles, next to their English equivalents.

EXAMPLE: **ένας πατέρας** — a father

a man
a garden
a teacher
a cashier
a friend
a student
a customer
a mirror

How to Form the Plural

When **masculine** nouns become **plural**, two things will change: the **definite article** and the **noun's ending**. (The plural for the indefinite article will be discussed later.)

• The **plural definite article** changes from ο to οι.
• The **ending** for each noun (ας, ος or ης) will change according to the noun group.

In the first group, the nouns that end in **ας** in the singular ...
... will end in **ες** in the plural.

So, **the man** — ο άνδρας becomes ...
...**the men** — οι άνδρες
(Note the change in the definite article and the noun's ending.)

Using the above example, write the plurals here of:

ο πατέρας   οι _πατέρες_   ο ταμίας   οι _____

In the second group, the nouns that end in **ος** in the singular ...
... will end in **οι** in the plural.

So, **the teacher** — ο δάσκαλος becomes ...
... **the teachers** — οι δάσκαλοι
(Note the change in the definite article and the noun's ending.)

Using the above example, write the plurals here of:

ο κήπος   οι _κήποι_   ο φίλος   οι _____

In the third group, the nouns that end in **ης** in the singular ...
... will end in **ες** in the plural.

So, **the student** — ο μαθητής becomes ...
... **the students** — οι μαθητές
(Note the change in the definite article and the noun's ending.)

Using the above example, write the plurals here of:

ο πελάτης   οι _πελάτες_   ο καθρέφτης   οι _____

Now let's look at **feminine nouns**. Their endings fall into three main categories, with some minor groups and exceptions.

Major Categories of Endings: α, η, ος

α as in	**μαθήτρια**	(female student)
	γυναίκα	(woman or wife)
	δασκάλα	(female teacher)
η as in	**ανάγκη**	(need)
	διακοπή	(interruption)
	νύφη	(bride)
ος as in	**μέθοδος**	(method)
	είσοδος	(entrance)
	Βίβλος	(Bible)

The **definite article** for singular, feminine nouns is **η**. Write each of the nouns listed above with its definite article, next to its English equivalent.

EXAMPLE: **η μαθήτρια** — the female student

the woman
the teacher
the need
the interruption
the bride
the method
the entrance
the Bible

The **indefinite article** for **feminine nouns** is **μια**. Write the same nouns with their indefinite articles, next to their English equivalents.

EXAMPLE: **μια μαθήτρια** — a student

a woman
a teacher
a need
an interruption
a bride
a method
an entrance
a Bible

How to Form the Plural

When **feminine** nouns become **plural**, again, two things will change: the **definite article** and the **noun's ending**.

* The **definite article** changes from **η** to **οι**.
* The **ending** for each noun (**α, η** or **ος**) will change according to the noun group.

In the first group, the nouns that end in **α** in the singular ...
                    ... will end in **ες** in the plural.

So, **the woman** — **η γυναίκα** becomes ...
   ... **the women** — **οι γυναίκες**
(Note the change in the definite article and the noun's ending.)

Using the above example, write the plurals here of:

η μαθήτρια   οι _____   η δασκάλα   οι _____

In the second group, the nouns that end in **η** in the singular ...
                    ... will also end in **ες** in the plural.

So, **the bride** — η νύφη becomes …
… **the brides** — οι νύφες
(Note the change in the definite article and the noun's ending.)

Using the above example, write the plurals here of:

η ανάγκη   οι_____   η διακοπή   οι_____

There is another group of feminine nouns ending in η that behave slightly differently in the plural. Their plural ending is εις. Examples of these are:

η λέξη (word) becomes οι λέξεις in the plural.
η τάξη (class) becomes οι τάξεις in the plural.

Following this format, what would the plural be for η πόλη?
Write it here: πόλεις

The only way to learn these words is to memorize them as you go along. And you will!

In the third group, the nouns that end in ος in the singular …
…will end in οι in the plural.
(Note that this change is the same as the change for the masculine nouns that end in ος.)

So, **the method** — η μέθοδος becomes …
… **the methods** — οι μέθοδοι.
(Note the change in the definite article and the noun's ending.)

Using the above example, write the plural here of:

η είσοδος   οι _____

Note: There is no plural for η Βίβλος.

The last gender group is **neuter nouns**. There are three major categories that have different endings, with exceptions.

Major Categories of Endings: *o, ι, μα, ος*

o as in	βιβλίο	(book)
	κτίριο	(building)
	σχέδιο	(plan)
ι as in	σπίτι	(house)
	γυαλί	(glass)
	ταξίδι	(trip)
μα as in	δράμα	(drama)
	ρήμα	(verb)
	σώμα	(body)
ος as in	έθνος	(nation)
	κράτος	(government)
	μέρος	(place — also slang for "bathroom")

The **definite article** for **neuter nouns** is το. Write each of the nouns listed above with its definite article, next to its English equivalent.

EXAMPLE: το βιβλίο — the book

the building
the plan
the house
the glass
the trip
the drama
the verb
the body
the nation
the government
the place

The **indefinite article** for **singular, neuter nouns** is ένα. Write the same nouns with the indefinite article, next to their English equivalents.

EXAMPLE: ένα βιβλίο — a book

a building
a plan
a house
a glass
a trip
a drama
a verb
a body
a nation
a government
a place

How to Form the Plural

When **neuter** nouns become **plural**, the same two things will change: the **definite article** and the **noun's ending**.

* The **definite article** changes from **το** to **τα**.
* The **ending** for each noun (**o, ι** or **μα**) will change according to the noun group.

In the first group, the nouns that end in **o** ...
                                    ... will end in **α**.

So, **the book** — **το βιβλίο** becomes ...
... **the books** — **τα βιβλία**
(Note the change in both the definite article and the noun's ending.)

Using the above example, write the plurals here of:

το κτίριο   τα _Κτίρια_   το σχέδιο   τα _____

In the second group, the nouns that end in ι will *add* an α at the end of the word.

So, **the house** — το σπίτι becomes ...
... **the houses** — τα σπίτια.
(Note the change in both the definite article and the noun's ending.)

Using the above example, write the plurals here of:

το γυαλί   τα _γυαλία_ (accent moves to the last syllable)
το ταξίδι   τα _____

In the third group, the nouns that end in μα will *add* the syllable τα at the end of the word.

So, **the drama** — το δράμα becomes ...
... **the dramas** — τα δράματα.
(Note the change in both the definite article and the noun's ending.)

Using the above example, write the plurals here of:

το ρήμα   τα _ρήματα_   το σώμα   τα _____

In the fourth group, the nouns that end in ος will drop that ending and add η.

So, **the nation** — το έθνος becomes ...
... **the nations** — τα έθνη.
(Note the change in both the definite article and the noun's ending.)

Using the above example, write the plurals here of:

το κράτος   τα _____   το μέρος   τα _____

Now you know the basics of genders, definite and indefinite articles and how they function in Greek, you can try this little exercise:

Look at the nouns listed below and, based on what you have learned about recognizing genders,

- write the **gender in the left-hand column**
- write the noun with its **definite article**
- write the same noun with its **indefinite article**
- write the noun in the **plural**, with its **plural article**, making sure to change the noun's ending to reflect the plural article.

(In this exercise, there are no feminine or neuter nouns that end in **ος**.)

The first line is an example.

	GENDER	NOUN W/ DEF. ART.	NOUN W/INDEF. ART.	PL. NOUN W/PL. ART.
τρόπος (way, means)	masc.	ο τρόπος	ένας τρόπος	οι τρόποι
παλάμη (palm)	fem	η παλάμη	μια παλάμη	οι παλάμες
ενθύμιο (souvenir)	neu	το ενθύμιο	ένα ενθύμιο	τα ενθύμια
ιδιοκτήτης (owner)	masc	ο ιδιοκτήτης	ένας ιδιοκτήτης	οι ιδιοκτήτες
πτώμα (corpse)	fem	η πτώμα	μια πτώμα	οι πτώματα
όνειρο (dream)	neu	το όνειρο	ένα όνειρο	τα όνειρα
τρίχα (small hair)	fem	η τρίχα	μια τρίχα	οι τρίχες
αξίνα (pickaxe)	fem	η αξίνα	μια αξίνα	οι αξίνες
σημάδι (sign)	neu	το σημάδι	ένα σημάδι	τα σημάδια
ταμίας (cashier)	masc	ο ταμίας	ένας ταμίας	οι ταμίες

Now that you have learned the basic rules about forming the plural, you will need to know the following rule. (This is where rules about the **plural** and rules about **accents** overlap):

No Greek noun can be accented beyond the third syllable from the end.

I will illustrate this with some neuter nouns first:

The word το πρόσχημα (excuse) is accented on the third syllable from the end. When the word becomes plural and the syllable τα is added, the accent has to move from the first vowel (ο) to the next one (η): τα προσχήματα.

Let's try this with another word: το κατάστημα (shop). When we add the syllable τα to form the plural, the accent moves. Now the word looks like this: τα καταστήματα.

Now let us look what happens to feminine nouns when the accent falls on the third to last syllable.

With the word η περίπτωση (condition), the plural will be ...
    ... οι περιπτώσεις.

Let us look at what has happened here:

1. The accent has moved from the ι to the ω.
2. The ending η has dropped off and has been replaced with εις.

Here is another illustration:

If the singular is η υπόθεση (hypothesis), the plural will be ...
    ... οι υποθέσεις.

Try this exercise with these nouns whose **accents change position** in the plural. Make sure that you make the appropriate changes to the endings of the nouns.

Singular	Plural
η κατάχρηση (excess)	οι _Κατα χρήσεις_
το διάστημα (distance)	τα _διαστήρατα_
το σύνθημα (signal)	τα _σύνθήματα_
η διεύθυνση (address)	οι _διευθύνση_
το αίσθημα (feeling)	τα _αισθήματα_
η μεταάφραση (translation)	οι _μεταφράσεις_

Use of the Definite Article:

The definite article is used in some ways that are different from the ways in which it is used in English.

You may have noticed in the vocabulary lists that there is a definite article **before the names of countries and cities**, as in **η Νέα Υόρκη** (New York) and **η Αγγλία** (England). The definite article is also used **before the names of people** when we are speaking *about* them. For instance, if we were speaking about Anna, we would refer to her as "**η 'Αννα.**" If we spoke of Nikos, we would refer to him as "**ο Νίκος.**" Notice that Anna has referred to her art teacher as "**ο κύριος Τζούμας,**" using the definite article.

The definite article is used before nouns when we are making general statements, such as Nikos' comment that English is difficult; he calls English "**η αγγλική γλώσσα.**" He could also have said "**τα αγγλικά.**"

As you progress in Greek, you will notice usage of articles that will be new to you. Eventually, it will all become quite natural.

A Note on the Indefinite Article:

Unlike English, Greek does not use the indefinite article when saying someone is in a particular profession. If we are saying someone is *a teacher*, we leave out the "a" and just say (literally) he or she "is teacher": είναι δάσκαλος or είναι δασκάλα. This also applies for an author, an artist, a student, etc.

You may remember that in the first dialogue, Anna asks Nikos, "Are you a student here?" which translates as "Είστε μαθητής εδώ;" Notice that no indefinite article is used.

Personal Pronouns and the First Verb You'll Need

Set out below is a table of personal pronouns along with the conjugated verb, "to be," which is είμαι. Generally, in speaking, we do not use the pronoun with the verb, except for emphasis or to avoid ambiguity. But we still need to know what these pronouns are. First, let's look at them:

SINGULAR   PLURAL

1st person   εγώ (I)   1st person   εμείς (we)
2nd person   εσύ (you)   2nd person   εσείς (you)
3rd person   αυτός (he)   3rd person   αυτοί (they, masc.)
3rd person   αυτή (she)   3rd person   αυτές (they, fem.)
3rd person   αυτό (it)   3rd person   αυτά (they, neut.)

IMPORTANT: Note that *he, she, it* and *they* can also refer to nouns, not just people. You will understand this better when you read the section called The Words "it" and "they," later in this chapter.

Let us look for a moment at the two words for *you*:

εσύ, the 2nd person singular, is used when speaking to someone you know on a first name basis or to a child.

εσείς, the 2ⁿᵈ person plural, (also called the *polite form*) is used when you are speaking to someone with whom you would be more formal, i.e., a teacher, an older person. But it is also used when speaking to a group. In that sense, it is the plural of εσύ.

And now here is your first verb:

EIMAI — to be

SINGULAR   PLURAL

1ˢᵗ p. εγώ είμαι (I am)	1ˢᵗ p. εμείς είμαστε (we are)
2ⁿᵈ p. εσύ είσαι (you are, fam.)	2ⁿᵈ p. εσείς είσαστε (you are, pol.)
3ʳᵈ p. αυτός είιναι (he is)	3ʳᵈ p. αυτοί είναι (they are, masc.)
3ʳᵈ p. αυτή είναι (she is)	3ʳᵈ p. αυτές είναι (they are, fem.)
3ʳᵈ p. αυτό είναι (it is)	3ʳᵈ p. αυτά είναι (they are, neut.)

Note these important grammatical points:

All forms of the verb have the same common root: ει, but the different persons have different endings. This is a basic concept when conjugating any verb.

The **endings of the pronouns** for the <u>third persons singular and plural</u> (he, she it, they) are the same as those for the corresponding definite articles which you have just learned (ος, η, ο, οι, ες, α).

The Words "it" and "they"

Because we do not generally use the pronoun in a simple sentence where the nominative case is used, we do not see the words "it" and "they," but we know that they are there. For example, if we say "It is here," that translates as "**Είναι εδώ.**" (Of course, this could also mean "They are here.") There is no way to know from the words "**Είναι εδώ**" what the number and gender of the subject is. We would only know that from the context.

(If the verb είναι were followed by an adjective, the adjective would reveal the number and gender of the subject, and you will learn about this later.)

Whatever the "it" or "they" that you are talking about, it has a gender, even if it does not show. If your "it" is a *garden* (ο κήπος) it is a *masculine* "it." In a sense, you are really calling the garden "he." If you say, for example:

"It (*the garden*) is here," you are really saying:
"[Αυτός — he] είναι εδώ," but the Αυτός doesn't show.

If you were talking about more than one garden, you would say:
"[Αυτοί — they] είναι εδώ," but the Αυτοί would not show. In a sense, you are calling the gardens "they."

If your "it" is an *entrance* (η είσοδος), it is a *feminine* "it." You are really calling the entrance "she." If you say, for example:

"It (*the entrance*) is here," you really saying:
"[Αυτή — she] είναι εδώ," although the Αυτή doesn't show.

It is always a good idea to learn a noun's gender as you build your vocabulary!

Exercises with είμαι:

Now that you know how to conjugate είμαι, you can express many things, not just about people, but also about nouns whose genders you know.

Using the vocabulary that you have so far, you can translate the following sentences into Greek. Refer to the two dialogues for some of the sentence structures.

1. The student is from New York. Οι μαθητές είναι απο της N Y
2. The men are here. Οι ανδρες ειναι εδω
3. We are from Greece. Εμεις Απο της Ελλάδα
4. Do you like New York? (refer to dialogue #1)
5. The woman is a teacher.

Now try and translate the following sentences into English:
(<u>Note</u>: You have not yet learned the word **την**, which you see in sentence #6, below. For now, just treat it as a definite article.)

1. **Το σπίτι μας είναι πολύ μικρό.** Our class is very small
2. **Γιατί είστε εδώ;** Why are you here?
3. **Μαθαίνω ελληνικά και είμαι από την Νέα Υόρκη.** I study Greek and I'm from N.Y.
4. **Σπουδάζετε τέχνη και θεατρικά έργα;** Do you study art and theater?
5. **Η μαθήτρια είναι από τις Ηνωμένες Πολιτείες.** She is from the US
6. **Ο κύριος Παύλος και η μητέρα μου είναι από την Αθήνα.** MPaulos and my mother are from Athens

CULTURAL TIP

Greek Drama

The world drama that Nikos longs to study is the fruit of the seeds of drama that were planted in ancient Greece thousands of years ago. World drama as we know it today has gone through many phases of evolution over the centuries, adding and subtracting in each of those phases various aspects and elements. We know that liturgical drama, mystery plays, epic theatre, symbolism, expressionism, naturalism, etc. all share some common traits, yet they are distinctly different art forms. Let us look back briefly to ancient Greece to consider the origin of these art forms.

It is probable that some form of drama predated the drama of ancient Greece, perhaps as tribal storytelling or religious ceremonies for fallen heroes. Archaeological findings reveal that drama in the formal sense began in the 500s B.C., when it took on the form of a singing and dancing component of festivals honoring the god Dionysius. Around 534 B.C., actual plays with tragic plots appeared and were presented during these festivals. Contests for tragedy-writing were held and awards were given for the best play.

Only a fraction of the works of the ancient tragedians is extant today and most of those that have survived are the works of Aeschylus, Sophocles and Euripides. Each of these playwrights' works, while falling into the broad category of ancient Greek drama, is characterized by differences in the playwrights' own philosophy, the types of characters in the play, the way in which those characters develop, the use of a chorus, and the structure of the play.

Some rules, however, were basic to all plays. Few actors were used, and all of them were men. Men played women's parts and each actor interpreted multiple roles. There were never more than three actors on stage at once. They wore masks, long garments and ornate headdresses and their lyric singing was enhanced by the chanting and dancing of a chorus.

During the 400s B.C., a dramatic genre later referred to as Old Comedy emerged. The most well known comedic playwright is Aristophanes, whose plays reflect the political and social tenor of the times. As time went on, comedy gained popularity and tragedy faded in importance. Then something called New Comedy emerged. Menander is the most notable playwright of this genre. New Comedy, and particularly Menander's plays, are concerned less with political themes and more with day-to-day life in middle class Athens.

Today, if you stand on the Acropolis in Athens, you can get a marvelous view of the Theatre of Dionysius on the hillside below. The amphitheatre construction is remarkably intact; it offers the spectator a clear idea of what it must have been like to be seated there, along with about 14,000 other attendees, watching the drama on the raised, circular platform (called "the orchestra") which today would be the stage.

In Greece, several festivals each year feature performances of ancient drama. From June to September, there is the Athens Festival, from July to September there is the Epidaurus Festival. In July and August one can attend the Philippi and Thassos Festival and the Dodoni Festival.

LESSON 3

ο Διάλογος:

Anna has dropped in on her friend, Daphne, and they chat over coffee.

Άννα: Καλησπέρα, Δάφνη!

Δάφνη: Καλησπέρα, Άννα! Παρακαλώ, έλα μέσα! θέλεις ένα ποτό; Έχω πορτοκαλάδα, νερό, τσάι...

Άννα: Έχεις καφέ;

Δάφνη: Μάλιστα! Θέλεις ζάχαρη;

Άννα: Ναι, θέλω, ευχαριστώ. Στην Νέα Υόρκη παίρνω τον καφέ μου με γάλα, αλλά εδώ...

Δάφνη: Καταλαβαίνω. Είναι διαφορετικά εδώ. Σ'αρέσουν τα φαγητά στην Ελλάδα;

Άννα: Ναι! Μ'αρέσουν πολύ! Δεν έχουμε τέτοια φαγητά στις Ηνωμένες Πολιτείες.

Δάφνη: Όχι; Πώς είναι τα φαγητά εκεί;

Άννα: Δεν είναι τόσο καλά, αλλά είναι εντάξει. Στην Ελλάδα τα φαγητά είναι τέχνη!

Dialogue:

Anna: Good evening, Daphne!

Daphne: Good evening, Anna! Please come in. Do you want a drink? I have orange juice, water, tea ...

Anna: Do you have coffee?

Daphne: Certainly! Do you want sugar?

Anna: Yes, I would, thank you (literally: I want it, thank you). In New York I take my coffee with milk, but here ...

Daphne: I understand. It's different here (literally: Things are different here.) Do you like the food in Greece?

Anna: Yes, I do! We don't have such food in the United States.

Daphne: No? How is the food there?

Anna: It is not so good, but it's O.K. In Greece, food is an art form!

VOCABULARY

το γάλα	milk
εκεί	there
εντάξει	O.K.
η ζάχαρη	sugar
καλός	good
ο καφές	coffee
μέσα	inside
το νερό	water
παίρνω	to take, to have (with regard to food)
Παρακαλώ	Please (also: You're welcome)
η πορτοκαλάδα	orange juice
το ποτό	drink
τέτοιος	such
το τσάι	tea
το φαγητό	food

SMALL BUT IMPORTANT WORDS FOR SENTENCE BUILDING

δεν	not (this word negates the verb)
με	with
όχι	no
τόσο	so (as in "so good")

USEFUL EXPRESSIONS AND COMPOUND WORDS

έλα μέσα	come in
Καλησπέρα	Good evening

GRAMMATICAL NOTES AND EXERCISES

Negating a Sentence:

We have seen the word δεν in the last sentence of the dialogue above. It comes before the verb (είναι) and together they translate as "it is not." The word δεν before any verb will negate the verb.

Place the word δεν before each verb in the sentences from Lesson 2, thereby making them negative.

1. Το σπίτι μας είναι πολύ μικρό. Το σπίτι μας δεν είναι πολύ μικρο
2. Μαθαίνω ελληνικά και είμαι από την Νέα Υόρκη. (There are two verbs in this sentence.)
3. Σπουδάζετε τέχνη και θεατρικά έργα;
4. Η μαθήτρια είναι από τις Ηνωμένες Πολιτείες.
5. Ο κύριος Παύλος και η μητέρα μου είναι από την Αθήνα.

Verbs: The Present Tense:

In English, we have three ways of expressing the present tense of a verb. Take, for example, the verb TO STUDY. We can say "I study," "I am studying," or "I do study." These sentences are all in the present tense.

In Greek, the present tense of the verb expresses all three of these present tense forms. So how do we know *which* form is being expressed? We know by the context.

In the previous dialogues, you have seen these two verbs:

έχω — to have and θέλω — to want. These are both regular verbs and both are conjugated the same way. Look at the tables below and note the endings for each person.

ΕΧΩ — to have

<u>SINGULAR</u>

εγώ έχω (I have)
εσύ έχεις (you have, fam.)
αυτός, αυτή, αυτό έχει
    (he, she, it has)

<u>PLURAL</u>

εμείς έχουμε (we have)
εσείς έχετε (you have, pol.)
αυτοί, αυτές, αυτά έχουν
    (they—3 genders—have)

The endings for these verbs are the endings for all the verbs in the first group of regular verbs: ω, εις, ει, ουμε, ετε, ουν.

Now we will look at the verb θέλω (to want). The endings are the same, but this verb will be shown *without* pronouns.

ΘΕΛΩ — to want

θέλω   θέλουμε
θέλεις   θέλετε
θέλει   θέλουν

Using these two verbs and the vocabulary you have so far, you can translate these sentences into Greek.

1. Do you have orange juice? (fam. and pol. forms)
2. No, I do not have orange juice but I have tea.
3. They want coffee with milk.
4. Thank you, I do not want water.
5. She has coffee and tea but we want milk.
6. Does he want a drink?

ΑΡΕΣΩ — to please, to be pleasing:

We have seen this verb used in the dialogues. It is a regular verb in that it uses the same endings as those for other regular verbs, but it is different in that it is really only used in the 3<u>rd</u> persons singular and plural.

As we have seen with **αρέσω**, the *person* in the sentence is not the *subject*, but rather, the *indirect object*.

If you want to say "**I like milk**," you actually say:
"[The] milk is pleasing *to me*": **Το γάλα μ'αρέσει** or
Μ'αρέσει το γάλα. (the **μ'** is the "to me")

Note that the verb is in the 3rd person singular, because the subject of this sentence is **the milk** (or **it**).

For now, we will just work with the constructions we have learned in the dialogues:

μ'αρέσει — I like (The **μ'** is really **με**, which means "to me.")
σ'αρέσει — you like [or "Do you like?"] (The **σ'** is really **σε**, which means "to you.")

Later, we will learn the indirect object pronouns for the other persons, i.e., he likes, we like, they like, etc. which are really "to him," "to her," "to us," etc.

Translate these simple sentences, using **αρέσω**:

1. I like tea very much. μ' αρέσει πολύ Τσάι
2. Do you like the book? σ'αρέσει το Βιβλίο;
3. Yes, I like coffee with sugar. Ναι, μ'αρέσει καφέ με ζάχαρη
4. Do you like Athens? Σ'αρέσει Αθήνα;

What if the subject of the sentence is plural, as in our dialogue? Daphne asks Anna if she likes Greek food. The word for "food" is **το φαγητό**, which is a singular, neuter noun, but in the dialogue, the word is used in the plural (**τα φαγητά**), which translates as "the dishes."

Since the subject (**τα φαγητά**) is in the 3rd person plural, the verb also has to be in the 3rd person plural. That is why Daphne asks Anna, "**Σ'αρέσουν τα φαγητά;**" (Are *the dishes* pleasing to you?). Note the ending **ουν**, which indicates the 3rd person plural.

Following this model, translate these simple sentences:

1. I like the food in the United States. (use plural of "food")
2. You like theatrical works. Σ'αρέσουν θεατρικά έργα
3. I like the teachers here. Μ' αρέσουν οι δασκάλες εδώ
4. Do you like the students?

Now try some sentences in the negative. The word **δεν** will go *before* the indirect object pronoun:

<u>EXAMPLES</u>: I do not like tea. Δεν μ'αρέσει το τσάι.

Don't you like the food? Δεν σ'αρέσουν τα φαγητά;

1. I do not like tea with milk.
2. Don't you like art?
3. I don't like the houses here.
4. Do you like drama? No, I don't. ("No, it doesn't please me.")

The Verbs You Know so Far:

All of the verbs that you have seen in the dialogues so far (except for **είμαι**) are regular in the present tense. Now that you know the endings, you can conjugate these verbs. Practice writing them here:

<u>EXAMPLE</u>: **μαθαίνω** — to learn

| singular: | **μαθαίνω** | **μαθαίνεις** | **μαθαίνει** |
| plural: | **μαθαίνουμε** | **μαθαίνετε** | **μαθαίνουν** |

σπουδάζω — to study
singular: σπουδάζω   σπουδάζεις   σπουδάζει
plural: σπουδάζουμε   σπουδάζετε   σπουδάζουν

ξέρω — to know
singular: ξέρω   ξέρεις   ξέρει
plural: ξέρουμε   ξέρετε   ξέρουν

παίρνω — to take, to have
singular:
plural:

καταλαβαίνω — to understand
singular:
plural:

νομίζω — to think
singular: νομίζω   νομίζεις   νομίζει
plural: νομίζουμε   νομίζετε   νομίζουν

θέλω — to want
singular: θέλω   θέλεις   θέλει
plural: θέλουμε   θέλετε   θέλουν

έχω — to have
singular: έχω   έχεις   έχει
plural: έχουμε   έχετε   έχουν

For practice in conjugating, translate these simple sentences.

1. He takes tea with milk. Παίρνω τσάι με γάλα
2. She doesn't understand the book. Δεν καταλαβαίνει το βιβλίο
3. I don't understand English. Δεν καταλαβαίνω αγγλικά
4. Our teacher doesn't have the books.
5. I don't know the child. (the child — το παιδι)
6. Peter and Anna don't know theatrical works.
7. Are you studying here? (fam. and pol. forms)
8. Come in! We are not studying.
9. He is learning well.
10. Do you think so? (fam. form)
[Only one word is needed to make this sentence! If you don't know it, check the dialogue in Lesson 2.]

Interrogative Sentences:

A sentence can be turned into a question by simply putting a question mark at the end of it. Here are two simple examples:

You understand.	Καταλαβαίνετε.
Do you understand?	Καταλαβαίνετε;

He is learning Greek.	Μαθαίνει ελληνικά.
Is he learning Greek?	Μαθαίνει ελληνικά;

(Of course, if you were speaking, the intonation of the voice would be different for the question than for the statement.)

Some sentences require question words. Let's expand your knowledge of sentence construction by learning how to use these. (You already know the first three.)

γιατί;	why?
πώς;	how?
ποιος;	who?
ποιος;	which?
πού;	where?
πότε;	when?
τίνος;	whose?
τι;	what?
πόσο;	how much
πόσος;	how many?

(We will learn "whom" later.)

These words work very much the same way as they do in English, but some require a little more work. Let's look at each of them and see how they are used. You will note that the word order in the sentences is often the same as in English.

1. γιατί;   why?

Why do you study drama?	Γιατί σπουδάζετε δράμα;
Why doesn't Maria want coffee?	Γιατί δεν θέλει η Μαρία καφέ;

2. πώς;   how?

How do you like our class?   Πώς σ'αρέσει η τάξη μας;
(literally: How does our class please you?)
How do you take the tea?   Πώς παίρνεις το τσάι;

3. ποιος;   who?

This word has six forms:
SINGULAR: ποιος, ποια, ποιο
PLURAL: ποιοι, ποιες, ποια

ποιος changes according to the number and gender of the subject. You already know these endings. For example:

MASC: Who is our teacher?   Ποιος είναι ο δάσκαλός μας;
Note: The gender of ποιος matches that of ο δάσκαλος.
         The ending of ποιος matches that of ο δάσκαλος.

         Who are our teachers?   Ποιοι είναι οι δάσκαλοί μας;
Note: The gender of ποιοι matches that of οι δάσκαλοι.
         The ending of ποιοι matches that of οι δάσκαλοι.

This rule applies for the two other genders, as below.

FEM: Who is she?   Ποια είναι αυτή;
        Who are they?   Ποιες είναι αυτές;

NEUT: Who is the child?   Ποιο είναι το παιδί;
        Who are they (the children?)   Ποια είναι τα παιδιά;

4. ποιος;   which?

This word has the same six forms as "who":
SINGULAR: ποιος, ποια, ποιο
PLURAL: ποιοι, ποιες, ποια

It changes according to the number and gender of the subject. For example:

MASC: Which [one] is my coffee?   Ποιος είναι ο καφές μου;
FEM: Which soup do you like?   Ποια σούπα σ'αρέσει;
NEUT: Which book do you want?   Ποιο βιβλίο θέλεις;

For the plural, you will need to adjust the endings as you do for "who."

MASC: Which men are here?   Ποιοι άνθρωποι είναι εδώ;
FEM: Which women are teachers?   Ποιες γυναίκες είναι δασκάλες;
NEUT: Which books does she read?   Ποια βιβλία διαβάζει;

5. πού;   where?

Where is the house?   Πού είναι το σπίτι;
Where do the students study?   Πού σπουδάζουν οι μαθητές;

6. πότε;   when?

When does Peter read?   Πότε διαβάζει ο Πέτρος;
When do you have [a] lesson?   Πότε έχετε μάθημα;

7. τίνος;   whose?

This word does not change according to the gender. It is *always* the same.

Whose house is it?   Τίνος σπίτι είναι αυτό;
Whose orange juice is it?   Τίνος πορτοκαλάδα είναι αυτή;

8. τι;   what?

What do you want?   Τι θέλεις;
What are you studying here?   Τι σπουδάζετε εδώ;

9. πόσο;   how much

This word is used for general questions of "how much?" such as:

How much does it cost?   Πόσο κάνει;

How much do you like it?   Πόσο σ'αρέσει;
(Since this word is not quantifying any item, it does not change.)

However, the *next* word, πόσος, (how many?) is declined in the six forms
that you have learned for "who" and "which." It has to agree in number and
gender with the item it is quantifying.

10. πόσος;   how many?

The six forms are:
SINGULAR: πόσος, πόση, πόσο
PLURAL: πόσοι, πόσες, πόσα

EXAMPLES:

How much water do you want?   Πόσο νερό θέλεις;
How many women are here?   Πόσες γυναίκες είναι εδώ;
How much money (τα λεφτά) do you have?   Πόσα λεφτά έχεις;

Note: The question words that change according to number and gender
(what, which, how much, how many) will also make other changes in other
grammatical constructions. In the next chapter, you will learn how to make
some of these changes.

Practice the question words you have just learned by constructing these *very*
basic sentences in Greek. (Don't forget the definite article before names!):

1. Where is Maria?   Πού είναι η Μαρία
2. Where does Nikos read?
3. Why don't you understand?   Τιατί δεν Καταλαβαίνεις;
4. Why does Anna study here?
5. What do you think?   Τι νομί ζεις;
6. What does Nikos read?
7. Who is Maria?   ποια η Μαρία
8. Who are you? (fam. and pol. forms)   ποιος είσαι;
9. When do they study?
10. How do you take the tea?   Πώς σπουδάζεις το Τσαί
11. How do they take the tea?

12. Which woman is Anna?
13. Which man is he?
14. Which student is Nikos?
15. Whose student is Nikos?

CULTURAL TIP

The Delights of Greek Food

Greek cuisine lends itself to convivial gatherings around tables with good friends and family. It marries well with humble wines, mingles well with outdoor settings and helps to create lovely memories.

But there is a paradox to this cuisine: on the one hand, some of its staple foods are the ancient, reliable components: grains, olive oil, legumes, yogurt, vegetables, lemon and fish, but at the same time, Greek dishes incorporate the delicate, fragrant elements of a cuisine born beyond the Greek mainland, dishes flavored with cinnamon, oregano, sesame and pine nuts.

How did this mixture occur? Greeks lived for millennia in Asia Minor, and so their cuisine was influenced by that of the ancient kingdoms of Arabia, Byzantium and Persia. This created a blending of Oriental and Occidental dishes and served only to improve everyone's experience of eating.

What we eat in Greece today is a combination of the complex, multi-layered dishes of the east, such as moussaka, and simple "shepherd's fare" of the mainland: grilled lamb, fresh vegetables, feta cheese. Greek cuisine utilizes a wide spectrum of homegrown ingredients and seasons them with what were once exotic, foreign ingredients, thus delighting the palate with surprising and stimulating flavors.

Eating is an ongoing celebration in Greece, where the year is punctuated by religious celebrations and festivals. Some special occasions feature a traditional bread or sweet which can sometimes hide a tiny surprise: a gold coin, a good luck charm. Some breads and cakes are decorated with charming motifs that add a precious quality to the lovingly made confection.

Lucky is the traveler who spends Easter in Greece, for he can enjoy lamb grilled outdoors on a spit, and can eat it in a sunlit garden accompanied by fresh tomatoes and young wine. Yes, as our friend Anna has said, in Greece, food is an art form. From the enchanting appetizers of eggplant caviar, fried smelts, phyllo puffs and stuffed grape leaves, through the sumptuous main courses seasoned with fresh herbs and aromatic spices, to the magnificent desserts: rich cakes sitting in pools of syrup, phyllo-wrapped sweets that evoke narrow, tiled passageways of the Middle East, or thick creamy yogurt garnished with walnuts and a drizzle of honey, a Greek meal allows us to savor a daily pleasure in the very highest way.

LESSON 4

ο Διάλογος:

Nikos returns home and is glad to see that Anna has been visiting with Daphne.

Νίκος: Γειά σου, 'Αννα! Τι κάνεις;

'Αννα: Καλά, ευχαριστώ, κι'εσύ;

Νίκος: Πολύ καλά. Πού είναι η Δάφνη;

'Αννα: Είναι στην κουζίνα. Κάνει καφέ.

Νίκος: Καλά! Κι'εγώ θέλω καφέ. Ξέρεις ότι είναι μια παράσταση απόψε στο θέατρο;

'Αννα: Ναι, το ξέρω. 'Εχουν Ελληνικούς χορούς.

Νίκος: Η Δάφνη κι'εγώ πηγαίνουμε με τους φίλους μας. Εσύ;

'Αννα: Δεν νομίζω. Μ'αρέσουν πολύ τέτοιοι χοροί, αλλά έχω πολλή δουλειά για το σχολείο.

Νίκος: Κι'εμείς έχουμε πολλή δουλειά αλλά είναι μια πάρα πολύ καλή παράσταση. Γιατί δεν πηγαίνουμε μαζί;

'Αννα: Εντάξει, αφήνω την δουλειά μου για αύριο.

Νίκος: Καλή ιδέα!

Dialogue:

Nikos: Hello, Anna! How are you?

Anna: Fine, thank you, and you?

Nikos: Very well. Where's Daphne?

Anna: She's in the kitchen. She's making coffee.

Nikos: Good! I'll also have some coffee. Do you know that there is a performance tonight at the theatre?

Anna: Yes, I know [it]. They're presenting (<u>literally</u>: having) Greek dances.

Nikos: Daphne and I are going with our friends. Are you going? (<u>literally</u>: And you?)

Anna: I don't think so. I really like these kinds of dances but I have a lot of work for school.

Nikos: We also have a lot of work but the performance is very, very good. Why don't we go together?

Anna: O.K., I'll leave my work for tomorrow.

Nikos: Good idea!

VOCABULARY

απόψε	tonight
αύριο	tomorrow
αφήνω	to leave (trans. verb)
η δουλειά	work
ελληνικός	Greek (adj.)
το θέατρο	theatre
η ιδέα	idea
η κουζίνα	kitchen
μαζί	together
η παράσταση	performance
πηγαίνω	to go
πολύς	much
το σχολείο	school
ο φίλος	friend
ο χορός	dance

SMALL BUT IMPORTANT WORDS FOR SENTENCE BUILDING

για   for
ότι   that (as in "I know *that* he is ...")

USEFUL EXPRESSIONS AND COMPOUND WORDS

δεν νομίζω	I don't think so
Γειά σου	Hello (fam. form)
πάρα πολύ (+ adjective)	very, very (+ adjective)
το ξέρω	I know

GRAMMATICAL NOTES AND EXERCISES

Two Important Words: τέτοιος and πολύς

These two words appear in the previous dialogue. Let us see what rules apply to them.

τέτοιος, which means "such" (or "this kind of, these kinds of"), is declined according to number and gender. Like ποιος, it agrees in number and gender with the noun that follows it. When it is declined, τέτοιος looks like this:

τέτοιος	τέτοιοι
τέτοια	τέτοιες
τέτοιο	τέτοια

Here are some examples:

Τέτεια θεατρικά έργα μ'αρέσουν πολύ.
I like these kinds of theatrical works very much.
(Notice that the ending of τέτοια agrees in number and gender with θεατρικά έργα.)

Δεν καταλαβαίνω τέτοια τέχνη.
I don't understand this kind of art.

UNDERLINE: After determining the number and gender of each noun, place the correct form of τέτοιος in front of the noun.

τέτειος κήπος		_τέτοιο_ σχέδιο
τέτοιες μαθητές		_τέτοια_ βιβλία
τέτοια μαθήτρια		_τέτοιοι_ άνθρωποι

πολύς means "much," and in its plural form it means "many." It is slightly irregular in its declension. Here are the six forms:

πολύς	πολλοί
πολλή	πολλές
πολύ	πολλά

Here are some examples:

πολύς καφές	a lot of coffee
πολλοί άνθρωποι	many people
πολλή ζάχαρη	much sugar
πολλές τάξεις	many classes
πολύ νερό	a lot of water
πολλά μαθήματα	many lessons

EXERCISE:

Place the correct form of πολύς in front of the noun.

Πολύς θόρυβος (noise)		*Πολλοί* δάσκαλοι
Πολλή πορτοκαλάδα		*Πολύ* αίμα (blood)
Πολλά σπίτια		*Πολλές* ανάγκες

The Accusative Case:

The accusative case is the form that an article and noun take if they are the direct object of a verb.

Here are some examples of sentences with direct objects; the underlined words are the *direct objects* of the verbs.

He is reading a book.
I am buying the shoes.
She doesn't understand the story.

We're looking at <u>George</u>.
Anna knows <u>Daphne</u>.

A verb that takes an object is called a *transitive* verb. Let's look at some sentences that contain <u>transitive verbs</u> and <u>direct objects</u>. All of these sentences are using the **accusative case**.

In some of the sentences, you will see changes in the definite article, indefinite article and the ending of noun (direct object). In some sentences there will be no change. We will learn the rules by going through each gender group, with an example from each category of endings within the group. We will learn this for the singular and plural.

'<u>Masculine Singular Nouns</u>: (you have learned that they can end in ας, ος and ης)

Sentences w/ definite article:

I know the teacher.	Ξέρω τον δάσκαλο.
They know the student.	Ξέρουν τον μαθητή.
He knows my father.	Ξέρει τον πατέρα μου.

What has happened here?

1. The definite article, which, for **δάσκαλος, μαθητής** and **πατέρας** would be **ο** in the nominative case, has changed to **τον** in the accusative case.
2. All three nouns have lost the final ς.

Sentences w/ indefinite article:

I want a tray.	θέλω έναν δίσκο. (tray — ο δίσκος)
I have a mirror.	Έχω έναν καθρέφτη.
She has a husband.	Έχει έναν άνδρα.

In these sentences, the indefinite article, **ένας**, has changed to **έναν**, and the final ς has dropped off the nouns.

Summary of <u>masculine singular accusative</u> rules:

1. The definite article **ο** becomes **τον**.
2. The indefinite article **ένας** becomes **έναν**.
3. The final **ς** drops off all nouns.

<u>Masculine Plural Nouns</u>:

For the group of nouns ending in **ος**, here is what happens:

I know the teachers.	Ξέρω τους δασκάλους.
I don't have the trays.	Δεν έχω τους δίσκους.

1. The plural definite article changes from **οι** to **τους**.
2. The noun's ending **οι** has changed to **ους**.

Note that the placement of the accent has changed in **δασκάλους**. This is because "**ους**" is a *long sound*, and a noun that ends in a long sound should not be stressed on the third from last syllable. (However, you *may* hear speakers of colloquial Greek place the accent on the third from the last syllable.)

For the group of nouns ending in **ας** and **ες**, here is what happens:

They know the students.	Ξέρουν τους μαθητές.
She's leaving the men there.	Αφήνει τους άνδρες εκεί.

1. The plural definite article changes from **οι** to **τους**.
2. The nouns' endings are the same as they are in the plural of the nominative case.

Summary of <u>masculine plural accusative</u> rules:

1. Definite article **οι** becomes **τους**.
2. Nouns ending in **ος** (in the nominative) end in **ους**.
3. Nouns ending in **ας** or **ης** (in the nominative) end in **ες**. (Same as nominative plural.)
4. If the word is originally stressed on the third from last syllable, the accent mark will move one space to the <u>right</u> because of the *long sound* **ους**.

Try these sentences for practice:

1. I am leaving the tray here. (to leave — **αφήνω**) *αφήνω του δίσκο εδώ*
2. She is leaving a tray here.
3. We are leaving the trays here.
4. They don't know our father.
5. Do you know the men? (use **άνδρας**) *Ξέρεις τους άνδρες*
6. She doesn't have the mirrors.
7. Do you know the customer? (customer — **ο πελάτης**)
8. Are you buying a mirror?
9. Does he understand the students? *Καταλαβαίνετε τους μαθητές*

<u>Feminine Singular Nouns</u>: (you have learned that they can end in **α**, **η** or **ος**.)

Sentences w/ definite article:

For the group of nouns ending in **α** and **η**, here is what happens:

I am learning the language.   **Μαθαίνω την γλώσσα.**
Do you know the bride?   **Ξέρεις την νύφη;**

The definite article **η** has changed to **την**. That's all!

For the group of nouns ending in **ος**:

I do not understand the method.   **Δεν καταλαβαίνω την μέθοδο.**

1. The definite article **η** has changed to **την**.
2. The word **μέθοδος** has lost its final **ς**.

Sentences w/ indefinite article:

Do you have a friend (fem. form) here?   **Έχεις μια φίλη εδώ;**
I want a chair.   **θέλω μια καρέκλα.**
Does the store have an entrance?   **Έχει μια είσοδο το μαγάζι;**

There is no change in the indefinite article and nouns ending in **ος lose the final ς** (as in the case of the word **η είσοδος**.)

Summary of <u>feminine singular accusative</u> rules:

1. becomes **την**
2. **μια** stays the same.
3. The final **ς** drops off of nouns that end **ος** in the nominative.

<u>Feminine Plural Nouns</u>:

For the group of nouns ending in **α** and **η**, here is what happens:

We know the teachers (fem. form). **Ξέρουμε τις δασκάλες.**
Do you know the friends? **Ξέρεις τις φίλες;**

1. The plural definite article **οι** has changed to **τις**. The rest is the same.

For the group of nouns ending in **ος**:

I don't understand the methods. **Δεν καταλαβαίνω τις μεθόδους.**

1. The plural definite article **οι** has changed to **τις**.
2. The ending of the noun has changed from **οι** to **ους**.

(Note that in this case, the placement of the accent has changed. This, as with the word **δασκάλους**, is because a noun ending in the *long sound* **ους** should not be stressed on the <u>third from the last</u> syllable.)

Summary of <u>feminine plural accusative</u> rules:

1. **οι** becomes **τις**.
2. Nouns ending in **α** and **η** will end the same way they do in the nominative case.
3. Nouns that end in **ος** will end in **ους**.
4. If the word is originally stressed on the third from last syllable, the accent mark will move one space to the <u>right</u> because of the *long sound* **ους**.

Try these sentences:

1. Does he have a chair? *Έχει μια* Καρέκλα
2. We are leaving the chair here.
3. We have a friend in Athens. (στην Αθήνα) Εχουμε μια φίλη στην Αθήνα
4. She doesn't know the language. Δεν ξερει την γλώσσα
5. We don't know the student (fem. form).
6. They are reading the cards. (card — η κάρτα)
7. He doesn't know the women. Δεν ξερει τις γυναικες
8. You don't know the methods.

Neuter Singular Nouns: (You have learned that they can end in **o, ι, μα**
                        and **ος**.)

Sentences w/ definite article:

I am reading the book.   Διαβάζω το βιβλίο.
Do you know the child?   Ξέρετε το παιδί;
Do they know the drama?   Ξέρουν το δράμα;
He understands the government.   Καταλαβαίνει το κράτος.

In the accusative case, the articles and nouns are the same as they are in the
nominative case; there are no changes.

Sentences w/ indefinite article:

Do you have a house here?   Έχετε ένα σπίτι εδώ;
I have a plan.   Έχω ένα σχέδιο.
Every sentence has a verb.   Κάθε πρόταση έχει ένα ρήμα.
                                    (sentence — η πρόταση)
The restaurant has a bathroom.   Το εστιατόριο έχει ένα μέρος.

Everything is the same as in the nominative case.

Neuter Plural Nouns:

We don't study theatrical works.	Δεν σπουδάζουμε τα θεατρικά έργα.
Are you reading the books?	Διαβάζετε τα βιβλία;
Are they learning the verbs?	Μαθαίνουν τα ρήματα;
He is studying the governments.	Σπουδάζει τα κράτη.

The important thing to remember with the neuter gender is that the nominative and the accusative cases are the same.

Try these sentences:

1. I know the work.
2. We are buying the milk. (to buy — αγοράζω)
3. She doesn't understand the child.
4. He wants a drink.
5. We are making a trip (ένα ταξίδι) together.
6. We don't understand Greek. (Use the plural neuter form of "Greek.")
7. They are buying the houses.
8. Do you know the verb?

The Accusative Case with Prepositions:

The accusative case is also used with certain *prepositions.* You already know some of these: με (with), από (from) and για (for).

Whenever we use one of these words, the accusative case must follow. In the following examples, the preposition is underlined; note the accusative form of the article and noun that follow it:

We are going <u>with</u> our friends.	Πηγαίνουμε με τους φίλους μας.
I am studying <u>with</u> a teacher.	Σπουδάζω μ'έναν δάσκαλο.
He is <u>from</u> London.	Είναι από το Λονδίνο.
	(London — το Λονδίνο)

We have a letter <u>from</u> our friends.	Έχουμε ένα γράμμα από τις φίλες μας.
I have a book <u>for</u> my teacher.	Έχω ένα βιβλίο για τον δάσκαλό μου.
Do you have work <u>for</u> the class?	Έχεις δουλειά για την τάξη;

The preposition **σε** (in, at, to, on) is a little different in that it <u>combines</u> with the accusative form of the article. With the *definite* article it looks like this:

SINGULAR
(σε + τον) = στον
(σε + την) = στην
(σε + το) = στο

PLURAL
(σε + τους) = στους
(σε + τις) = στις
(σε + τα)   = στα

Naturally, the article has to agree in number and gender with the direct object. Here are some examples:

SINGULAR:

στον κήπο	in the garden (Notice that there is no ς on κήπος.)
στην τάξη	in the class
στο σπίτι	at home (literally "in the house")

PLURAL:

στους κήπους	in the gardens
στις τάξεις	in the classes
στα σπίτια	in the houses

When **στο** combines with the *indefinite* article, it looks like this:

σ'έναν κήπο	in a garden
σε μια τάξη	in a class
σ'ένα σπίτι	in a house

Now translate these sentences, using these prepositions and the accusative case.

1. I want milk in the tea.
2. I think that he is a friend from school.
3. Why are you buying the books for my mother?
4. Tonight we have a letter from our teacher.
5. Maybe the women are not in the kitchen.
6. Whose children are in the class?
7. There is *a lot* of sugar in the coffee.
8. When is he going with the men to the office? (office — το γραφείο)
9. Is there a performance at the theatre tonight?

Summary of Changes — Nominative to Accusative Case

Gender	Type of Article	Articles Nom.	Accus.	Nominative Noun Group Ending	Accusative Change in Ending
masc.	def. sing.	ο	τον	ος, ας, ης	ς drops off
masc.	indef. sing.	ένας	έναν	ος, ας, ης	ς drops off
masc.	plural	οι	τους	οι	ους
masc.	plural	οι	τους	ας, ης	ες
fem.	def. sing.	η	την	α, η	no change
fem.	def. sing.	η	την	ος	ς drops off
fem.	indef. sing.	μια	μια	α, η	no change
fem.	indef. sing.	μια	μια	ος	ς drops off
fem.	plural	οι	τις	α, η	no change
fem.	plural	οι	τις	ος	ους
neut.	def. sing.	το	το	ο, ι, μα, η, ος	no change
neut.	indef. sing.	ένα	ένα	ο, ι, μα, η, ος	no change
neut.	plural	τα	τα	ο, ι, μα, η, ος	no change

The Accusative Case with Declined Words:

You already know that words that modify nouns, such as ποιος (who and which), τέτοιος (such), πολύς (much, many) and πόσος (how much, how many) always have to agree in number and gender with the nouns they modify. These types of words also have to change to the accusative case when the sentence calls for it.

Here are their <u>declined accusative forms</u> and some examples of their use in sentences with direct objects and prepositions that require the accusative case:

<u>much:</u>

πολύ	πολλούς
πολλή	πολλές
πολύ	πολλά

I don't have a lot of coffee.   Δεν έχω πολύ καφέ.
(Notice that the masculine, singular form, πολύς, and the word καφές, have both lost the final ς.)

We know a lot of people here.   Ξέρουμε πολλούς ανθρώπους εδώ.
(Notice the ους ending on the two words in this sentence.)

<u>whom:</u>

ποιον	ποιους
ποια	ποιες
ποιο	ποια

From whom is the letter?   Από ποιον είναι το γράμμα;

which:

Which stories are you reading?   Ποιες ιστορίες διαβάζεις;

Which students do you know?   Ποιους μαθητές ξέρετε;

such:

τέτοιον	τέτοιους
τέτοια	τέτοιες
τέτοιο	τέτοια

Do you understand these kinds of stories? (story — η ιστορία)
Καταλαβαίνεις τέτοιες ιστορίες;

I do not eat this kind of food.
Δεν παίρνω τέτοια φαγητά.

how many, how much:

πόσον	πόσους
πόση	πόσες
πόσο	πόσα

For how many classes are you studying?
Για πόσες τάξεις σπουδάζεις;

How much sugar do you want in the tea?
Πόση ζάχαρη θέλεις στο τσάι;

Translate these sentences using the accusative case. Pay careful attention to the number and gender of the direct objects.

1. In which street is the house? (street — ο δρόμος)
2. In which streets are the stores? (the store — το μαγαζί)
3. With which teachers are you studying?

4. For which children are the toys? (the toy — το παιχνίδι)
5. We don't have a lot of chairs in our garden but I have a chair in the house.
6. I am buying a lot of milk for the children.
7. How many chairs do you have?
8. Do you think that he wants a lot of orange juice?
9. I do not understand these kinds of dramatic works.
10. I do not buy these kinds of books.
11. Which books do you buy for school?
12. He knows that you have many ideas.
13. We do not have a lot of money.

Note: Now that you have worked so hard to learn these accusative forms and endings, here is another piece of information: it is not always necessary to use the ν on words like δεν, τον, την and words that are declined like them. The letter ν only needs to be placed at the end of these words when the word comes before a vowel or the word starts with κ, ξ, π, τ, τσ or ψ. But because this is a *basic* grammar book, we will use ν every time to *avoid ambiguity* with the neuter gender. Later in this book, we will drop it.

CULTURAL TIP

Greek Folk Dancing

Like all the world's regional dancing, Greek folk dancing springs from a spontaneous desire to express joy. It rises up to enhance any celebration, be it the humblest family gathering in a tree-shaded garden to a serious, yet joyous religious festival.

While there is some debate on this topic, it has been said that much of Greek folk and traditional dancing comprises steps and sequences of dances that were practiced in ancient Greece. These dances would be done by both men and women and the dainty, light movements such as shuffling, dragging, gentle hopping, cross-over steps and pivoting on one foot are considered to be reflections of ancient Greek steps. Such steps are often syncopated with the lyrics sung by musicians, as in days of old when the Greek chorus and dancers accompanied one another.

By contrast, the men's dances that originated in craggy, mountainous areas are characterized by more vigorous leaping steps. These dances are the forerunners of the urban folk dance and music that were born in the mid-20th century, known as *Rembetika*, in which the leader of the dance showcases his expertise, engaging in impressive springing steps and vivacious twirling. *Rembetika*, which were popularized by the music of Manos Hatzidakis (*"Never on Sunday"*) and Milis Theodorakis (*"Zorba the Greek"*) and are now danced by many a tourist in tavernas, include well-known trademarks—the dangling handkerchief and the frequently broken plate.

Regional dances are many in Greece, and their origins are taken seriously. Costume plays an important role, and a regional dance troupe will only perform with the costumes appropriate to their particular region. The costume is largely dictated by the traits of the area in which the dance was born: the climate, terrain, even the trades in which the original dancers were engaged, all influenced the choice of clothing.

In some regions, dancers wear layers of clothing, such as apron-like garments over tapered pants. These might be heavily embroidered, with underlayers of white crocheted or lace-edged sleeves or skirts peeking out. Women sometimes wear remarkably elaborate ornamentation made up of beautifully made gold chains from which many coins are suspended, and complicated jeweled neck pieces, all clinking gently as the dancers move. Footwear could vary from sturdy boots to soft pigskin slippers, with everything in between, depending on the nature of the dance.

Apart from the visible and audible characteristics of Greek dancing, many secrets and traditions are couched in the arrangement of dancers on the stage, secrets that are usually not apparent to the spectator. When watching a performance, the viewer may not realize that the positioning of the dancers in the circle or in the line follows the dictates of an intricate hierarchy that has developed over time and is determined by age, gender, or birth order in the family. These "rules" have been handed down with the dances from one generation to the next.

Today there are several troupes that perform traditional dance, the most well known being Dora Stratou, a troupe which performs both in Greece and abroad. Traditional dancing and folk dancing are both art forms that Greeks treasure and strive to keep vibrant as modern life continues to evolve.

LESSON 5

ο Διάλογος:

On Friday night, Daphne calls Anna and they discuss their plans for the weekend.

'Αννα: Εμπρός!

Δάφνη: Γειά σου, 'Αννα! Είμαι η Δάφνη. Τι κάνεις;

'Αννα: 'Ετσι κι'έτσι. Είμαι λίγο κουρασμένη. Πρέπει να τελειώσω την δουλειά μου για το σχολείο. 'Εχω ένα μεγάλο πρόγραμμα αύριο.

Δάφνη: Αλήθεια; Τι θα κάνεις;

'Αννα: Θέλω να πάω στην Πλάκα. Είμαι στην Αθήνα έναν μήνα και δεν την ξέρω ακόμη.

Δάφνη: Θα σ'αρέσει. Η Πλάκα είναι πολύ ενδιαφέρουσα. 'Εχει μικρά μαγαζιά, μουσικούς στους δρόμους, καλά εστιατόρια και καφενεία. Με ποιον θα πας;

'Αννα: Θα πάω με μια φίλη από την γειτονιά μου. Πρέπει να αγοράσω μερικά ενθύμια, δώρα από την Ελλάδα για τους φίλους μου στην Νέα Υόρκη. Θέλεις να μας συνοδέψεις;

Δάφνη: Δυστυχώς, δεν είμαι διαθέσιμη αύριο. Ο Νίκος κι'εγώ θα πάμε στην εξοχή με την οικογένειά μας. Αλλά την άλλη φορά, ίσως θα πάμε μαζί.

'Αννα: Μάλιστα! Την άλλη φορά.

Δάφνη: Λοιπόν, να περάσεις καλά.

'Αννα: Επίσης. Καληνύχτα!

Dialogue:

Anna: Hello!

Daphne: Good evening, Anna! It's Daphne. How are you?

Anna: So-so. I am a little tired, but I have to finish my work for school. I have a big program for tomorrow.

Daphne: Really? (literally: the truth?) What will you be doing?

Anna: I want to go to the Plaka. I have been (literally: I am) in Athens two months and still have not seen it. (literally: and I still am not familiar with it.)

Daphne: You'll like it! The Plaka is very interesting! It has small shops, musicians in the streets, good restaurants and cafés. With whom will you go?

Anna: I will go with a friend of mine from the neighborhood. I have to buy a few souvenirs, gifts from Greece for my friends in New York. Do you want to come with us?

Daphne: Unfortunately, I am not available tomorrow. Nikos and I are going to the country with our family. But next time, perhaps, we can go to the Plaka together.

Anna: Of course! Next time.

Daphne: Well then, have a good time.

Anna: You, too. Good night!

VOCABULARY

ακόμη	yet, still
η αλήθεια	truth
διαθέσιμος	available
δυστυχώς	unfortunately
το δώρο	gift
η γειτονιά	neighborhood
ενδιαφέρων	interesting
το ενθύμιο	souvenir
το εστιατόριο	restaurant
η εξοχή	the country(side)
το καφενείο	café
κουρασμένος	tired
μεγάλος	big
μερικός	some, a few
ο μήνας	month
ο μουσικός	musician
η οικογένεια	family
πρέπει	to have to (must)
το πρόγραμμα	program
συνοδεύω	to accompany
τελειώνω	to finish

SMALL BUT IMPORTANT WORDS FOR SENTENCE BUILDING

λίγο   a little
λοιπόν   well, then

USEFUL EXPRESSIONS AND COMPOUND WORDS

Αλήθεια;	Really?
Εμπρός!	Hello! (for the telephone)
Επίσης	You too
έτσι κι'έτσι	so-so
Να περάσεις καλά	Have a good time
την άλλη φορά	next time
Καληνύχτα	Good night

GRAMMATICAL NOTES AND EXERCISES

The Future Tense:

Set out below are the present and future forms of some regular verbs. Since you already know how to conjugate the present tense of regular verbs, you can add some new verbs to your vocabulary.

Most regular verbs make only a small spelling change when they move from the present to future tense. The verbs below are grouped in "families" according to the spelling change that occurs in the future tense.

To form the future tense:

1. Make the necessary small spelling change in the verb, as indicated below.
2. Add the ending to the verb that agrees with the *person*. These will be the same endings you have used in the present tense: ω, εις, ει, ουμε, ετε, ουν.
3. Place the particle **θα** before the *future form* of the verb.

(All examples are given in the first person singular.)

In the first verb group, the **ζ** changes to a **σ**. This is very easy! After the first two examples, you can fill in the future tense yourself.

ENGLISH	PRESENT	FUTURE
I read	διαβάζω	θα διαβάσω
I buy	αγοράζω	θα αγοράσω
I celebrate	γιορτάζω	
I think	νομίζω	
I study	σπουδάζω	
I clean	καθαρίζω	
I return	γυρίζω	

Practice sentences:

1. Where will they study tomorrow?
2. What will she buy for the class?
3. Thank you, but I will not celebrate with the children tonight. (place δεν before θα)

In the second group, the ζ changes to a ξ in the future.

ENGLISH	PRESENT	FUTURE
I look at	κοιτάζω	θα κοιτάξω
I change	αλλάζω	θα αλλάξω
I play	παίζω	
I frighten	τρομάζω	
I shake off	τινάζω	

Practice sentences:

1. Will the children play in the neighborhood?
2. Why will you change the program?
3. Unfortunately, I will not look at the book tonight.

In the third group, the υ changes to a ψ in the future.

ENGLISH	PRESENT	FUTURE
I travel	ταξιδεύω	θα ταξιδέψω
I cook	μαγειρεύω	θα μαγειρέψω
I believe	πιστεύω	
I work	δουλεύω	
I accompany	συνοδεύω	

Practice sentences:

1. Will the restaurant cook for the family?
2. Will you work at the café tonight?
3. Will he believe the stories?

In the fourth group, the φ changes to a ψ in the future.

ENGLISH	PRESENT	FUTURE
I write	γραφω	θα γράψω
I nod	γνέφω	θα γνέψω
I describe	περιγράφω	

Practice sentences:

1. How will they describe the performance?
2. Will you write to our friends in the country?
3. Will she nod?

In the fifth group, the ν changes to a σ in the future.

ENGLISH	PRESENT	FUTURE
I leave	αφήνω	θα αφήσω
I pay	πληρώνω	θα πληρώσω
I lift	σηκώνω	
I finish	τελειώνω	

Practice sentences:

1. I will pay the bill at the restaurant. (bill — ο λογαριασμός)
2. They will not lift the books.
3. We will leave the souvenirs here.

In the last group, there is no change at all!

ENGLISH	PRESENT	FUTURE
I know	ξέρω	θα ξέρω
I have	έχω	θα έχω
I want	θέλω	
I do	κάνω	
I am	είμαι	
It is pleasing	αρέσει (3rd person only for this verb, singular or plural)	

Practice sentences:

1. What will we do tomorrow with Anna?
2. They will want coffee.
3. You will not like the food there. (θα comes before personal pronoun σ')

There are many more verbs in each of these categories, and you will be learning them as you move along.

Many verbs have irregular future forms. These simply have to be memorized. Some of the verbs that you learned earlier are irregular in the future tense. They are:

ENGLISH	PRESENT	FUTURE
to learn	μαθαίνω	θα μάθω
to understand	καταλαβαίνω	θα καταλάβω
to take, to get	παίρνω	θα πάρω
to go	πηγαίνω	θα πάω

EXERCISE:

Change the following sentences from present to future.

1. Μαγειρεύουμε το φαγητό στην κουζίνα.
2. Νίκος δεν πιστεύει την ιστορία.
3. Οι φίλοι μας παίρνουν τον καφέ τους μαζί. (τους means "their")
4. Τι σπουδάζετε στο σχολείο;
5. Η παράσταση μ'αρέσει πολύ.
6. Κοιτάζεις το παιχνίδι; (the game — το παιχνίδι)
7. Τρομάζετε τα παιδιά.
8. Μαθαίνουν την μουσική για την παράσταση.
9. Καταλαβαίνει την γλώσσα;

Since πηγαίνω is quite irregular in the future, it is shown here in all persons:

θα πάω	θα πάμε
θα πάς	θα πάτε
θα πάει	θα πάνε

Translate:

1. Where will we go tomorrow?
2. Will you go to the theatre with the class?
3. The musicians will go to the countryside together.

Special note: Another use of **πηγαίνω**:

This verb can also be used as a transitive verb to mean to *take someone somewhere*, as in "I am taking my mother to the doctor." This would translate as:

Πηγαίνω την μητέρα μου στον γιατρό.

Because **πηγαίνω** is a transitive verb in this sentence, you must remember to use the accusative case. Notice that in the above sentence, **η μητέρα** and **ο γιατρός** are both in the accusative form.

In the following sentences, you can practice the present and future forms of **πηγαίνω**:

1. She is taking the child to (the) school in the neighborhood.
2. She will take the child to school tomorrow.
3. We are taking Anna to the store because she wants to buy souvenirs.
4. Unfortunately, they will not take Anna to the theatre.
5. I'm taking the family home. (home — **στο σπίτι**)
6. Well then, I will take the family home.

A Special Case: when, if, as soon as

There are certain words which, when they introduce a clause that *implies* the future, eliminate the need for the word **θα**. These words are:

όταν, αν, μόλις and **άμα**

1. όταν   when

When I go to the store, I will buy the groceries.
Όταν πάω στο μαγαζί, θα αγοράσω τα τρόφιμα.

The first verb, which is preceded by όταν, does not need θα.

2. αν   if

If he works tomorrow, he will not go to the theatre.
Αν δουλέψει αύριο, δεν θα πάει στο θέατρο.

3. μόλις   as soon as

As soon as we return, we will write the letter.
Μόλις γυρίσουμε, θα γράψουμε το γράμμα.

4. άμα means all three of the above: when, if, or as soon as

Just for practice, write the above sentences substituting άμα for the other three words.

The Continuous Future

The future tense, as we have just learned it, is for cases in which the future action will only take place one time. If an action will be continuous, for example, "I will be living in Paris" (indicating *from now on*) or "He will study in this room" (indicating a permanent change in the study location), we use the continuous future.

The continuous future is formed by using the *present tense* of the verb with the particle θα in front of it. Here are two examples:

I will be working at the bank.   Θα δουλεύω στην τράπεζα.

She will be writing to my friend.   Θα γράφει στην φίλη μου.

Translate:

1. You will leave your books here when you go to (the) work.
2. He will be buying the gifts for the family.

Helping Verbs: to want to, to have to (must)

(When we use helping verbs, we go back to our knowledge of the *future* form of the verb.)

When a sentence contains a *helping verb*, such as "I want" or "I must," the next thing that follows is another verb in an infinitive form. For example:

I want **to go** into the garden with the children.
There are two verbs in this sentence. In Greek it looks like this:
Θέλω να πάω στον κήπο με τα παιδιά.

Q: How do we form the infinitive "to go" when it follows a conjugated verb (θέλω)?

A: The verb to go is formed by using the particle **να** followed by the future form of the verb πάω (first person singular in this case). The result is **να πάω**.

In other words: we use the *future* form of a verb with the particle **να** to form the infinitive that follows a *helping verb*.

Here are some more examples of this construction. The conjugated (helping) verb is underlined and the infinitive is bold:

I want **to write** a book.
Θέλω να γράψω ένα βιβλίο.

He wants **to go** into the garden with the children.
Θέλει να πάει στον κήπο με τα παιδιά.

<u>They want</u> **to go** into the garden with the children.
Θέλουν να πάνε στον κήπο με τα παιδιά.

Notice that in each of these sentences, the verbs agree with the subject. That is because the subject is performing both actions.

If we add another <u>person</u>, each verb has to agree with its respective agent. For example:

He wants *us* to go into the garden with the children.
Θέλει να πάμε στον κήπο με τα παιδιά.

Notice that the first verb, "he wants" is conjugated in the third person singular (to agree with the subject, *he*), but the verb "to go" is conjugated in the <u>first person plural</u> because it is about <u>us</u>. Whomever the verbs apply to dictates the way in which the second verb will be conjugated.

More examples:

We want *you* (fam. form) to go into the garden with the children.
Θέλουμε να πάς στον κήπο με τα παιδιά.
(Note that θέλουμε agrees with the subject, *we*, and πάς agrees with *you*.)

She wants *me* to go into the garden with the children.
Θέλει να πάω στον κήπο με τα παιδιά.

They want *him* to go into the garden with the children.
Θέλουν να πάει (αυτός) στον κήπο με τα παιδιά.
(If you wish to avoid ambiguity with the verb πάει—which could apply to <u>him</u>, <u>her</u> or <u>it</u>—it is all right to include the pronoun, which, in this case, is αυτός.)

In all the sentences, note the agreements of the verbs with their pronouns.

Now we will use some other verbs. After looking at the examples, try translating the rest of these sentences using the construction we have just learned.

EXAMPLES:

She wants me to buy the house.
Θέλει να αγοράσω το σπίτι.

I want her to write the letter.
Θέλω να γράψει το γράμμα. (Or *with* the pronoun: Θέλω να γράψει <u>αυτή</u> το γράμμα.)

We want her to look at the photographs.
Θέλουμε να κοιτάξει τις φωτογραφίες.

Translate:

1. She wants him to go to the stores in our neighborhood.
2. I think that he wants me to make coffee for the musicians.
3. She wants us to celebrate together the next time.
4. He knows that we want them to pay the bill at the café.
5. I don't know why you want her to come back tomorrow.
6. We want to take Anna to the theatre but unfortunately, she has a lot of work for school.
7. Please come in ... we want you (fam.) to lift the chairs.

<u>Another helping verb</u>: to have to (must)   πρέπει

This verb is a special case because it is <u>not conjugated</u>. It is always the same, although it can change tense.

It is easy to say:

I must go to the bank.
Πρέπει να πάω στην τράπεζα.

All we need do is place the *infinitive form* of the verb (**να** + the future form) after **πρέπει**.

He has to buy the groceries.
Πρέπει να αγοράσει τα τρόφιμα.

Translate:

1. She has to clean the house.
2. We have to return to Paris. (Paris — **το Παρίσι**)

In the *negative*, it looks like this:

He doesn't have to buy the groceries.
Δεν πρέπει να αγοράσει τα τρόφιμα.

Translate:

1. You don't have to pay the bill.
2. He doesn't have to change the plan.

If we want to express this idea in the *future*, we place **θα** in front of **πρέπει**:

I will have to go to the bank tomorrow.
Θα πρέπει να πάω στην τράπεζα αύριο.

Translate:

1. Unfortunately, you will have to write to the school.
2. We will have to buy gifts from Paris.

In the *negative* in the *future*, it will look like this:

I will not have to go to the bank tomorrow.
Δεν θα πρέπει να πάω στην τράπεζα αύριο.

Translate:

1. We will not have to describe the performance.
2. He will not have to lift the books for the women.

Practice Sentences using πρέπει:

1. We must study the Bible together.
2. We will have to study the Bible together tomorrow.
3. Nikos and Anna have to go to the theatre tonight.
4. They will have to go to the theatre tomorrow.
5. You do not have to buy the groceries.
6. You will not have to buy the groceries tomorrow.

The verb πρέπει can also be translated as "should." How would you say:

1. Maybe he should go to the store with my friend.
2. Each person should clean the house.
3. We should not change the program.
4. You should not frighten the children.

We can use this same structure with the verb αρέσω, except that with this verb, we use the *continuous future*. If we want to say "I like to write letters to my friends," the first verb is conjugated and next is in the continuous future. This sentence translates as:

Μ'αρέσει να γράφω γράμματα στους φίλους μου.
(literally: Writing letters to my friends pleases me.)

MORE EXAMPLES:

Do you like to travel?
Σ'αρέσει να ταξιδεύεις;
(literally: Does traveling please you?)

Why don't you like to study English?
Γιατί δεν σ'αρέσει να μαθαίνεις αγγλικά;
(literally: Why doesn't studying English please you?)

Can you say…?

1. I like to work at home because there is a lot of noise at school.
2. Why don't you like to play in the garden?
3. Do you like to read books in Greek? (in Greek — στα ελληνικά)

Two important verbs

to start: αρχίζω
to continue: συνεχίζω

These two verbs are a special case, like αρέσω, because when they are used
as helping verbs, the verb that follows must be in the continuous future.

EXAMPLES:

I am starting to study Greek.   Αρχίζω να μαθαίνω ελληνικά.

We are continuing to study Greek. Συνεχίζουμε να μαθαίνουμε
                                   ελληνικά.

Notice that, in both cases, **μαθαίνω** is in the continuous future.

The future forms: **θα αρχίσω** and **θα συνεχίσω**

CULTURAL TIP

The Plaka

The Plaka, a district which represents the original core of the city of Athens, is a welcome oasis in a busy, modern metropolis. It sits at the foot of the Acropolis and offers one the opportunity to stroll, shop and eat in a placid and unfrenzied atmosphere.

The Plaka is a nicely laid out grid of streets that are lined with ornate 19th century buildings. At street level, there are shops for tourists that sell souvenirs and artifacts: postcards, pottery, cotton drawstring pants with matching tunics, hand-knit sweaters, silver jewelry and scale-model replicas of sculptures and Greek buildings of antiquity. Although many of the stores carry precisely the same items, one can always find something unique that is only available in that particular store.

More upmarket shops carry 18 karat gold jewelry with designs based on mythical and ancient Greek motifs. Window after window dazzles the eye with sumptuous creations, all very tempting for jewelry lovers.

Despite the attractiveness of the Plaka as a tourist spot, somehow it is never difficult to navigate its quaint streets. There always seems to be room for shoppers, visitors and street musicians. The Plaka has some charming, early 20th century cafés where one can enjoy many varieties of coffee: cold, hot, frothy or plain with varying quantities of milk. Of course one would not want to miss the experience of sampling the Greek pastries. You can also have lunch in one of the tavernas in the mottled shade of a gnarled, old tree. As you sit there, curious, tidbit-seeking cats may approach you and nod hopefully. The sun, the shadows, the cats, the breeze—they are all part of the afternoon atmosphere of the Plaka.

At night, the district is lively with restaurants that are always well patron-ized. It is like one long party that never ends. Don't miss it!

LESSON 6

ο Διάλογος:

Nikos calls Anna to see how her day went at the Plaka.

Νίκος: Γειά σου, 'Αννα! Λοιπόν, πώς σ'άρεσε η Πλάκα;

'Αννα: Μ'άρεσε πολύ. Πήγαμε σε πολλά ενδιαφέροντα μέρη!

Νίκος: Για παράδειγμα;

'Αννα: Ψωνίσαμε σε όλα τα μικρά μαγαζιά και αγόρασα μερικά δώρα.

Νίκος: Ωραία! Μετά τι κάνατε;

'Αννα: Αποφασίσαμε να πάμε στο Καφενείο Κωτσόλης γιατί ήμαστε λίγο κουρασμένες. Μ'άρεσε πολύ εκείνο το καφενείο γιατί είχε μουσική. Μετά, συνεχίσαμε να κοιτάζουμε τα χειροτεχνήματα.

Νίκος: Αυτή η φίλη σου γνωρίζει καλά την Αθήνα;

'Αννα: Ναι. Είναι Ελληνίδα.

Νίκος: Την άλλη φορά, ίσως η Δάφνη κι'εγώ θα σας συνοδέψουμε. Θέλω να πάμε μαζί στην Ακρόπολη. Η θέα από εκεί είναι θαυμάσια!

Dialogue:

Nikos: Hello, Anna! Well, how did you like the Plaka?

Anna: I liked it very much. We went to a lot of interesting places.

Nikos: For example?

Anna: We shopped in all the little stores and I bought several gifts.

Nikos: Great! Then what did you do?

Anna: We decided to go to the Kotsolis Café because we were a little tired. I liked that café very much because it had music. Then we continued looking at handicrafts.

Nikos: Does this friend of yours know Athens well?

Anna: Yes. She is Greek.

Nikos: The next time, perhaps Daphne and I can accompany you. I want us to go together to the Acropolis. The view from there is wonderful!

VOCABULARY

η Ακρόπολη	the Acropolis
αποφασίζω	to decide
αυτός	this (one)
εκείνος	that (one)
η Ελληνίδα	Greek woman
θαυμάσιος	wonderful
η θέα	view
μετά	then, afterwards
τα χειροτεχνήματα	handicrafts
ψωνίζω	to shop

SMALL BUT IMPORTANT WORD FOR SENTENCE BUILDING

ὅλος   all

USEFUL EXPRESSIONS AND COMPOUND WORDS

για παράδειγμα for example
Ωραία!   Great!

GRAMMATICAL NOTES AND EXERCISES

The Simple Past

The simple past is used to describe an action that has taken place and has finished. For example:

She wrote a letter to her friends.
The boy went to the store.

Since you already know how to form the future tense, it will be easy to form the simple past for the groups of verbs you have learned.

You can derive the simple past by starting with the *future* tense. You will need to make these changes:

1. remove the particle θα.
2. move the accent back one syllable.
3. append the new set of endings (see below).

Let us see what happens to the verb διαβάζω (1ˢᵗ person sing.) as it moves from the present to the future to the past.

PRESENT	FUTURE	PAST
διαβάζω	θα διάβασω	διάβασα

Notice what has happened:

1. the word θα has disappeared.
2. the change from ζ to σ has been retained.
3. the accent has shifted back one syllable.
4. a new ending has appeared.

Here is what the verb **διαβάζω** looks like in the past for all persons:

διάβασα	διαβάσαμε
διάβασες	διαβάσατε
διάβασε	διάβασαν

Note the endings for the past tense: **α, ες, ε, αμε, ατε, αν**

Notice that in the past tense, the accent always falls on the antepenultimate (second to the last) syllable. For the 1ˢᵗ and 2ⁿᵈ persons plural (we, you pl.), the accent stays where it was in the future because it was *already* on the antepenultimate syllable.

Let us look at another verb:

PRESENT: **κοιτάζω**   FUTURE: **θα κοιτάξω**

PAST:

κοίταξα	κοιτάξαμε
κοίταξες	κοιτάξατε
κοίταξε	κοίταξαν

Note that the same changes have occurred.

Here is a slightly irregular verb:

PRESENT: **καταλαβαίνω**   FUTURE: **θα καταλάβω**

PAST:

κατάλαβα	καταλάβαμε
κατάλαβες	καταλάβατε
κατάλαβε	κατάλαβαν

As you have seen, it is easy to get to the past tense by looking at the future tense and making the simple changes.

EXERCISE: Can you change these future forms to the simple past?

You will have to: a) remove the word θα;
b) determine in which person the verb is conjugated;
c) append the correct ending to the verb;
d) move the accent to the antepenultimate syllable, if it is not there already.

FUTURE	PAST	ENGLISH TRANSLATION
1. θα σπουδάσεις		
2. θα συνοδέψουμε		
3. θα πιστέψω		
4. θα παίξετε		
5. θα αλλάξουν		
6. θα γιορτάσεις		
7. θα τελειώσω		
8. θα αφήσουν		

How would you say...?

1. We studied together at my office and then we accompanied our friends to the Acropolis.
2. Unfortunately, the Greek woman did not believe the story.
3. When did he change the money?
4. Why did you decide to go to New York (η Νέα Υόρκη)? (use the *helping verb* construction to conjugate "to go")
5. For example, how many children celebrated together?
6. Did you finish the handicrafts for school?
7. We finished the work and then we shopped at the store.
8. We did not accompany Anna to the entrance.

Now start from the present tense and construct the future and the past tenses:

PRESENT   FUTURE   PAST

1. μαγειρεύεις
2. κοιτάζουν
3. σηκώνω
4. αρχίζετε
5. νομίζει
6. αγοράζω
7. καταλαβαίνουν
8. περιγράφεις

Try translating these sentences:

1. Did she understand the story?
2. Did you buy a mirror at the store?
3. She described the view very well.
4. We cooked the soup for the man.
5. Great! But did the Greek woman like the soup?
6. She began to read. (remember the rule about "to begin!")
7. I lifted the table.
8. Did you look at the view? (pol. form)

Q: How can we put an accent on the antepenultimate syllable when the verb only has two syllables?

A: We will *add* an extra syllable at the *beginning* of the word, when necessary, to carry the accent! Let us look at some examples, using verbs that you know:

PRESENT: μαθαίνω   FUTURE: θα μάθω

PAST:

έμαθα   μάθαμε
έμαθες   μάθατε
έμαθε   έμαθαν

Notice that the 2nd and 3rd persons plural (μάθαμε and μάθατε) do not need the extra syllable at the beginning of the verb because they already have a sufficient number of syllables.

Let us try this with another verb:

PRESENT: γράφω   FUTURE: θα γράψω

PAST:

έγραψα   γράψαμε
έγραψες   γράψατε
έγραψε   έγραψαν

Try this exercise yourself with the verbs κάνω and θέλω, which operate the same way.

PRESENT: κάνω   FUTURE:

PAST (all forms):

PRESENT: θέλω   FUTURE:

PAST (all forms):
ήθελα   θάλαμε

How would you say…?

1. He did not want to write to my friend in the country.
2. What did you do in the Plaka?
3. How much did you learn at school?
4. She wrote so many cards.
5. For example, what did the teachers do with the class?
6. They wrote a book but I didn't like it. (literally: "… but it didn't please me.")
7. How much work did the children do at home?

The past tense of **πρέπει**:

An extra syllable has to be added to the beginning of **πρέπει**, which will become **έπρεπε** in the past. The verb following **έπρεπε** is conjugated with **να** + future form of the verb.

EXAMPLE: I had to write to the women. Έπρεπε να γράψω στις γυναίκες.

Can you translate …

1. She had to go to the bank in our neighborhood.
2. We did not have to read these kinds of books.
3. Did you have to cook the soup for the children?

Now we will look at the irregular verbs you have learned and learn their past tense forms. Since these past tenses are not derived from the future, we will not show the future tense here.

PRESENT		PAST (all forms)	
to go:	πηγαίνω	πήγα	πήγαμε
		πήγες	πήγατε
		πήγε	πήγαν
to take:	παίρνω	πήρα	πήραμε
		πήρες	πήρατε
		πήρε	πήραν
to be:	είμαι	ήμουν	ήμαστε
		ήσουν	ήσαστε
		ήταν	ήταν
to have:	έχω	είχα	είχαμε
		είχες	είχατε
		είχε	είχαν

Translate the following sentences using the above verbs:

1. The musicians were not in the street. Really? Where were they?
2. Did you get coffee at the café?
3. I was not at home because I took my friend to the store.
4. Where were you? (both forms).
5. We went with our friends to the theatre.
6. She took the child to school. Really? Did you go together?
7. He took the books to the office.
8. What did you get when you went to the store tonight?

HELPFUL HINT: The best thing you can do right now is make yourself a separate verb chart where you can log in new verbs as you learn them. Hold the paper horizontally and make columns from left to right, labeled:

ENGLISH   PRESENT   FUTURE   PAST

Write in the verbs and tenses that you already know; as you move along, you can add the verbs you learn in future chapters.

Four Important Words: όλος, άλλος, μερικός, λίγος

όλος	all
άλλος	other, next
μερικός	a little, some, a few
λίγος	a little, some, a few

These useful little words are declined (just as ποιος is) to agree in number, gender and case. You will recognize these endings:

όλος	όλοι	άλλος	άλλοι
όλη	όλες	άλλη	άλλες
όλο	όλα	άλλο	άλλα

(It may be difficult for speakers of English to remember that όλος and not άλλος means "all.")

μερικός	μερικοί	λίγος	λίγοι
μερική	μερικές	λίγη	λίγες
μερικό	μερικά	λίγο	λίγα

(These endings are those that are used for almost all adjectives. We will study adjectives in the next chapter.)

Simply decline the word to match the number and gender of the noun it is modifying. If the noun is a direct object or is preceded by a preposition that requires the accusative, adjust the ending accordingly.

Let us look at a few examples, in sentences using both nominative and accusative case, of how these words can be used:

NOM: All of the children decided to buy handicrafts.
        Όλα τα παδιά αποφάσισαν να αγοράσουν χειροτεχνήματα.

ACC: We went to the Acropolis with all of the students.
        Πήγαμε στην Ακρόπολη με όλους τους μαθητές.

NOM: The other café has music.
        Το άλλο καφενείο έχει μουσική.

ACC: He is working with the next customer.
        Δουλεύει με τον άλλον πελάτη.

NOM: A few families wrote cards to the students at school.
        Μερικές οικογένειες έγραψαν κάρτες στους μαθητές στο σχολείο.

ACC: I want to learn a few dances.
        Θέλω να μάθω μερικούς χορούς.

NOM: Only a few dishes in the restaurant are good.
        Μόνο λίγα φαγητά στο εστιατόριο είναι καλά.

ACC: I have few (not many) ideas.
        Έχω λίγες ιδέες.

A note on the word λίγο: You have used this word before in its underlined form, as in "a little tired": λίγο κουρασμένος. When λίγο is modifying an adjective, it does not change.

Demonstrative Articles and Pronouns

This and That, These and Those
This one and That one, These and Those

To express *this*, *that*, *these* and *those* before a noun (in the nominative case), as in "this car," "that man," "these children," "those women," etc., do the following:

For *this* and *these*: Place the form of **αυτός** that agrees in number and gender with the noun before the noun and its article:

EXAMPLES:	the car	το αμάξι
	this car	αυτό το αμάξι
	the children	τα παιδιά
	these children	αυτά τα παιδιά

Let us start with an exercise using **αυτός**: follow the model and make the change in the sentence using the right form of **αυτός**.

The coffee is very good.	Ο καφές είναι πολύ καλός.
This coffee is very good.	Αυτός ο καφές είναι πολύ καλός.

The neighborhood is old.	Η γειτονιά είναι παλιά.
This neighborhood is old.	Αυτή η γειτονιά είναι παλιά.

The students are in school.	Οι μαθητές είναι στο σχολείο.
These students are in school.	Αυτοί οι μαθητές είναι στο σχολείο.

Now you try it:

The book is on the table.
This book is on the table.

The story is interesting. (ενδιαφέρουσα)
This story is interesting.

The musicians are in the restaurant.
These musicians are in the restaurant.

Now let's see what happens when we change from the nominative to the accusative case, that is, when the noun is the object rather than the subject:

NOM: This coffee is very good.
        Αυτός ο καφές είναι πολύ καλός.

ACC: I want this coffee.
        Θέλω αυτόν τον καφέ.

NOM: This neighborhood is old.
        Αυτή η γειτονιά είναι παλιά.

ACC: They have a house in this neighborhood.
        Έχουν ένα σπίτι σ'αυτήν την γειτονιά.

NOM: These methods are difficult.
        Αυτές οι μέθοδοι είναι δύσκολες.

ACC: I do not understand these methods.
        Δεν καταλαβαίνω αυτές τις μεθόδους.

So we can conclude that αυτός has to reflect the number and gender of the noun it is modifying, and it has to obey the rules of the case as well.

The word **αυτός**, in its declined form, can also stand on its own to mean "this one." For example:

This coffee is good.	**Αυτός ο καφές είναι καλός.**
This one is good.	**Αυτός είναι καλός.**
I want this coffee.	**Θέλω αυτόν τον καφέ.**
I want this one.	**Θέλω αυτόν.**

EXERCISE: Translate both sentences in each set; the first uses the nominative case, the second uses the accusative. Make all necessary changes:

1. We like this restaurant.
   We are going to this restaurant.

2. The theatre is doing (use "having") a performance.
   We are going to this theatre.

3. These women are my friends.
   I know these women.

4. These friends (masc.) want to travel.
   I want to travel with these friends.

5. This woman is my mother.
   Do you know this woman?

6. This student (masc.) is very clever. (**έξυπνος**)
   I am studying with this student.

7. These students (fem.) are at school.
   We will write to these students.

8. These plans are on the table.
   I have to look at these plans.

9. These customers are shopping at the store.
   I will accompany these customers to the door. (η πόρτα)

10. These performances will end late. (αργά)
    We will not go to these performances.

Now that you know how to use αυτός, you need only apply the same principles to say *that* and *those*: Place the form of εκείνός that agrees in number and gender with the noun before the <u>noun and its article</u>:

EXAMPLES: the man   ο άνθρωπος
             that man   εκείνος ο άνθρωπος

             the women   οι γυναίκες
             those women   εκείνες οι γυναίκες

And now with the accusative:

Did you look at that book?
Κοίταξες εκείνο το βιβλίο;

I want to work with those men.
Θέλω να δουλέψω με εκείνους τους ανθρώπους.

To strengthen your skills, substitute αυτός with εκείνος in the previous exercise.

Here are 15 questions to translate that will make use of many of the concepts you have learned thus far: number, gender, case, tense, and special rules you have learned about certain words and expressions:

1.   As soon as she reads these books, she will know the truth.
2.   Who will start to lift those chairs?
3.   If I buy a lot of groceries, will you (fam.) make the food? (dishes).
4.   How many children will play in these streets?
5.   When will you learn each verb?
6.   He does not like these kinds of gifts.

7. How much sugar was there in the drinks?
8. She doesn't know that a few children want to play here.
9. How will we pay these bills?
10. We bought these toys for those children.
11. All the students wanted to study at this school.
12. You do not have to buy the groceries for this family.
13. We want to go to the next performance.
14. Do you think that this café is good?
15. This man is not my father.

CULTURAL TIP

Greek Handicrafts

Greece is a treasure trove of handicrafts that offer true insight into a way of life that is fast fading. The production of handicrafts, like folk dancing, was more widely and assiduously practiced by previous generations and, unfortunately, does not hold the same appeal for younger people. This may be because of the attractiveness that mass produced, imported items have in today's world. But that does not mean that you, the traveler, cannot find beautiful and tastefully made handmade and homegrown items to bring back.

Crafts, especially those of the Greek islands, were born out of a true need of island dwellers to produce useful utensils, clothing or housewares in places that were relatively isolated. The individual chains of islands still produce their own particular motifs. Some are bold, vigorous and geometric. Other designs are more serpentine and flowery. These motifs are found on vases, plates or pots, or they may be used in embroidery, on table linens, aprons or curtains.

The beauty of crafts is that they are fashioned out of local materials, local woods, fibers, metals. Craft items were originally made for the artisan's own use and not intended to be sold as souvenirs to tourists. The crafts produced by men tend to be items that can take all day or several days to make: carved utensils, clay pots, metal vessels. Women's handicrafts, however, tend to be more lightweight, portable items: lace, embroidery or basketweaving; something that can be picked up but quickly laid down if the woman is called upon for other tasks.

Today, many crafts have evolved into souvenir items that are expressly intended for the tourist. This does not make them any less lovely to purchase and to place in one's own home or to use personally. Who would not want to bring home some of the sparkling white cotton lace tableware or clothing from Mykonos, or a well-tooled piece of leather or a hand-fashioned wood and brass ornament to adorn long hair? Even the items considered "tacky souvenirs," once they are taken out of context and are not standing among hundreds of others just like themselves, can adorn a shelf back home in a charming way. Painted plates with scenes from Greek mythology, white mini-sculptures of Greek gods, glass "worry" beads, silver and gold-embossed religious icons, miniature stained glass lanterns that hold candles, brightly painted wooden marionettes and silver jewelry can all become cherished mementos of a trip to the paradise that is Greece.

LESSON 7

ο Διάλογος:

Anna's classmate, Aliki, is curious about Anna's family and home in New York and her plans to travel with her family when school is over.

Αλίκη: Πού μένετε στην Νέα Υόρκη;

Άννα: Τώρα, μένουμε στην Τσέλση, που είναι μια γραφική περιοχή με πολλά παλιά σπίτια.

Αλίκη: Είναι παλιό το δικό σας σπίτι;

Άννα: Ναι. Είναι από τον περασμένο αιώνα. Έχει μεγάλα παράθυρα, πολλά δωμάτια, ένα σαλόνι και ένα(ν) μικρό κήπο πίσω. Το σαλόνι μας βλέπει στο(ν) δρόμο και το πρωί, ο ήλιος μπαίνει στα δωμάτια.

Αλίκη: Έχεις το δικό σου υπνοδωμάτιο;

Άννα: Ναι. Οι γονείς μου έδωσαν σε κάθε παιδί το δικό του υπνοδωμάτιο. Η αδελφή μου έχει το υπνοδωμάτιό της δίπλα στο δικό μου υπνοδωμάτιο. Ο αδελφός μας, που είναι ακόμη πολύ μικρός, έχει το υπνοδωμάτιό του κοντά στο λουτροδωμάτιο. Είναι ένα άνετο σπίτι.

Αλίκη: Αλήθεια, πότε θα ταξιδέψουν οι γονείς σου στην Ελλάδα;

Άννα: Ταξίδεψαν κιόλας πριν από δύο χρόνια και επίσης πέρσι. Ήταν τότε που ανακάλυψαν το σχολείο μας. Αυτήν τη(ν) φορά θα μείνουν στην Αθήνα για μία ή δύο εβδομάδες.

Αλίκη: Θα φτάσουν σύντομα;

Άννα: Όχι. Τον Ιούνιο.

Αλίκη: Θα νοικιάσουν ένα διαμέρισμα;

Dialogue:

Aliki: Where do you (pl.) live in New York?

Anna: Now we are living in Chelsea, which is a picturesque district with many old houses.

Aliki: Is your own house old?

Anna: Yes. It is from the last century. It has large windows, many rooms, a living room and a small garden in the back. Our living room looks out of the street and in the morning, the sun comes in the windows.

Aliki: Do you have your own bedroom?

Anna: Yes. My parents gave each child his own room (literally: "its own room," because "child" is neuter). My sister has her bedroom next to my bedroom. Our brother, who is still very young (literally: small), has his bedroom near the bathroom. It's a cozy house.

Aliki: By the way, when will your parents travel to Greece?

Anna: They already traveled here two years ago and last year too. It was then that they discovered our school. This time, they will stay in Athens for one or two weeks.

Aliki: Will they arrive soon?

Anna: No. In June.

Aliki: Will they rent an apartment?

Άννα: Όχι. Φέτος θα μείνουν σ'ένα ξενοδοχείο κοντά στο σχολείο. Μετά το σχολείο, δηλαδή, όταν τελεώσει το πρόγραμμα, θα πάμε στη(ν) Σαντορίνη.

Αλίκη: Ξέρετε κιόλας ένα καλό ξενοδοχείο εκεί;

Άννα: Θα νοικιάσουμε το ίδιο σπίτι που νοικιάσαμε πέρσι. Είναι ένα μάλλον μικρό, άσπρο σπίτι με γαλάζιες πόρτες. Βλέπει στη(ν) θάλασσα και κάθε υπνοδωμάτιο έχει μια θαυμάσια θέα! Αρέσει στη(ν) μητέρα μου η μεγάλη κουζίνα. Το απόγευμα, το χωριό είναι ήσυχο αλλά τη(ν) νύχτα, είναι γεμάτο από τουρίστες.

Αλίκη: Και πότε θα γυρίσετε στην Νέα Υόρκη;

Άννα: Θα γυρίσουμε τον Αύγουστο γιατί το Σεμπτέμβριο θα αρχίσω το πανεπιστήμιο!

Anna: No. This year they will stay in a hotel near the school. After school, that is when the program ends, we will go to Santorini.

Aliki: Do you already know a good hotel there?

Anna: We will rent the same house that we rented last year. It is a rather small, white house with blue doors. It looks out at the sea and every bedroom has a wonderful view! My mother likes the large kitchen. In the afternoon, the village is quiet but at night it is full of tourists.

Aliki: And when will you go back to New York?

Anna: We will go back in August because in September I will start university!

<u>Note</u>: In this chapter, we will start to drop the letter ν (by putting it in parenthesis) from the words τον, την, έναν and δεν (and their derivatives) before words starting in consonants that do not require it.

You have already learned that the ν is only needed before *vowels* and the letters κ, ξ, π, τ, τσ and ψ. One example is στο δρόμο, in Anna's second set of lines in this dialogue. Since ο δρόμος is a masculine word, the accusative article is really τον, but you do not need the ν before the letter δ. Eventually, we will drop the ν altogether when it is not required.

VOCABULARY

η αδελφή	sister
ο αδελφός	brother
ο αιώνας	century
άνετος	cozy, comfortable
ανακαλύπτω	to discover
το απόγευμα	afternoon
άσπρος	white
βλέπω	to look, to see
γαλάζιος	blue
γεμάτος (+ από)	full (of)
οι γονείς	parents
γραφικός	picturesque
το διαμέρισμα	apartment
ο δικός	own (followed by possessive)
δίνω	to give
δίπλα (+ στο or απο)	next to*
το δωμάτιο	room
η εβδομάδα	week
ο ήλιος	sun
ήσυχος	calm, quiet
η θάλασσα	sea
ο ίδιος	the same
κιόλας	already
κοντά (+ στο)	near*
το λουτροδωμάτιο	bathroom
μάλλον	rather, somewhat
μένω	to live, to stay
μπαίνω	to come in, to enter
νοικιάζω	to rent
η νύχτα	night
το ξενοδοχείο	hotel

*can also stand on its own to mean "nearby," as in "the house is nearby."

το πανεπιστήμιο	university
το παράθυρο	window
περασμένος	previous, last
η περιοχή	district
πέρσι	last year
πίσω	behind, in back of
η πόρτα	door
πριν	before, ago
το πρωί	morning
το σαλόνι	living room
σύντομα	soon
τότε	then, at that time
ο τουρίστας, η τουρίστρια	tourist
τώρα	now
το υπνοδωμάτιο	bedroom
φέτος	this year
η φορά	time (as in "this time")
φτάνω	to arrive
ο χρόνος	year (plural: τα χρόνια)
το χωριό	village

SMALL BUT IMPORTANT WORD
FOR SENTENCE BUILDING

ή   or

USEFUL EXPRESSIONS AND COMPOUND WORDS

αλήθεια	by the way
αυτήν τη(ν) φορά	this time
βλέπω (+ σε)	to look out onto
πριν από δύο χρόνια	two years ago
τη(ν) νύχτα	at night
το απόγευμα	in the afternoon
το πρωί	morning, in the morning

GRAMMATICAL NOTES AND EXERCISES

New Verbs From This Lesson

You can add these to your log.

Regular Verbs:

ENGLISH	PRESENT	FUTURE	PAST
to discover	ανακαλύπτω	θα ανακαλύψω	ανακάλυψα
to rent	νοικιάζω	θα νοικιάσω	νοίκιασα
to arrive	φτάνω	θα φτάσω	έφτασα

Irregular verbs: (these are not as hard as they look!)

ENGLISH	PRESENT	FUTURE	PAST
to look, see	βλέπω	θα δώ	είδα
		θα δεις	είδες
		θα δει	είδε
		θα δούμε	είδαμε
		θα δείτε	είδατε
		θα δουν	είδαν
to come in, enter	μπαίνω	θα μπω	μπήκα
		θα μπεις	μπήκες
		θα μπει	μπήκε
		θα μπούμε	μπήκαμε
		θα μπείτε	μπήκατε
		θα μπουν	μπήκαν
to give (you can easily fill this one in)	δίνω	θα δώσω	έδωσα
to live, stay (and this one too!)	μένω	θα μείνω	έμεινα

Try some practice sentences with these verbs and some of the new vocabulary:

1. The sun does not come in the windows in this apartment.
2. Two years ago, we saw that picturesque district.
3. When did they arrive in Paris?
4. Did they give each child his own book this morning?
5. We will arrive there in the morning.
6. She will not give gifts to her friends this year.
7. She will not go into the restaurant with those people.
8. Will you (pl.) rent a house near the sea?
9. What do they want to see when they go to New York?
10. Did you (fam.) see the books that (που) I left here this afternoon?

A Useful Word: που

In the last sentence, we see this word used as a prepositional pronoun. It refers to something already mentioned. It can translate as "that," "who," "when," or "whom," depending on what you are referring to.

It can refer to a subject or object. In the above sentence #10, που refers to an <u>object</u> (books).

Did you see the books <u>that</u> I left here?
Είδες τα βιβλία <u>που</u> άφησα εδώ;

In the following sentence, <u>που</u> refers to a subject:

That is the man <u>who</u> reads to the children.
Εκείνος είναι ο άνθρωπος <u>που</u> διαβάζει στα παιδιά.

Let's look at some examples of sentences using που to refer to both subjects and objects:

That is the district <u>that</u> is so picturesque.
Εκείνη είναι η περιοχή <u>που</u> είναι τόσο πολύ γραφική.

That is the district that we saw on our trip.

Εκείνη είναι η περιοχή που είδαμε στο ταξίδι μας.

In this sentence, district is the object of the verb, because we saw it.

MORE EXAMPLES:

That is the man who reads to the children.

Εκείνος είναι ο άνθρωπος που διαβάζει στα παιδιά.

In this sentence, the man is the subject.

That is the man whom I saw yesterday.

Εκείνος είναι ο άνθρωπος που είδα χθές.

In this sentence, the man is the object, because I saw him.

Translate:

1. Do you like the chairs that they bought?
2. This is the book that I read.
3. That is the woman whom we know.
4. That is the teacher (fem.) who came into the school.
5. Those are the friends who go to this school.

The word που can also mean "when." Here are some examples:

That was the day when we went to the theatre.

Εκείνη ήταν η μέρα που πήγαμε στο θέατρο.

It was the night when you wrote the letter.

Ήταν η νύχτα που έγραψες το γράμμα.

Possessives

When we express the possessive, we place a possessive adjective after the noun.

For example: my book — **το Βιβλίο μου.**

You already know some possessive adjectives, but here is the complete table:

my	μου	our	μας
your	σου	your	σας
his or its	του	their	τους (for all genders)
(if the "it" is masculine)			
her or its	της		
(if the "it" is feminine)			
its	του		
(if the "it" is neuter)			

Unlike possessive adjectives in other languages, the Greek possessive does not change according to the number and gender of the *noun it is modifying.* So for "my house" or "my houses," the word "my" is always the same—**μου.**

my house = **το σπίτι μου**   my houses = **τα σπίτια μου**

As you see above, the definite article comes before the noun and the possessive adjective comes after the noun. Notice that the definite article and the nouns have changed, but the possessive has remained the same.

For practice, substitute the other possessive adjectives:

your house (fam.)
his house
her house
our house
your house (pl.)
their house

Note: When a possessive adjective follows a word of *three syllables or more*, the adjective is considered, in a sense, to be appended to the noun, thus adding a syllable. Since *no Greek word can be accented beyond the third from the last syllable*, you will need to <u>add an accent mark</u> at the end of the noun. You will remember this from these examples:

ο δάσκαλος = the teacher   ο δάσκαλός μας = our teacher

Add the possessives to these nouns and make the appropriate change in the accent:

the apartment	το διαμέρισμα	his apartment
the statue	το άγαλμα	their statue
the statues	τα αγάλματα	our statues
the room	το δωμάτιο	her room
the family	η οικογένεια	my family

Translate these nouns, using the possessive adjective:

my books
your (fam.) sister
your sisters
his brother
our children
your (pl). cards
their students

The Accusative Case and Possessives

In the *accusative case*, although the article and nouns can change, the *possessive adjective does not change*. For example:

Nom: This is my garden.
        Αυτός είναι ο κήπος μου.
Acc: I am working in my garden.
        Δουλεύω στον κήπο μου.

<u>Nom</u>:	They are their brothers.
	Είναι οι αδελφοί τους.
<u>Acc</u>:	They're going with their brothers.
	Πηγαίουν με τους αδελφούς τους.

The Word δικός — own

In the dialogue, we have seen the word **δικός** used to express the idea of "my own," "your own," etc. This word is an adjective and is declined according to number and gender of the noun it is modifying. Here are the forms of **δικός**:

ο δικός	οι δικοί
η δική	οι δικές
το δικό	τα δικά

To construct a phrase (in the nominative) with the word "own," the words are placed in the following order:

1. definite article   2. **δικός** (declined)   3. possessive   4. noun
     το   **δικό**   **μου**   **δωμάτιο**

<u>Examples</u>:

my own room	**το δικό μου δωμάτιο**
his own cars	**τα δικά του αμάξια**
our own neighborhood	**η δική μας γειτονιά**
your (pl.) own parents	**οι δικοί σας γονείς**

Notice how the form of **δικός** agrees in number and gender with the nouns in each phrase.

Try translating these:

her own doctor
our own language
your (fam.) own customers
their own families

The word **δικός** can also mean "mine," "yours," etc. For example, if you ask:

Whose car is this?   **Τίνος αμάξι είναι αυτό;**
The answer could be: It is *his*.   **Είναι το δικό του.**

Answer these questions, using the indicated possessive:

Τίνος παιδιά είναι αυτά;   **Είναι _____** (theirs).
Τίνος σούπα είναι αυτή;   **Είναι _____** (hers).

This is easy, because the answer is really in the question!

Now construct the question <u>and</u> the answer in Greek:

1. Whose money is this?   It is not mine.
2. Whose chairs are these?   I think they are yours (fam).
3. Whose gifts are these?   They are hers.

Of course, in the *accusative case*, you will have to make the necessary adjustments. The accusative forms of **δικός** are:

το(ν) δικό (+ possessive)   **τους δικούς**
τη(ν) δική   **τις δικές**
το δικό   **τα δικά**

(Note that the *neuter* forms are the same in the nominative and the accusative.)

Here are some examples, using the accusative:

She is studying with her own friends.
Σπουδάζει με τους δικούς της φίλους.

We have our own method.
Έχουμε τη(ν) δική μας μέθοδο.

I want my own photographs.
Θέλω τις δικές μου φωτογραφίες.

Change the examples given in the nominative to the accusative, making any necessary modifications:

in my own room
with his own cars
in our own neighborhood
with your own parents

Talking About Time

This chapter's dialogue contains a lot of time-related expressions and examples of how to express time. The first thing to know about expressing time in Greek is that it is always done in the *accusative case*. As you have seen, such expressions as "in the afternoon" (το απόγευμα) or "in the morning" (το πρωί) use the article and noun in the accusative; there is no need for the preposition "in," as there is in English.

Below is a list of the time-related words and expressions from the dialogue as well as some other useful ones. We will also learn the days of the week and months of the year, which are expressed in the accusative.

You already know ...

ακόμη	still
ο άλλος	next (also "other")
απόψε	tonight
αργά	late
αύριο	tomorrow
μετά	then, afterwards
ο μήνας	month
πότε	when

Time-Related Words and Expressions from the Dialogue

ο αιώνας	century
το απόγευμα	afternoon, in the afternoon
η εβδομάδα	week

κιόλας	already
η νύχτα	night
τη(ν) νύχτα	at night
περασμένος	previous, last
την περασμένη εβδομάδα	last week
πέρσι	last year
πριν	before, ago
δύο χρόνια πριν	two years ago
το πρωί	morning, in the morning
σύντομα	soon
τότε	then, at that time
τώρα	now
φέτος	this year
η φορά	time (as in "this time")
αυτήν τη(ν) φορά	this time
την άλλη φορά	next time
ο χρόνος	year (plural: τα χρόνια)

Using the time words and expressions that you know, try translating these sentences. They make use of other vocabulary and grammatical principles that you have already learned.

1. Last year, we discovered a hotel in an old district.
2. Two years ago, she saw your parents in New York.
3. Today we will see the picturesque villages in the countryside.
4. This year, we'll rent his apartment near the sea.
5. Next time, we want to rent the old house in the village.
6. Today I am starting university.
7. I like this apartment because in the afternoon the sun comes in through the windows.
8. Last night, a lot of tourists arrived in our village.
9. Is your house from this century or from the last century?
10. You're late—the program already started an hour ago.
11. In our neighborhood, there is often a lot of noise. That is why we don't like it (the neighborhood).
12. Next week, we will change the program.
13. Last week, we decided to stay with our own friends.

Months of the Year — Οι Μήνες

(They are all masculine nouns.)

Use the *accusative* to say …

ο Ιανουάριος	January	*in* January **τον Ιανουάριο**
ο Φεβρουάριος	February	*in* February **τον Φεβρουάριο**
ο Μάρτιος	March	*in* March **τον Μάρτιο**
ο Απρίλιος	April (fill in the rest)	
ο Μάϊος	May	
ο Ιούνιος	June	
ο Ιούλιος	July	
ο Αύγουστος	August	
ο Σεπτέμβριος	September	
ο Οκτώβριος	October	
ο Νοέμβριος	November	
ο Δεκέμβριος	December	

Translate:

1. In which month is your birthday? (τα γενέθλια — birthday)
2. My birthday is in April.
3. We will travel to New York in October.
4. She has to start studying in February.
5. I like London in May.

CULTURAL TIP

Rugged and Dramatic Santorini

At the southernmost edge of the island chain called the Cyclades lies the small but potent island of Santorini. You may have seen print advertisements that make use of the images of the luminous blue domes of Santorini's churches juxtaposed against the ice-white buildings and the equally blue sea.

This dramatic contrast characterizes the island: beaches of black sand that are reminders of volcanic activity, tall cliffs upon which small clusters of homes are built, and treacherously steep, serpentine roads that connect the ancient harbor with town life.

The two cornerstones of Santorini are the towns Fira and Ia, which lie at opposite ends of the island. Ideally, a traveler would stay at one end of the island and explore the winding and climbing roads that go from one end of Santorini to the other, taking in the natural beauty, open spaces and striking views.

The town of Fira is small and lively. Its streets are terraced, interconnected and chock-a-block with eateries and shops selling postcards, souvenirs and local crafts. The area around Fira offers an open vista of unspoiled, undeveloped land with scrubby brush and tall grasses. New, small-scale hotels are being built, thankfully, in a style consistent with that of the island's traditional architecture: whitewashed, two-storey buildings with balconies, blue doors, shutters and shaded front porches.

The ride to Ia will take you along steep, narrow roads that will lead you directly to the heart of a fantasyland: mazelike colonies of white buildings crowned by blue-domed churches. As you explore the hilly, open-air labyrinth of this town, you will weave in and out of pathways connected by courtyards and staircases of only three or four steps. You will most certainly come upon families of cats relaxing on cool tiles while comforting kitchen sounds emanate from within the thick, white walls.

The main street of Ia is narrow, cobbled and slightly undulating. You can walk it from one end to the other, stopping at quaint cafés for coffee, ice cream or fruit parfaits while you take in a view that you will never forget. It is at once intimate and all encompassing, like the view of a miniature world inside a sugar Easter egg: one of minute proportions that contains everything within it.

The opportunity to sit anywhere that offers a view while enjoying the stillness of a Santorini afternoon is a privilege to be valued. May you find your way there.

LESSON 8

ο Διάλογος:

Aliki and Anna continue their conversation about vacation plans:

'Αννα: Γενικά, πού κάνετε τις διακοπές σας εσύ και η οικογένειά σου;

Αλίκη: Μερικές φορές μας αρέσει να κάνουμε τις διακοπές μας εδώ στην Ελλάδα αλλά μερικές φορές προτιμούμε να ταξιδέψουμε στο εξωτερικό.

'Αννα: Πού, για παράδειγμα;

Αλίκη: Λοιπόν, πέρσι περάσαμε δεκαπέντε μέρες στην Ιταλία. Είδαμε τη Ρώμη, τη Φλορεντία και μερικές μικρές πόλεις. Φέτος, ζήτησα από τον πατέρα μου να περάσουμε δύο ή τρεις εβδομάδες στην Ισπανία.

'Αννα: Γιατί θέλεις να πάς εκεί;

Αλίκη: Θέλω να την δω. Λένε ότι οι παραλίες είναι όμορφες. Μπορούμε να νοικιάσουμε ένα αυτοκίνητο και να οδηγήσουμε στην εξοχή. Γνωρίζεις την Ισπανία;

'Αννα: 'Οχι, δεν την γνωρίζω ακόμη. Γνωρίζω καλά την Γαλλία και μιλώ λίγο γαλλικά. Μιλάς ισπανικά;

Αλίκη: Δεν τα μιλώ καθόλου, αλλά τα καταλαβαίνω λίγο.

'Αννα: Αλήθεια, επειδή μένεις στην Ελλάδα, πηγαίνεις καμιά φορά στα ελληνικά νησιά;

Αλίκη: Ναι. Κάπου-κάπου πηγαίνω το Σαββατοκύριακο στην Μύκονο.

Dialogue:

Anna: Generally, where do you and your family spend your vacation?

Aliki: Sometimes we like to spend our vacation here in Greece but sometimes we prefer to travel abroad.

Anna: Where, for example?

Aliki: Well, last year we spent fifteen days in Italy. We saw Rome, Florence and several small cities. This year I asked my father if we could spend (<u>literally</u>: I asked of my father that we spend) two or three weeks in Spain.

Anna: Why do you want to go there?

Aliki: I want to see it. They say that the beaches are beautiful. We can rent a car and drive into the countryside. Do you know Spain?

Anna: No, not yet. (<u>literally</u>: I don't know it yet.) I know France well and I speak a little French. Do you speak Spanish?

Aliki: No, not at all (<u>literally</u>: I don't speak it at all) but I understand it a little.

Anna: By the way, since you live in Greece, do you ever go to the Greek islands?

Aliki: Yes. Sometimes I spend the weekend in Mykonos.

Άννα: Μύκονος! Με προσκάλεσαν οι φίλοι μου να πάω εκεί τον Θεβρουάριο και να μείνω μαζί τους.

Αλίκη: Η Μύκονος είναι πολύ ενδιαφέρουσα, ιδιαίτερα για τους ξένους, αλλά το χειμώνα κάνει κρύο. Ίσως οι φίλοι σου μπορούν να πάνε την άνοιξη.

Άννα: Θα τους ρωτήσω.

Anna: Mykonos! My friends invited me to go there in February and stay with them.

Aliki: Mykonos is very interesting, especially for foreigners, but in the winter it is cold. Perhaps your friends could go in the spring.

Anna: I will ask them.

VOCABULARY

η άνοιξη	the spring
το αυτοκίνητο	automobile, car
η Γαλλία	France
τα γαλλικά	French (language)
γενικά	generally
οι διακοπές	vacation
τα ελληνικά νησιά	the Greek islands
ζητώ	to request, to ask
ιδιαίτερα	especially
η Ισπανία	Spain
τα ισπανικά	Spanish
η Ιταλία	Italy
καθόλου	not at all (used with the negative)
λέω	to say
μιλώ	to speak
μπορώ	to be able to
η Μύκονος	Mykonos
το νησί	island
ο ξένος	foreigner, stranger (also *guest*)
οδηγώ	to drive
όμορφος	beautiful
η παραλία	beach, coastline
περνώ	to spend, to pass (time)
προσκαλώ	to invite
προτιμώ	to prefer
η Ρώμη	Rome
ρωτώ	to ask
το Σαββατοκύριακο	weekend
η Φλορεντία	Florence
ο χειμώνας	winter

SMALL BUT IMPORTANT WORDS
FOR SENTENCE BUILDING

δεκαπέντε	fifteen
δύο	two
επειδή	since, because
τρεις	three

USEFUL EXPRESSIONS AND COMPOUND WORDS

καμιά φορά	sometimes, ever
κάνει κρύο	it's cold (weather)
κάπου-κάπου	sometimes
μαζί τους	with them
μερικές φορές	sometimes
στο εξωτερικό	abroad
την άνοιξη	in the spring
το χειμώνα	in winter

GRAMMATICAL NOTES AND EXERCISES

Direct Object Pronouns

The above dialogue illustrates the use of the direct object pronoun. The direct object pronoun is the "it" or "him" or "them" that we use in a sentence to refer to something already mentioned.

When Anna asks Aliki why she wants to got to Spain, Aliki answers, "I want to see <u>it</u>" (θέλω να <u>την</u> δω.) and the *it* refers to *Spain*. Because Spain is a feminine singular noun, it has a feminine singular pronoun (την) to replace it in the answer.

Let's look at all the direct object pronouns—some of them will look familiar to you.

me	με	us	μας
you (fam.)	σε	you (pol.)	σας
him	τον	them	τους, τις, τα
(or *it* for a masc. sing. noun.)		(depending upon the noun's gender)	
her	την		
(or *it*, for a fem. sing. noun)			
it	το		
(when the noun is neuter)			

Try this simple substitution drill, following the example:
(Notice that the direct object pronoun goes *before* the verb.)

EXAMPLE: Γνωρίζεις <u>την Ιταλία</u>; Ναι, <u>την</u> γνωρίζω καλά.

1. Βλέπεις <u>τους ανθρώπους</u>; Όχι, δεν _____ βλέπω καθόλου.
2. Μιλάς <u>(τα) ελληνικά</u>; Ναι, _____ μιλώ λίγο.
3. Κάνατε <u>τις διακοπές</u> σας στο εξωτερικό; Όχι. _____ κάναμε στην Ελλάδα.
4. Ο δάσκαλος <u>με</u> κοιτάζει; Ναι, _____ κοιτάζει.

5. Η Μαρία μας προσκαλάει στο σπίτι της; Ναι, _____ προσκαλάει στο σπίτι της.
6. Προσκαλούμε την Μαρία στο σπίτι μας; Μάλιστα, _____ προσκαλούμε!

Now translate these questions and answers, using direct object pronouns:

1. Do you know the Greek islands? Yes, I know them well.
2. Did you buy the toy for the child? Yes, I bought it.
3. Did Maria see the tourists in the neighborhood? Yes, she saw them.
4. Is she looking at Nikos? No, she's not looking at him.
5. Does he see the beaches? Yes, he sees them.
6. Whom (Ποιον) are you looking at? I am looking at you. (both forms.)
7. Does he see you? Yes, he sees me.

We have seen that in the present and past tenses, we put the direct object pronoun *before* the verb. Now let's see what happens in the future tense:

Will you see the children tonight?   Yes, I will see them tonight.
Θα δεις τα παιδιά απόψε;   Ναι, θα τα δω απόψε.

Notice that the direct object pronoun comes between the particle θα and the future form of the verb.

Try these two sets of sentences in the present and future:

Βλέπεις τους ανθρώπους; Όχι, δεν _____ βλέπω καθόλου.

Ο δάσκαλος με κοιτάζει; Ναι, _____ κοιτάζει.

Future:

Try translating these sentences, which use direct object pronouns in their answers:

1. Will you have the money tomorrow? No, I will not have it. (Remember that δεν always comes before θα.)
2. Will she buy the milk for the guests? Yes, she will buy it.

3. Did you take <u>the glass</u> from the kitchen? No, but I will take <u>it</u> now.
4. When will he finish <u>his work</u>? He will finish <u>it</u> on the weekend.
5. When will we clean <u>the car</u>? We will clean <u>it</u> now.

Contracted Verbs

In this dialogue, you have seen some verbs in forms that you probably do not recognize. They are contracted verbs, and they are conjugated slightly differently from the verbs you have learned so far. These verbs are:

ζητώ	to request, to ask, to ask for
μιλώ	to speak
μπορώ	to be able to
οδηγώ	to drive
περνώ	to pass, to spend (time)
προσκαλώ	to invite
προτιμώ	to prefer
ρωτώ	to ask

Within this verb group, there are subgroups, as you will see in the conjugations. Let us look at these verbs and learn how they work in the present, future and past:

ζητώ — to request, to ask, to ask for, to look for

ζητώ	ζητούμε (or ζητάμε)
ζητάς	ζητάτε
ζητάει	ζητούν

There are two ways to use ζητώ:

When we use this verb to mean "request," "look for" or "ask for," naturally, it will take the accusative because it will be followed by a direct object. For example:

He is asking for (or *looking for*) his mother.
Ζητάει την μητέρα του. (Notice the accusative article **την**.)

<u>But if we say</u>: He is asking his mother if he can go to the store:
Ζητάει <u>από</u> την μητέρα του να πάει στο μαγαζί....the verb is followed by
<u>από</u>, literally: He is asking <u>of</u> his mother that he can go to the store:

Similarly, when Aliki says that she has asked her father if they can go to
Spain, she follows the verb with "<u>από</u> τον πατέρα μου."

How would you say…?

1. She is requesting a room that looks out on the sea.
2. He is asking (of) his father if he can have a toy.
3. We are looking for the university.
4. What did you ask (of) your family?

Now let's see what happens when contracted verbs are conjugated in the
<u>future</u>:

θα ζητήσω   **θα ζητήσουμε**
θα ζητήσεις   **θα ζητήσετε**
θα ζητήσει   **θα ζητήσουν**

What has happened here? The original ending has dropped off and has been
replaced by an ending starting with **ήσ** + the personal endings.

Translate these:

1. She will request a room that looks out on the sea.
2. He will ask (of) his father if he can have a toy.
3. We will look for the university.

Let us look at a similarly conjugated verb:

ρωτώ — to ask

ρωτώ   **ρωτούμε** (or **ρωτάμε**)
ρωτάς   **ρωτάτε**
ρωτάει (or **ρωτά**) **ρωτούν**

This verb is most commonly used when we are asking someone a question. It is always followed by the *accusative* case.

You do not need any preposition with **ρωτώ**. You simply say, for example:

I am asking my friends.	**Ρωτώ τους φίλους μου.**
We're asking our teacher.	**Ρωτούμε την δασκάλα μας.**

The <u>future</u> form of **ρωτώ** is exactly the same as that of **ζητώ**. You can write out the rest of the future forms of **ρωτώ** here:

ρωτώ — future tense

θα ρωτήσω

Now combine your knowledge of *direct object pronouns* with the verb **ρωτώ**. (Remember that in the future, the direct object pronoun goes between the particle **θα** and the future form of the verb.)

She is asking him tonight.
She will ask him this year.

They are asking us now.
They will ask us next week.

I am asking them.
I will ask them tomorrow.

Are you asking me?
Will you ask me in March?

I think that she is asking him.
I think that she will ask him soon.

From our original list of contracted verbs, the other verbs that work the same way as **ζητώ** and **ρωτώ** are:

προτιμώ — to prefer
μιλώ — to speak

Based on what you know of **ζητώ** and **ρωτώ**, you can conjugate **προτιμώ** and **μιλώ** below in the present and the future. (**Μιλώ** has two forms for the 1ˢᵗ person singular.) You should also log all these verbs into your verb table.

to prefer	FUTURE
προτιμώ	**θα προτιμήσω**

to speak	FUTURE
μιλώ	**θα μιλήσω**
(also **μιλάω**)	

Now we will look at two other verbs on this list, which are a little different from one another. Look carefully to notice the slight differences from one verb to the next:

προσκαλώ — to invite

PRESENT		FUTURE	
προσκαλώ	**προσκαλούμε**	**θα προσκαλέσω**	**θα προσκαλέσουμε**
προσκαλείς	**προσκαλείτε**	**θα προσκαλέσεις**	**θα προσκαλέσετε**
προσκαλάει	**προσκαλούν**	**θα προσκαλέσει**	**θα προσκαλέσουν**
(**προσκαλεί**)			

οδηγώ — to drive

PRESENT		FUTURE	
οδηγώ	**οδηγούμε**	**θα οδηγήσω**	**θα οδηγήσουμε**
οδηγείς	**οδηγείτε**	**θα οδηγήσεις**	**θα οδηγήσετε**
οδηγεί	**οδηγούν**	**θα οδηγήσει**	**θα οδηγήσουν**

Sentences using **προτιμώ, οδηγώ, μιλώ** and **προσκαλώ**:

1. Sometimes we prefer to stay at a hotel near the sea.
2. Will you invite them?
3. Do you know how to drive?
4. She speaks Greek very well.
5. I prefer to invite my brothers to a restaurant.
6. When will they speak to the doctor?
7. Where will we drive next week?
8. I think that they will prefer to stay in the bedroom near the bathroom.
9. Soon we will be driving to France together.
10. They will not invite us tomorrow.
11. We are speaking to the class now.
12. They are not inviting my sister this time.
13. Do you prefer to travel in the spring or in the winter?
14. I don't think that she will invite me.
15. She does not like to speak Spanish.

The verb **περνώ** — to pass, to spend (time)

περνώ

PRESENT		FUTURE	
περνώ	περνούμε	θα περάσω	θα περάσουμε
περνάς	περνάτε	θα περάσεις	θα περάσετε
περνάει	περνούν	θα περάσει	θα περάσουν
(περνά)			

Here are some examples of sentences with this verb:

She is spending the weekend in Paris.
Περνάει το Σαββατοκύριακο στο Παρίσι.

Where will you spend your vacation?
Πού θα περάσεις τις διακοπές σου;

We will spend Sunday together.
Θα περάσουμε την Κυριακή μαζί.

Translate these sentences, which make use of **περνώ** in the present and future tense:

1. Where are they spending their vacation?
2. Where will they spend the weekend?
3. This year we are spending the winter in Athens.
4. Last year we spent the winter in New York.
5. Generally, I spend weekends at home.
6. I will spend next weekend in the country.

A new helping verb: **μπορώ** — to be able to

μπορώ

PRESENT		FUTURE	
μπορώ	μπορούμε	θα μπορέσω	θα μπορέσουμε
μπορείς	μπορείτε	θα μπορέσεις	θα μπορέσετε
μπορεί	μπορούν	θα μπορέσει	θα μπορέσουν

As you know, helping verbs are always combined with **να** + the future form of another verb. For example:

I can see the ocean from my window.
Μπορώ να δώ την θάλασσα από το παράθυρό μου.

Can you read this book to the children?
Μπορείς να διαβάσεις αυτό το βιβλίο στα παιδιά;

Now you can say …

1. I cannot see well at night.
2. When can we begin?
3. Can you speak to the doctor tomorrow?

Are you ready? Now we are going to put all of these contracted verbs into the past tense. Here is the formula:

1. Remove the particle **θα**.
2. Move the accent one syllable to the left, <u>except</u> for the 1ˢᵗ and 2ⁿᵈ persons plural.
3. Drop the future tense endings and replace them with the past tense endings.

I will demonstrate with the verb **ζητώ**:

ζητώ

<u>FUTURE</u>

θα ζητήσω	θα ζητήσουμε
θα ζητήσεις	θα ζητήσετε
θα ζητήσει	θα ζητήσουν

<u>PAST</u>

ζήτησα	ζητήσαμε
ζήτησες	ζητήσατε
ζήτησε	ζήτησαν

Now you can fill in the past tense for the rest of the persons for:

μιλώ:
μίλησα

μπορώ:
μπόρεσα

οδηγώ:
οδήγησα

περνώ:
πέρασα

προσκαλώ:
προσκάλεσα

προτιμώ:
προτίμησα

ρωτώ:
ρώτησα

Sentences to translate using contracted verbs in the past tense:

1. Two years ago, they invited my parents to their house in the Greek islands.
2. Last spring we drove to France and we stayed there for fifteen days.
3. Unfortunately we did not spend the afternoon at the beach.
4. Last July we looked for an apartment in Mykonos but we did not want to rent it.
5. Maybe she preferred to stay at the hotel.
6. He already spoke to the foreigners and asked them if they bought a lot of souvenirs.
7. Three months ago I spent a week in Spain.
8. She went to school in New York and afterwards, she spent the summer there. (το καλοκαίρι — summer)
9. As soon as I spoke to the musician, he knew that I wanted to request a song. (το τραγούδι — song)
10. They were not able to enter the house.
11. Last year we were able to travel abroad.
12. In the morning, a few friends in the neighborhood invited us to their house.
13. The last time that I drove there, I had a good time. (περνώ καλά — to have a good time)
14. Last May I asked my father to pay my bill, but at that time did he not have the money.
15. Where did they spend last summer?
16. He invited me to see his house but I preferred to shop in the stores.

The Verb λέω

We also have one irregular, very useful verb in this dialogue:

λέω — to say, to tell

λέω	λέμε
λές	λέτε
λέει	λένε

This verb is particularly useful when expressing "my name is," "your name is," etc. The formula is simple, now that you know the direct object pronouns:

Q: **Πώς σε λένε?** or **Πώς σας λένε?**
What is your name? (literally: How do they call you?)

A: **Με λένε Νίκο.**
My name is Nikos.
(Notice that the final ς is gone from **Νίκος** because the name is the direct object of the verb, so the accusative case is used.)

Πώς τον λένε;	What is his name?
Πώς την λένε;	What is her name?

Using your <u>direct object pronouns</u>, how would you say…?

1. What are their names? (masc. plural)
2. What are their names? (fem. plural)

And how would you answer:

1. His name is Peter.
2. Her name is Maria.
3. My name is Anna.
4. Their names are Daphne and Aliki.
5. Their names are John and Peter. (**Γιάννης** — John)
   (Don't forget to drop the ς on these names!)

The verb **λέω** has irregular future and past forms:

<u>FUTURE:</u>		<u>PAST:</u>	
θα πω	**θα πούμε**	είπα	είπαμε
θα πεις	**θα πείτε**	είπες	είπατε
θα πει	**θα πουν**	είπε	είπαν

For practice, translate each of the following sentences into Greek, then change them to the future and then to the past:

1. What is she saying?
2. What will she say?
3. What did she say?
4. Is he telling the story?
5. Will he tell the story?
6. Did he tell the story?
7. Are we telling the truth?
8. Will we tell the truth?
9. Did we tell the truth?
10. What are you saying to the child? (do this in both forms of <u>you</u>)
11. What will you say to the child?
12. What did you say to the child?
13. Are they saying something? (something — κάτι)
14. Will they say something?
15. Did they say something?
16. I am not telling the truth.
17. I will not tell the truth.
18. I did not tell the truth.

Time-Related Expressions

Here are a few more, including some from the dialogue.

αργότερα	later
το βράδυ	the evening
για την ώρα	for now
καμιά φορά	sometimes, ever
κάπου-κάπου	sometimes
η μέρα	day
μερικές φορές	sometimes
νωρίς	early
πάντοτε	always
σήμερα	today
σπάνια	seldom

στην ώρα	on time
συνήθως	usually
συχνά	often
χθες	yesterday
η ώρα	hour

Special Cases:

| το μέλλον | the future |
| το παρελθόν | the past |

As you know, time-related expressions that refer to <u>specific times</u> require only the accusative case and no preposition. But "future" and "past" refer to indefinite times, and so need to take the preposition σε. So, if we want to say:

| "in the future," we would say: | στο μέλλον |
| "in the past," we would say: | στο παρελθόν |

πριν — before (followed by future form of the verb in order to create a gerund)

<u>EXAMPLES</u>:

Πριν <u>πάει</u> στο σπίτι, ο Γιάννης μίλησε με τη(ν) Μαρία.
Before <u>going</u> home, John spoke with Mary.

Πριν <u>μιλήσω</u> με τον Πέτρο, θα μιλήσω με την μητέρα του.
Before <u>speaking</u> with Peter, I will speak with his mother.

Translate the sentences below, which make use of these time-related expressions:

1. In the future, you (fam.) will have to finish your work on time.
2. Where did you go with your friends yesterday?
3. Do you go often to Paris?
4. She usually stays at a rather old hotel when she travels to London.
5. Do I have to stay in that bedroom today? For now, yes.

6. In the past, we stayed at our own house near the university.
7. The next time, I want you to arrive on time or early.
8. In our neighborhood, there is often a lot of noise.
9. Sometimes we like to travel abroad, but for now, we will spend our vacation in Athens.
10. I want to ask you something later.
11. She always eats before going to school.
12. We are always home in the evening.

Days of the Week

They are all feminine except for Saturday, which is neuter.

Use accusative to say ...

Sunday	η Κυριακή	*on* Sunday	την Κυριακή
Monday	η Δευτέρα	*on* Monday	τη(ν) Δευτέρα
Tuesday	η Τρίτη	*on* Tuesday	την Τρίτη
Wednesday	η Τετάρτη fill in	*on* Wednesday	
Thursday	η Πέμπτη	*on* Thursday	
Friday	η Παρασκευή	*on* Friday	
Saturday	το Σάββατο	*on* Saturday	

and don't forget: the weekend, on the weekend — **το Σαββατοκύριακο**

Translate:

1. Do you have plans for Saturday?
2. I am going to the theatre on Tuesday.
3. On Friday, our friends will arrive in Athens.
4. I have to work on Monday.
5. Where will you go on the weekend?

CULTURAL TIP

A Quick Look at Mykonos

Seeing Mykonos is a worthwhile experience if you are in Greece, for although the island cannot boast any historical or archaeological attractions in the conventional sense, its structure, layout and lifestyle are phenomena in themselves.

You may stay in a guesthouse where you'll never meet the owner. She'll leave you your breakfast and expect you to leave her the money at the end of your stay, and it is possible that the only company you will have as you come and go is the dog and cat who live in the courtyard.

Mykonos is like a beehive, buzzing unceasingly, but not noisily, with tourists and natives who seem to be in constant motion. The main hub of the island is an inscrutable maze of smoothly paved, cobbled pathways lined with cube-like, white dwellings. Everything is connected to everything else by brightly painted wooden stairways, miniature verandahs and balconies.

Everyone in Mykonos appears to be moving from one lovely spot to another: from café to shop to waterfront restaurant, in and out of doorways, disappearing around corners, climbing up and down steps adorned with red, turquoise or orange banisters, into back alleys or shaded patios. The whole place is like one tremendous game of Hide and Seek that takes you past glittering showcases of gold and gemstones, open-air shops selling only white lace, and stopping-off places where you can have ice cream and coffee and try to decipher the map. You may pass the same place many times on your walk but you cannot get lost. Mykonos is so small, it is only a matter of a few steps before you are greeted once again by the sea.

Beyond the hub, where there is more space between things, there are soothing country restaurants where you'll feel truly at home. At your rustic wooden table that overlooks the Aegean, you can sit and sip wine and enjoy the woody scent of your chicken grilling—no doubt, someone will want to chat with you about the purpose of your journey. It will be one of those times when everything in the world seems perfect. . . .

LESSON 9

ο Διάλογος:

Aliki and Anna are exchanging news about their friends who are studying in other countries.

Αλίκη: Έχεις πολλούς φίλους που σπουδάζουν στο εξωτερικό;

Άννα: Ναι! Πολλοί φίλοι μου έφυγαν από την Νέα Υόρκη για να σπουδάσουν σε άλλες χώρες.

Αλίκη: Από τότε που είσαι στην Ελλάδα, έλαβες πολλά γράμματα απ'αυτούς;

Άννα: Ναι. Τους γράφω συχνά και τους στέλνω φωτογραφίες επίσης. Χθες, έλαβα τέσσερα γράμματα από τέσσερεις διαφορετκούς φίλους!

Αλίκη: Πού είναι και τι σπουδάζουν;

Άννα: Μία μου έγραψε από την Ελβετία. Αυτό που είπε για το σχολείο της είναι πολύ ενδιαφέρον. Και ένας άλλος φίλος μου μού έστειλε φωτογραφίες από το σχολείο του στη Γαλλία, που σπουδάζει γαλλική λογοτεχνία.

Αλίκη: Δεν έχεις μια αδελφή που μένει τώρα στο Λονδίνο;

Άννα: Ναι. Της γράφω συνήθως κάθε εβδομάδα, αλλά δεν συνηθίζει να μου απαντάει κανονικά. Θα πρέπει να της τηλεφωνήσω. Είναι μόνη της, χωρίς τους γονείς μας. Κ'εσύ, έχεις φίλους στο εξωτερικό;

Αλίκη: Ναι. Ένας καλός φίλος μου πήγε στην Γερμανία για να σπουδίσει ιστορία. Του γράφω με το κομπιούτερ. Είναι πιο εύκολο και πιο γρήγορο. Έτσι, μπορούμε να στείλουμε φωτοφραφίες επίσης.

Dialogue:

Aliki: Do you have a lot of friends who are studying abroad?

Anna: Yes! Many friends of mine left New York in order to study in other countries.

Aliki: Since you have been in Greece, have you received many letters from them?

Anna: Yes. I write to them often and I send them photographs too. Yesterday I received four letters from four different friends!

Aliki: Where are they and what are they studying?

Anna: One of them wrote to me from Switzerland. What she said about her school is very interesting. And another friend of mine sent me photographs from his school in France where he is studying French literature.

Aliki: Don't you have a sister who is living in London now?

Anna: Yes. I usually write her every week but she is not in the habit of answering me regularly. I will have to call her. She is alone, without our parents. And you, do you have friends abroad?

Aliki: Yes. A good friend of mine went to Germany (in order) to study history. I write him via the computer. It is easier and quicker. We can send photos that way, too.

Άννα: Το κομπιούτερ είναι θαυμάσιο. Νομίζω ότι είναι απίστευτο πως μπορούμε να "μιλήσουμε" με τόσους διαφορετκούς τρόπους, παντού στον κόσμο, αν και εγώ προτιμώ μια κάρτα ή ένα γράμμα.

Αλίκη: Έχεις δίκιο. Το κομπιούτερ ειίναι χρήσιμο αλλά ένα γράμμα είναι περισσότερο προσωπικό.

Anna: The computer is wonderful. I think it's unbelievable that we can "talk" in many different ways everywhere in the world, although *I* prefer a card or a letter.

Aliki: You're right. The computer is useful but a letter is more personal.

VOCABULARY

απαντώ	to answer
απίστευτος	unbelievable
αυτό που	what (in the sense of "that which")
γρήγορος	fast, rapid
εύκολος	easy
κανονικά	regularly
το κομπιούτερ	computer
ο κόσμος	world
λαβαίνω	to receive
η λογοτεχνία	literature
με	with, by, by means of
μία	one (fem. form)
μόνος του	alone
παντού	everywhere
περισσότερο (+ adj.)	more
προσωπικός	personal
στέλνω	to send
συνηθίζω (+ να)	to be in the habit of
τέσσερεις, τέσσερα	four
τηλεφωνώ	to telephone, to call
ο τρόπος	way, method, means, manner
η χώρα	country
χρήσιμος	useful
χωρίς	without
φεύγω	to go out, to leave (intrans.)

SMALL BUT IMPORTANT WORDS FOR SENTENCE BUILDING

έτσι	thus, that way
τόσος	so much, so many

USEFUL EXPRESSIONS AND COMPOUND WORDS

από τότε που (+ verb)	since the time that ... (+ verb)
αν και	although
για να (+ verb in future form)	in order to
Έχεις δίκιο	You're right

GRAMMATICAL NOTES AND EXERCISES

Let's look at several new concepts that have been introduced in this dialogue:

Indirect Object Pronouns

The first important one is <u>indirect object pronouns</u> (*to* him, *to* them, etc.). This is also called the <u>Dative Case</u>.

As in the case of direct object pronouns, there is a little table to memorize:

to me	**μου**	to us	**μας**
to you (fam.)	**σου**	to you (pol.)	**σας**
to him	**του**	to them	**τους, τις, τους**

(or *to it* for a masc. sing. noun.) (depending upon the gender)
to her   **της**
(or *to it* for a fem. sing. noun)
to it   **του**
(when the noun is neuter)

You already know some verbs that you can use with indirect object pronouns: to give (**δίνω**), to write (**γράφω**), to say (**λέω**), to read (**διαβάζω**), to buy (**αγοράζω**), to speak (**μιλώ**).

Here are some simple examples:

She is writing <u>to her</u> today.
<u>**Της**</u> **γράφει σήμερα.**

We are speaking <u>to them</u> about their vacation.
<u>**Τους**</u> **μιλούμε για τις διακοπές τους.**

My teacher gave (to) <u>me</u> a book.
Ο δάσκαλος μου <u>**μού**</u> **έδωσε ένα βιβλίο.**

(Notice how in this sentence, **μου** appears twice: once as a <u>possessive</u> and once as an <u>indirect object pronoun</u>. An accent is placed on the second one to differentiate between two different parts of speech.)

With the addition of indirect object pronouns to your vocabulary, you can complete your knowledge of the verb **αρέσω**, which you learned earlier:

I like	**μ'αρέσει (μου αρεσει)**	We like	**μας αρέσει**
You like	**σ'αρέσει (σου αρεσει)**	You like	**σας αρέσει**
He likes	**του αρέσει**	They (masc.) like	**τους αρέσει**
She likes	**της αρέσει**	They (fem.) like	**τις αρέσει**
It likes	**του αρέσει**	They (neut.) like	**τους αρέσει**

Of course, depending on what the <u>subject</u> of the sentence is, the verb could also be **αρέσουν**. If you are saying, "I like Spain," the subject in a *Greek* sentence is *Spain*, which is <u>singular</u>: "Spain pleases me." **Η Ισπανία μ'αρέσει.**

But if the sentence is "I like children" ("Children are pleasing to me."), then the subject of the sentence is <u>plural,</u> and you would have to say: **Τα παιδιά μ' αρέσουν.**

How would you say…?

1. She does not like to travel.
2. They (fem.) like the food in Greece.
3. We do not like music.
4. They (masc.) like books.

Now you can translate these sentences using indirect object pronouns and other verbs:

1. What did she say to you? (both forms of <u>you</u>)
2. He is buying her a car.
3. We are reading to them (the children).
4. When did he write to us?

The dialogue contains some more verbs that you can use with indirect object pronouns: to answer (**απαντώ**), to send (**στέλνω**), and to telephone (**τηλεφωνώ**). Here are the basics of their conjugations. You can fill in the rest:

απαντώ

PRESENT

απαντώ	απαντούμε
απαντας	απαντάτε
απαντά(ει)	απαντούν

FUTURE

θα απαντήσω

PAST

απάντησα

It is important to remember:

ρωτώ takes a **direct** object pronoun: She asks me. **Με ρωτάει.**

απαντώ takes an **indirect** object pronoun: She answers me. **Μου απαντάει.**

στέλνω — regular in the present

FUTURE

θα στείλω

PAST

έστειλα

τηλεφωνώ — regular in the present

FUTURE

θα τηλεφωνήσω

PAST

τηλεφώνησα

When using indirect object pronouns (i.o.p.) in sentences containing <u>helping</u> <u>verbs</u>, notice that the i.o.p. is placed between the word **να** and the verb.

I have to write <u>to him</u> tomorrow.	**Πρέπει να** <u>**του**</u> **γράψω αύριο.**
She wants to answer <u>you</u>.	**Θέλει να** <u>**σου**</u> **απαντήσει.**

Translate these:

1. We want to send him the books.
2. They have to read to them (the women).
3. She wanted to speak to me yesterday.
4. She cannot answer them (the men).
5. Do you have to send the money to her?
6. You must not call him.
7. Do you want to buy me a few groceries?
8. She can give you coffee later.

Let's see what happens when a sentence contains both a direct object pronoun (d.o.p.) and an i.o.p. We will do a substitution drill:

She gives you <u>coffee</u>.	*change to*:	She gives <u>it</u> to you.
Σου δίνει καφέ.		**Σου το(ν) δίνει.**

He sent her <u>the money</u>.	*change to*:	He sent <u>it</u> to her.
Της έστειλε τα λεφτά.		**Της τα έστειλε.**

Notice that the i.o.p. comes before the d.o.p.!

<u>Substitution drill</u>: Change each sentence by first replacing the indirect object with an i.o.p. Then replace the direct object with a d.o.p. Follow the 3-part example:

She is reading the books <u>to the children</u>.
Διαβάζει τα βιβλία <u>**στα παιδιά**</u>.

She is reading the books <u>to them</u>.
<u>**Τους**</u> **διαβάζει τα βιβλία.**

She is reading <u>them</u> (the books) to them.
Τους <u>τα</u> διαβάζει.

He is sending the letters to his mother.
He is sending her the letters.
He is sending them to her.

They are buying your sister (to your sister) a car.
They are buying her a car.
They are buying it for her.

She sent her father (to her father) some gifts.
She sent him some gifts.
She sent them to him.

Did she read a story to the children?
Did she read (to) them a story?
Did she read it to them?

αυτό που — that which

The next important grammatical idea is the use of the words αυτό που, which means <u>what</u> in the sense of "that which."

In the dialogue, Anna tells Aliki that *that which (or what)* her friend wrote her about the school in Switzerland is very interesting. When we use the word "what" to refer to something we have already mentioned, we are really saying "that which."

Examples of sentences in which "what" means "that which" are:

Do you know <u>what</u> he said to me yesterday?
Ξέρεις <u>αυτό που</u> μου έιπε χθες;

I like <u>what</u> he bought at the store.
<u>Αυτό που</u> αγόρασε στο μαγαζί μ'αρέσει.
(<u>If</u> the implication is that *that which* consists of multiple "things," you can also say <u>αυτά</u> που.)

I don't understand <u>what</u> (things) he wrote in the letter.
Δεν καταλαβαίνω <u>αυτά που</u> έγραψε στο γράμμα.

Translate:

1. Did he understand what she wanted?
2. This dish is not what I asked for.
3. Did they receive what they requested?

Borrowed Words

το κομπιούτερ (computer) is a word that has been borrowed from English. Borrowed words are spelled phonetically and are neuter in gender. The Greek language has many words borrowed from other languages; you will learn to recognize them because of their singularly un-Greek look! Borrowed words do not change in the accusative or the plural.

Some New Verbs

συνήθιζω (+ να) — to be in the habit of

This is a very useful verb which you can combine with the *present tense* of another verb to mean that something is done regularly, or that one is <u>in the habit</u> of doing it. This verb follows the same rule that you know for "to start" and "to continue"—the particle **να** is followed by the <u>continuous future</u> form of the of verb.

EXAMPLES:

Συνηθίζω να σπουδάζω κάθε μέρα.
I am in the habit of studying every day.

Συνηθίζει να μιλάει στην γυναίκα του πριν φύγει.
He makes a habit of speaking to his wife before he goes out.

How would you say...?

1. Are you in the habit of writing to your parents regularly?
2. We are in the habit of buying the groceries before we go home.
3. They are not in the habit of calling their parents at night.

This verb is regular in the future: **θα συνηθίσω** and regular in the past: **συνήθισα**

λαβαίνω — to receive — regular in the present

FUTURE: **θα λάβω**, etc.   PAST: **έλαβα**, etc.
                                    (Remember, you do not need to add
                                    the first syllable ε in the 1st and
                                    2nd persons plural!)

φεύγω — to go out, to leave — regular in the present

FUTURE: **θα φύγω**, etc.   PAST: **έφυγα**, etc.
                                    (Again, you do not need to add
                                    the first syllable ε in the 1st and
                                    2nd persons plural!)

Special use of the preposition **με** — with, by, by means of

This is the preposition to use when you are talking about transportation:

by bus	**με το λεωφορείο**
by train	**με το τρένο**
by car	**με το αμάξι**
by plane	**με το αεροπλάνο**

A new word: **ο τρόπος** — way, method, means, is also used with the preposition **με**. For example:

By what means (in what way) did he finish the work?
Με ποιον τρόπο τελείωσε τη δουλειά;
(Note that the accusative case is used here.)

από τότε που — since the time that (+ verb in present with applicable person)

EXAMPLE (from the dialogue):

Από τότε που είσαι στην Ελλάδα ... Since you have been in Greece ...

Try combining this expression with some other verbs to make sentences:

1. Since you have been studying French, did you go to France?
2. Since the time he has known them, has he told them about his family?
3. Since she has started her lessons, has she learned a lot?

Numbers 0–20

0	μηδέν
1	ένας, μία, ένα (this number has three genders)
2	δύο
3	τρεις, τρεις, τρία (this number has three genders)
4	τέσσερεις, τέσσερεις, τέσσερα (this number has three genders)
5	πέντε
6	έξι
7	επτά
8	οκτώ
9	εννέα
10	δέκα
11	ένδεκα
12	δώδεκα

13	δεκατρείς, δεκατρείς, δεκατρία
14	δεκατέσσερεις, δεκατέσσερεις, δεκατέσσερα
15	δεκαπέντε
16	δεκαέξι
17	δεκαεπτά
18	δεκαοκτώ
19	δεκαεννέα
20	είκοσι

The numbers one, three and four (and their compound numbers) have more than one form. The neuter form is used for counting and as a neuter article. The masculine and feminine forms are used as articles and agree with the noun they are modifying.

EXAMPLE:

three men	τρεις άνθρωποι
three women	τρεις γυναίκες
three children	τρία παιδιά

How would you say...?

four men
four women
four children

Try some simple sentences using these numbers.

1. We have four friends who are studying abroad.
2. I traveled to Brazil four or five times.
3. We have only one bathroom in our apartment.
4. They are taking fifteen children to the performance.

Review

Days of the Week and Months of the Year

Answer the following questions in Greek:

1. Ποια μέρα έχετε μάθημα;
2. Ποιο(ν) μήνα έχετε τις διακοπές;
3. Ποια μέρα ψωνίζετε τα τρόφιμα; (ψωνίζω τα τρόφιμα — to go
   grocery shopping)
4. Ποια μέρα είναι σήμερα;
5. Ποια μέρα ήταν χθες;
6. Ποιο(ν) μήνα είναι τα γενέθλιά σας; (τα γενέθλια — birthday)
7. Ποιες μέρες δεν πρέπει να δουλέψετε;
8. Ποιο(ν) μήνα αρχίζει η άνοιξη;

The Seasons — Οι Εποχές

winter	ο χειμώνας
spring	η άνοιξη
summer	το καλοκαίρι
autumn, fall	το φθινόπωρο

Translate these sentences about the seasons: (Remember—you do not need
a preposition with time expressions—just use the accusative case.)

1. Will you begin studying at the university in the summer or in the fall?
2. I do not like the winter in New York and that's why I travel to Spain.
3. I prefer to spend the springtime in Paris.
4. What will you do this summer?

Words About the Home

Take another look at the dialogue in Lesson 7 and review the words used to describe the home. Then answer these questions in Greek:

1. Μένετε σ'ένα διαμέρισμα ή σ'ένα σπίτι;
2. Είναι μεγάλο ή μικρό το υπνοδωμάτιό σας;
3. Σε ποιο δωμάτιο μαγειρεύετε το φαγητό;
4. Πόσα λουτροδωμάτια είναι στο σπίτι σου;
5. Είναι μεγάλο το σαλόνι;
6. Μπαίνει ο ήλιος στα παράθυρα το απόγευμα;
7. Βλέπει το σαλόνι στο(ν) δρόμο ή στον κήπο;
8. Είναι παλιό το σπίτι σας;

Adjectives

Adjectives are words that modify nouns, such as *big*, *different*, *blue*, *short*, etc. In Greek, in the nominative case, every adjective has six forms: singular (three genders) and plural (three genders).

You already learned something about how to decline adjectives when you learned the words for "such," "which," "own," etc. It will not be hard for you to understand how these rules are applied to other adjectives.

Let's look at some of the adjectives that you have already seen in the dialogues and exercises so far. The first few are laid out in the six nominative forms. Notice that you have learned these endings before, when you learned the definite article.

απίστευτος — unbelievable	απίστευτοι
απίστευτη	απίστευτες
απίστευτο	απίστευτα
άσπρος — white	άσπροι
άσπρη	άσπρες
άσπρο	άσπρα

You can fill in these:

γεμάτος (+ απο) — full (of)
γραφικός — picturesque
διαθέσιμος — available
δύσκολος — difficult
ελληνικός — Greek
έξυπνος — clever
εύκολος — easy
ήσυχος — calm, quiet
θεατρικός — theatrical
καλός — good
κουρασμένος — tired
μεγάλος — big
μικρός — small
όμορφος — beautiful
περασμένος — previous, last
προσωπικός — personal
χρήσιμος — useful

Oftentimes, adjectives that have a <u>vowel</u> before the ος ending take an α ending (instead of an η) in the feminine singular form.

γαλάζιος — blue   γαλάζιοι
γαλάζια   γαλάζιες
γαλάζιο   γαλάζια

Using this principle, you can fill in these:

παλιός — old
ίδιος — the same
θαυμάσιος — wonderful

Important rules for adjectives:

<u>Mixed Genders</u>: When a group of items or people contains a mixture of genders, masculinity dominates. For example, if we are talking about a group of students in which some are female and some are male, the students are described in the <u>masculine plural</u>.

<u>Speaking in Generalities</u>: When we speak in non-specific terms, such as "It is *important* that you go ..." or "It is *easy* to do it this way," where the *it* is not really defined, we always use the adjective in the <u>neuter singular</u> gender. This is because the *it* is really substituting for the word το πράγμα, which means the *thing*.

Notice some of the examples of this in the dialogue:

Αυτό που είπε για το σχολείο της είναι πολύ <u>ενδιαφέρον</u>.
What she said about her school is very interesting.

Είναι πιο <u>εύκολο</u> και πιο <u>γρήγορο</u>.
It is easier and quicker.

Νομίζω ότι είναι <u>απίστευτο</u> πως μπορούμε ...
I think that it is unbelievable that ...

How would you say...?

1. It is difficult to understand why they are going away.
2. It is not good for you to go home too late. (πάρα πολύ — too)

<u>Special Cases</u>: these simply have to be learned separately.

The word **alone**: Notice how this adjective appends itself to the indirect object pronoun.

PERSON	MASCULINE	FEMININE	NEUTER
I	μόνος μου	μόνη μου	μόνο μου
you	μόνος σου	μόνη σου	μόνο σου
he, she, it	μόνος του	μόνη της	μόνο του
we	μόνοι μας	μόνες μας	μόνα μας

| you | μόνοι σας | μόνες σας | μόνα σας |
| they | μόνοι τους | μόνες τις | μόνα τους |

The *ending* of **μόνος** changes, based on the gender and number of the party.

<u>EXAMPLES</u>:

1. The children cannot go to the theatre alone.
   Τα παιδιά δε μπορούν να πάνε μόνα τους στο θέατρο.

2. I like to study alone.
   Μ'αρέσει να σπουδαζω μόνος μου. (masc.)
   Μ'αρέσει να σπουδαζω μόνη μου. (fem.)

3. The women are alone in the house tonight.
   Οι γυναίκες είναι μόνες τις στο σπίτι απόψε.

4. We are not alone this afternoon. (masc.)
   Δεν είμαστε μόνοι μας αυτό το απόγευμα.

Translate:

1. Do you (fem. pl.) like to go shopping alone?
2. The small child is alone in the garden.
3. We (fem.) like to be alone.
4. They (masc.) are used to (in the habit of) being alone.

The adjective **interesting**: It has a rather irregular form!

ενδιαφέρων	ενδιαφέροντες
ενδιαφέρουσα	ενδιαφέρουσες
ενδιαφέρον	ενδιαφέροντα

How would you say…?

1. This book is not interesting.
2. Her story was very interesting.
3. The lessons at school are very interesting.

Adjectives in the accusative case:

You will have to make the appropriate spelling changes in the accusative case. Simply drop the final ς in the masculine singular and change the ιο to ους in the masculine plural. (Of course, the article will change too.) Unlike words such as τέτειος or ποιος, adjectives do not take the final ν on the masculine, singular accusative form.

EXAMPLES:

I am studying with a very clever student.
Μαθαίνω μ'έναν πολύ έξυπνο μαθητή.

We are studying with some very clever students.
Μαθαίνουμε με μερικούς έξυπνους μαθητής.

The adjective ενδιαφέρων has a slight change in the accusative. Can you find it?

ενδιαφέροντα	ενδιαφέροντες
ενδιαφέρουσα	ενδιαφέρουσες
ενδιαφέρον	ενδιαφέροντα

Translate these sentences, which contain adjectives. Be careful to look for those that require the accusative and make the necessary adjustments:

1. The sea is blue and calm.
2. We like to look at the calm, blue sea.
3. I know a clever, young student (female).
4. We have many good friends.
5. They are looking at the beautiful young women.
6. He drives an old, white car.
7. We want to see the picturesque beaches in Spain.
8. We're looking for a few available students (mixed group).
9. Did you see many theatrical performances?

Countries, Nationalities, Languages and Adjectives

To add to your knowledge of adjectives, here is a table that will provide you with a sampling of names of countries, their citizens (both male and female), and the adjective used to describe things, such as food, literature, customs, etc.

The table is laid out to read, for example:

COUNTRY	NATIONALITY	LANGUAGE	ADJECTIVE
Greece	Greek (male) Greek (female)	Greek	Greek (for things)

As you can see, in English it is very simple—almost all the words are the same. But in Greek, each of these words is slightly different, including the use of upper and lower case letters.

COUNTRY	NATIONALITY	LANGUAGE	ADJECTIVE
η Βραζιλία (Brazil)	ο Βραζιλιάνος	τα πορτογαλικά	βραζιλιάνικος
η Κίνα (China)	ο Κινέζος η Κινεζα	τα κινεζικά	κινεζικός
η Αγγλία (England)	ο Άγγλος η Αγγλίδα	τα αγγλικά	αγγλικός
η Γαλλία (France)	ο Γάλλος η Γαλλίδα	τα γαλλικά	γαλλικός
η Γερμανία (Germany)	ο Γερμανός η Γερμανίδα	τα γερμανικά	γερμανικός
η Ελλάς η Ελλάδα (Greece)	ο Έλληνας η Ελληνίδα	τα ελληνικά	ελληνικός
η Ολλανδία (Holland)	ο Ολλανδός η Ολλανδή	τα ολλανδικά	ολλανδικός

η Ιρλανδία (Ireland)	ο Ιρλανδός η Ιρλανδή	τα αγγλικά	ιρλανδικός
η Ιταλία (Italy)	ο Ιταλός η Ιταλίδα	τα ιταλικά	ιταλικός
η Ιαπωνία (Japan)	ο Ιάπωνας η Ιαπωνέζα	τα ιαπωνέζικα τα ιαπωνικά	ιαπωνικός ιαπωνέζος
η Πορτογαλία (Portugal)	ο Πορτογάλος η Πορτογαλίδα	τα πορτογαλικά	πορτογαλικός
η Ισπανία (Spain)	ο Ισπανός η Ισπανίδα	τα ισπανικά	ισπανικός
η Ελβετία (Switzerland)	ο Ελβετός η Ελβετη	τα ιταλικά τα γερμανικά τα γαλλικά	ελβετικός
η Τουρκία (Turkey)	ο Τούρκος η Τουρκάλα	τα τουρκικά	τουρκικός

οι Ηνωμένες Πολιτείες (see below)
(The United States)

η Αμερική (America)	ο Αμερικανός η Αμερικανίδα	τα αμερικανικά	αμερικανικός

Here are some sentences to translate. They will help to reinforce the information you have just learned and to manipulate adjectives.

1. In the United States, many people speak Spanish.
2. She is studying French literature at the university in Paris.
3. Do all Swiss people speak several languages?
4. Have you studied Japanese art?
5. Yes, and I have traveled to Japan several times.
6. Why do Brazilians speak Portuguese?

CULTURAL TIP

Memories of Studying Abroad

Some of us had the chance, when we were young, to pack up and go to foreign countries, to study that country's language or to immerse ourselves in a discipline that seemed well suited to a particular place: art history in Italy, literature in France, architecture in Greece, music in Spain. For some, it was just an opportunity to see another way of life, to meet new friends, or to bond with a place to which we might later return as adults, working people, people with families and with other adventures behind us.

For most, studying abroad usually included a post-studies trip that took us to lands adjacent to those in which we had spent the junior year, the semester or the summer. We went backpacking, hiking, tooling around with a Eurailpass, all in an attempt to soak up more of what had been available to us during our school time. We hoped to find more opportunities awaiting us— opportunities to learn about language, culture, currencies, and to discover pieces of ourselves that seemed to be more at home in foreign cultures than in our own American backyards.

The benefit of all of this was, of course, a widening of our horizons, an expansion of our view of who we were and who we could be. Learning another language was a piece of the adventure, but learning about the people was the main dish. The language provided a closer look into these unknown territories—it gave us access to a way of thinking that was different from our own.

Later in life, we can reflect back upon the value gained by these experiences of our youth: the freshness and curiosity with which we watched the view from the train window, the eagerness to know everything.

As we move forward in our Greek journey, let us recall or create that energy and bring it to the mastery of this language.

LESSON 10

ο Διάλογος:

Anna drops in on Nikos, who invites her to come with him and his family on a day trip.

Νίκος: Καλώς την 'Αννα! 'Ελα μέσα! Τι κάνεις;

'Αννα: Πολύ καλά, ευχαριστώ. Δε σου μίλησα για σχεδόν δύο εβδομάδες.

Νίκος: Το ξέρω! Σου τηλεφώνησα προχθές και σου άψησα ένα μήνυμα. Το έλαβες;

'Αννα: Ναι, αλλά ήμουν πολύ απασχολημένη με την δουλειά! Δεν είχα καμιά ευκαιρία να σου απαντήσω.

Νίκος: Καταλαβαίνω. Και οι δυό μας, η Δάφνη και εγώ, ήμαστε επίσης πολύ απασχολημένοι. Ελπίζω να μπορέσεις να σταματήσεις την δουλειά σου το Σαββατοκύριακο.

'Αννα: Γιατί;

Νίκος: Γιατί θέλουμε να σε προσκαλεσούμε να περάσεις την Κυριακή με μας και την οικογένειά μας.

'Αννα: Ω; Θα περάσουμε τη μέρα εδώ, στο σπίτι σας;

Νίκος: 'Οχι. Θα πάμε με το αυτοκίνητο στην εξοχή, στο Σούνιο. Θέλουμε να σου το δείξουμε, εκτός αν το επισκέφτηκες κιόλας.

'Αννα: 'Οχι. Δεν το ξέρω καθόλου.

Νίκος: Η παραλιακή διαδρομή είναι όμορφη, ιδιαίτερα όταν φεύγουμε από την πόλη και ο θόρυβος και η κίνηση εξαφανίζονται. Και καθοδόν, αν ο καιρός είναι καλός, μπορούμε να φάμε στο ύπαιθρο σε μια χωριάτικη ταβέρνα.

Dialogue:

Nikos: Welcome, Anna! Come in! How are you?

Anna: Very well, thank you. I haven't spoken to you for almost two weeks.

Nikos: I know! I called you the day before yesterday and left you a message. Did you get it?

Anna: Yes, but I was very busy with work! I did not have an opportunity (a chance) to answer you.

Nikos: I understand. The two of us, Daphne and I, were also very busy. I hope that you can stop your work for the weekend.

Anna: Why?

Nikos: Because we want to invite you to spend Sunday with us and our family.

Anna: Oh? Will we spend the day here at your house?

Nikos: No. We'll go out to the country by car, to Sounion. We want to show it to you, unless you have already been there. (literally: unless you have already visited it.)

Anna: No. I don't know it at all.

Nikos: The coastal route (ride) is beautiful, especially when we leave the city and the noise and the traffic disappear. And on the way, if the weather is good, we can eat outdoors in a country taverna.

Άννα: Πού βρίσκεται το Σούνιο;

Νίκος: Βρίσκεται νότια της Αθήνας, στο τέλος της χερσονήσου, σε μια εξαιρετική θέση. Εκεί υπάρχει ένας αρχαίος, ερειπομένος ναός που βλέπει προς την θάλασσα. Μπορούμε να περπατήσουμε και να βγάλουμε φωτογραφίες.

Άννα: Δεν τραβώ πολύ καλά φωτογραφίες ...

Νίκος: Εντάξει, τουλάχιστο μπορείς να κάνεις μια προσπάθεια! Βέβαια, δεν θέλεις να χάσεις αυτήν την ευκαιρία.

Άννα: Εντάξει, πότε πρέπει να ετοιμαστώ την Κυριακή;

Νίκος: Θα ερθούμε στο σπίτι σου στις δέκα η ώρα περίπου.

Άννα: Θα είμαι έτοιμη. Αλήθεια ... ποιος άλλος έρχεται;

Νίκος: Οι τρεις μας και οι γονείς μου. Ο θείος μου, η θεία μου, ο γιός τους και η κόρη τους, δηλαδή, οι εξάδελφοί μου, θα πάνε με το δικό τους αυτοκίνητο.

Άννα: Θα μ'αρέσει πολύ να περάσω τη μέρα με την συντροφιά σας. Ευχαριστώ πολύ!

Νίκος: Παρακαλώ! Λοιπόν, έφαγες;

Άννα: Ναι, έφαγα, αλλά διψώ λίγο. Μπορούμε να πιούμε κάτι;

Νίκος: Μάλιστα! Εγώ πεινώ και διψώ. Ας πάμε να βρούμε τη Δάφνη. Και οι τρεις μας μπορούμε να πάρουμε κάτι και μετά μπορούμε να κάνουμε μια βόλτα.

Άννα: Καλή ιδέα! Ας πάμε!

Anna: Where is Sounion?

Nikos: It is south of Athens at the end of the peninsula, in a beautiful
spot. There is an ancient, ruined temple there that looks out
toward the sea. We can walk around and take pictures.

Anna: I don't take very good pictures. (literally: I don't take pictures
very well.)

Nikos: Well, at least you can make an attempt! Certainly, you don't
want to miss this opportunity.

Anna: O.K. And when do I have to be ready on Sunday?

Nikos: We will come to your house at about 10:00.

Anna: I'll be ready. By the way, who else is coming?

Nikos: The three of us and my parents. My uncle, my aunt, their son
and their daughter, that is, my cousins, will go in their own car.

Anna: It will give me great pleasure to spend the day in your
company. Thank you very much!

Nikos: You're welcome! So, have you eaten?

Anna: Yes, I ate, but I am a little thirsty. Can we get something to drink?

Nikos: Of course! *I* am hungry and thirsty.* Let's go find Daphne. The
three of us can get something and then we can take a walk.

Anna: Good idea! Let's go!

---

*In the Greek sentence, the pronoun (εγώ) is used for emphasis.

VOCABULARY

αρχαίος	ancient
απασχολημένος	busy
βέβαια	certainly
βρίσκομαι	to be, to be located
βρίσκω	to find
ο γιός	son
δείχνω	to show
η διαδρομή	ride, route
διψώ	to be thirsty
ελπίζω	to hope
ο εξάδελφος, η εξαδέλφη	cousin
εξαιρετικός	extraordinary
εξαφανίζομαι	to disappear
ερειπομένος	ruined
έρχομαι	to come
επισκέπτομαι	to visit
ετοιμάζομαι	to get ready
έτοιμος	ready
η ευκαιρία	opportunity, chance
η θεία	aunt
ο θείος	uncle
η θέση	spot, place
καθοδόν	on the way
ο καιρός	the weather
καμιά	none, not one
η κίνηση	traffic
η κόρη	daughter
το μήνυμα	message
ο ναός	temple
παραλιακός	coastal
πεινώ	to be hungry
περίπου	about, more or less
περπατώ	to walk around
πινώ	to drink

η πόλη	city
προχθές	the day before yesterday
σταματώ	to stop
η συντροφιά	company
σχεδόν	almost
η ταβέρνα	tavern (casual restaurant)
τουλάχιστο	at least
τρώω	to eat
υπάρχω	to be, to exist (usually used only in 3rd per. sing. and pl.)
χάνω	to lose, to miss
η χερσόνησος	peninsula
χωριάτικος	rural, country-style

SMALL BUT IMPORTANT WORD FOR SENTENCE BUILDING

προς   toward

USEFUL EXPRESSIONS AND COMPOUND WORDS

Ας πάμε!	Let's go!
βγάζω φωτογραφίες	to take pictures
εκτός αν	unless
και οι δύο	both
και οι δυό μας	the two of us
Καλώς την	welcome
κάνω μια βόλτα	to take a walk
κάνω μια προσπάθεια	to make an attempt
νότια της Αθήνας	south of Athens
οι τρεις μας	the three of us
ποιος άλλος	who else
στις δέκα η ώρα	at ten o'clock
στο τέλος	at the end
στο ύπαιθρο	outdoors
τραβώ φωτογραφίες	to take pictures

GRAMMATICAL NOTES
AND EXERCISES

Prepositional Pronouns

When Nikos says "… we want to invite you to spend Sunday with <u>us</u> …" he is using a prepositional pronoun. These are the pronouns such as *me*, *him*, *us*, etc., that come after prepositions such as "for," "from," "without," etc.

Let's use the same kind of table we have used to learn other pronouns. These are the prepositional pronouns used before the prepositions such as για, από, με, and σε:

me	μένα	us	μας
you (fam.)	σένα	you (pol.)	σας
him	αυτόν	them	αυτούς, αυτές, αυτά
(or *to it* for a masc. sing. noun.)		(depending upon the gender)	
her	αυτήν		
(or *to it* for a fem. sing. noun)			
it	αυτό		
(when the noun is neuter)			

When the preposition ends in a consonant, as in the word χωρίς (without), we need to add the letter ε in front of μένα, σένα, μας and σας, making them εμένα, εσένα, εμάς and εσάς. As you try to pronounce these combinations, you will see why the added syllable is used.

Translate these sentences, using prepositional pronouns:

1. Do you want to go with us to the Greek islands this summer?
2. She decided to go to the performance without me.
3. Did he do the work for them (mixed group) this afternoon?
4. When will I receive a letter from you (pl.)?
5. The students (fem.) are not here and I cannot continue the lesson without them.
6. Where are the children? I have something for them.

Reflexive Verbs and the Passive Voice

You have seen a new kind of verb in this dialogue. These are **reflexive** verbs and they are conjugated differently from the two other kinds of verbs you have learned so far.

Reflexive verbs convey the idea of something being done to the agent, as in "getting oneself ready" or "washing oneself." They also convey the *passive voice*, where the agent is not named. An example of this would be:

The restaurant <u>is located</u> on Main Street (which really means "The restaurant locates itself ...").

Reflexive verbs are a little more complicated, but if you follow the formula, you will soon find that you can conjugate them quite naturally.

There are a few types of reflexive verbs. Each category is classified by its own set of endings. In this chapter, we will learn how to conjugate those verbs that end in **ομαι**. In the next two chapters, we will learn the rest.

The reflexive verbs in this dialogue are:

βρίσκομαι	to be, to be located
επισκέπτομαι	to visit
ετοιμάζομαι	to get ready
εξαφανίζομαι	to disappear
έρχομαι	to come

Let us look at the conjugations, noticing the endings and learning the patterns.

επισκέπτομαι — to visit

επισκέπτ<u>ομαι</u>	επισκεπτ<u>όμαστε</u>
επισκέπτ<u>εσαι</u>	επισκεπτ<u>όσαστε</u>
επισκέπτ<u>εται</u>	επισκέπτ<u>ονται</u>

Practice this verb by translating these sentences:

1. Are you visiting your cousins in England?
2. We are visiting your sister in order to celebrate her birthday.
3. Are your parents visiting the Greek Islands?

In the <u>future tense</u>, the endings drop off and are replaced by new ones:

θα επισκεπτ<u>ώ</u>   θα επισκεπτ<u>ούμε</u>
θα επισκεπτ<u>είς</u>   θα επισκεπτ<u>είτε</u>
θα επισκεπτ<u>εί</u>   θα επισκεπτ<u>ούν</u>

Now change the sentences above to the future tense, adding the words below and subtracting any that are not appropriate:

1. This spring,
2. Tomorrow,
3. Next year,

In the past tense, we attach another set of endings:

επισκέπτ<u>ηκα</u>   επισκεπτ<u>ήκαμε</u>
επισκέπτ<u>ηκες</u>   επισκεπτ<u>ήκατε</u>
επισκέπτ<u>ηκε</u>   επισκέπτ<u>ηκαν</u>

(Notice how the accent mark changes position, based on the number of syllables in the word.)

Write these sentences, using the past tense:

1. Yesterday,
2. Last fall,
3. Last year,

Let's try another verb:

ετοιμάζομαι — to get ready

ετοιμάζομαι	ετοιμαζόμαστε
ετοιμάζεσαι	ετοιμαζόσαστε
ετοιμάζεται	ετοιμάζονται

In verbs where there is a ζ before the ομαι ending, the ζ changes to στ in the future and past. This is the future tense:

θα ετοιμα<u>στ</u>ώ	θα ετοιμα<u>στ</u>ούμε
θα ετοιμα<u>στ</u>είς	θα ετοιμα<u>στ</u>είτε
θα ετοιμα<u>στ</u>εί	θα ετοιμα<u>στ</u>ούν

In the <u>past tense</u>, the στ is retained and the past tense endings are appended:

ετοιμά<u>στ</u>ηκα	ετοιμα<u>στ</u>ήκαμε
ετοιμά<u>στ</u>ηκες	ετοιμα<u>στ</u>ήκατε
ετοιμά<u>στ</u>ηκε	ετοιμά<u>στ</u>ηκαν

Now translate these sentences, paying close attention to the tense being used:

1. I often get ready early.
2. She will get ready at about ten o'clock.
3. We did not get ready yesterday.

Based on what you have just learned, you can now conjugate the verb εξαφανίζομαι—to disappear. Only the first person singular is filled in. You do the rest!

PRESENT

εξαφανίζομαι	εξαφανιζ
εξαφανιζ	εξαφανιζ
εξαφανιζ	εξαφανιζ

Translate these sentences:

1. My money is disappearing.
2. The day is disappearing slowly. (slowly — **αργά**)
3. Sometimes a problem disappears easily.

FUTURE

θα εξαφανιστώ	θα εξαφανι
θα εξαφανι	θα εξαφανι
θα εξαφανι	θα εξαφανι

Using these verbs, change the above sentences to the future tense.

PAST

εξαφανίστηκα	εξαφανι
εξαφανί	εξαφανι
εξαφανί	εξαφανί

Using these verbs, change the above sentences to the past tense.

Some other verbs that function in the same way are:

χρειάζομαι	to need
κουράζομαι	to get tired
ενθουσιάζομαι	to become enthusiastic
εντυπωσιάζομαι	to be impressed
περιεργάζομαι	to watch, to be attentive
φαντάζομαι	to imagine

Try constructing some sentences on your own with all of these verbs. It will help reinforce the structure in your mind.

Irregular Reflexive Verbs:

Two of the reflexive verbs in the dialogue need to be learned separately. They are regular in the present, but are irregular in the future and past.

βρίσκομαι — to be, to be located, literally, "to find oneself"

βρίσκομαι	βρισκόμαστε
βρίσκεσαι	βρισκόσαστε
βρίσκεται	βρίσκονται

Practice sentences:

1. The train is in the station. (ο σταθμός — station)
2. Where are you today? (fam. form)
3. Where are you today? (pol. form)

FUTURE: Note that both the *stem* and the *endings* change. You will need to memorize this verb.

θα βρεθώ	θα βρεθούμε
θα βρεθείς	θα βρεθείτε
θα βρεθεί	θα βρεθούν

Now write the above sentences in the future tense.

PAST

βρέθηκα	βρεθήκαμε
βρέθηκες	βρεθήκατε
βρέθηκε	βρέθηκαν

And now write the above sentences in the past tense.

Another irregular verb:

έρχομαι — to come

έρχομαι	ερχόμαστε
έρχεσαι	ερχόσαστε
έρχεται	έρχονται

Write these sentences for practice:

1. He comes to my house often.
2. We are coming to visit our friends in Athens.
3. They are not coming here for the summer.

FUTURE

θά' ρθω	θά' ρθουμε
θά' ρθεις	θά' ρθετε
θά' ρθει	θά' ρθουν

Write the above sentences in the future:

1. Today,
2. This afternoon,
3. Soon,

PAST

ήρθα	ήρθαμε
ήρθες	ήρθατε
ήρθε	ήρθαν

Write these above sentences in the past:

1. The day before yesterday,
2. Last month,
3. Last year,

More Verbs from the Dialogue

Now we will get back to our study of verbs from the dialogue, regular and contracted:

Regular Verbs: Fill in the missing parts.

<u>PRESENT</u>   <u>FUTURE</u>

χάνω   χάνουμε   θα χάσω
χάνεις   χάνετε
χάνει   χάνουν

<u>PAST</u>

έχασα

Translate:

1. Unfortunately, she missed my birthday.
2. If we do not go with them to the country, we will miss an important opportunity. (important — **σπουδαίος**)
3. Did you lose something?
4. You are losing money in this situation. (situation — **η κατάσταση**)

ελπίζω — to hope

<u>PRESENT</u>   <u>FUTURE</u>   <u>PAST</u>

ελπίζω   θα ελπίσω   έλπισα

Translate:

1. We hope that you will come too.
2. I hope that the ride will be picturesque.
3. He hopes that his uncle and aunt will visit him next year.
4. I hope to stay with them, at least for now.

Irregular Verbs: You can fill these in based on your knowledge and the models you have. Any irregularities that are new are shown.

PRESENT	FUTURE		PAST	
δείχνω	θα δείξω		έδειξα	
βγάζω	θα βγάλω		έβγαλα	
πίνω	θα πιώ	θα πιούμε	ήπια	ήπιαμε
	θα πιείς	θα πιείτε	ήπιες	ήπιατε
	θα πιεί	θα πιούν	ήπιε	ήπιαν
βρίσκω	θα βρώ		βρήκα	

Translate these sentences, using these four new verbs:

1. If you are ready, I want to show you a beautiful spot where there is a ruined temple.
2. Do you take pictures well?
3. I am making an attempt to find her son for her.
4. We are drinking an extraordinary drink.
5. She doesn't want to miss the opportunity to show us this country taverna.
6. If the weather is good, we'll find our friends.

A special case: υπάρχω — to be, to exist (usually used only in 3rd persons sing. and pl.)

This verb expresses the idea "there is" or "there are" (which can also be expressed by **είμαι**). Keep in mind that **υπάρχω** carries with it more of a connotation of the *existence* or the *availability* of something. Therefore, it is usually only needed in the third person singular (it) and third person plural (them), shown here.

PRESENT	FUTURE	PAST
υπάρχει	θα υπάρξει	υπήρξε
υπάρχουν	θα υπάρξουν	υπήρξαν

How would you say...?

1. How many ancient temples are there in Rome?
2. There is a good hotel where you can stay with your family.
3. There are many buses in Athens.
4. Why are there so many good restaurants in this district?

Regular Contracted Verbs:

PRESENT	FUTURE	PAST
περπατώ	θα περπατήσω	περπάτησα
τραβώ	θα τραβήξω	τράβηξα
διψώ	θα διψάσω	δίψασα
πεινώ	θα πεινάσω	πείνασα

How would you say...?

1. I am always hungry in the morning.
2. We like to walk around in our own city.
3. Do you think the children will be thirsty later?
4. She will take all the pictures for you.
5. We will arrive early and I think we will be hungry.
6. They were not thirsty at all.

A special case: σταματώ — to stop

σταματώ   θα σταματήσω   σταμάτησα

Note that the verb **σταματώ** is used the same way as "to start," "to continue" and "to be in the habit of." It is followed by **να** and the <u>continuous future</u> of the verb.

You will remember: I <u>start</u> working.   Αρχίζω να δουλεύω.
                   I <u>continue</u> working.   Συνεχίζω να δουλεύω.

<u>And similarly</u>:   I <u>stop</u> working.   Σταματώ να δουλεύω.

Can you say…?

1. Why did you stop taking pictures?
2. He stopped talking all of a sudden. (all of a sudden — **άξαφνα**)
3. Every day they stop studying at two o'clock.
4. When will we stop traveling?

An Irregular Contracted Verb: τρώω — to eat

PRESENT		FUTURE		PAST	
τρώω	τρώμε	θα φάω	θα φάμε	έφαγα	φάγαμε
τρώς	τρώτε	θα φάς	θα φάτε	έφαγες	φάγατε
τρώει	τρώνε	θα φάει	θα φάνε	έφαγε	έφαγαν

Translate:

1. What did you eat today with the company?
2. What do they like to eat?
3. Do they eat this kind of food?
4. Certainly, we will eat something when we arrive there.
5. I do not eat in the morning.
6. She is not in the habit of eating before 10 o'clock.

The Imperative "Let's ..."

"Let's" refers to something *we* will do. To express this idea, we combine the word ας with the future form of the verb in the first person plural (we). Here are some examples:

Let's eat!	**Ας φάμε!**
Let's read!	**Ας διαβάσουμε!**
Let's make an attempt!	**Ας κάνουμε μια προσπάθεια!**

Try these:

1. Let's take pictures when we go to Spain.
2. Let's visit the United States.
3. Let's talk to the French woman about her trip.
4. Let's go in (**με**) the same car.

A new expression:

When Anna comes into Nikos' home, Nikos greets her by saying, "**Καλώς την!**" It is an idiom that means "Welcome here!"

The form we see above is the feminine form. The masculine form is "**Καλώς τον!**" and the neuter form is "**Καλώς το!**"

When the person is leaving, you can bid them good-bye with the very nice expression, "**Στο καλό!**" (This is good for all genders.) This is highly idiomatic, but roughly translated, it means, "Please go to places where all good things happen."

Review of Adjectives: Useful Adjectives and Their Opposites

You have already learned how to manipulate adjectives. Here is a list of 20 everyday adjectives and their opposites. You already know some of them:

good	καλός	bad	κακός
easy	εύκολος	difficult	δύσκολος
beautiful	όμορφος	ugly	άσχημος
young, new	νέος	elderly	ηλικιωμένος
(brand) new	καινούριος	old	παλιός
certain	βέβαιος	uncertain	αβέβαιος
healthy	υγιής*	sick	άρωστος
clean	καθαρός	dirty	βρωμικός
simple	απλός	complicated	περίπλοκος
curious	περίεργος	indifferent	αδιάφορος
interesting	ενδιαφέρων	boring	πληκτικός
clever	έξυπνος	stupid	βλάκας*
wide	πλατύς*	narrow	στενός
correct	σωστός	incorrect	εσφαλμένος
strong	γερός	weak	αδύνατος
light	φωτεινός	dark	σκοτείνος
thin	λεπτός	fat	παχύς*
wet	υγρός	dry	στεγνός
happy	χαρούμενος	sad	λυπημένος
tall	ψηλός	short	κοντός

*adjective with special declension

Νομ.		Acc.	
υγιής	υγιείς	υγιή	υγιείς
υγιής	υγιείς	υγιή	υγιείς
υγιές	υγιά	υγιές	υγιά
παχύς	παχοί	παχύ	παχιούς
παχιά	παχιές	παχύ	παχιές
παχί	παχιά	παχύ	παχιά
βλάκας	βλάκες	βλάκα	βλάκες
βλάκας	βλάκες	βλάκα	βλακες
βλάκας	βλάκες	βλάκα	βλάκες
πλατύς	πλατοί	πλατύ	πλατιούς
πλατιά	πλατιές	πλατιά	πλατιές
πλατύ	πλατιά	πλατύ	πλατιά

Numbers 20 – 100

21	εικοσιένας, εικοσιμία, εικοσιένα
22	εικοσιδύο
23	εικοσιτρείς, εικοσιτρείς, εικοσιτρία
24	εικοσιτέσσερεις, εικοσιτέσσερεις, εικοσιτέσσερα
25	εικοσιπέντε
26	εικοσιέξι
27	εικοσιεπτά
28	εικοσιοκτώ
29	εικοσιεννέα
30	τριάντα
31	τριανταένας, κ.τ.λ. (κ.τ.λ. = και τα λοιπά = and the rest. This is the Greek equivalent of *etc.*)
40	σαράντα
50	πενήντα
60	εξήντα
70	εβδομήντα
80	ογδόντα
90	ενενήντα
100	εκατό

Can you write out these numbers?

thirty-three
forty-seven
one hundred and ninety-six
eighty-eight
seventy-eight
fifty-one
one hundred and nineteen

CULTURAL TIP

A Drive Down the Coast

If you have only a few days to spend in Athens and want to shift, momentarily, out of the intensity of city life, take a drive down the coast to the southern tip of the Attic peninsula. The ride itself is uplifting, for you will breeze down the coast road along the shimmering water of the Adriatic, which is bordered by craggy cliffs covered with wildflower bushes. Your destination is Sounion, the site of the ruined temple of Poseidon, strategically placed atop a hill overlooking the sea.

En route, you may stop at any of several country tavernas and eat tasty roasted dishes garnished with sweet, fresh tomatoes and briny black olives. A delicious local wine completes the experience. Then sit back and breathe in the fragrant country air, whose scent is a mixture of salt and the vegetation all around you.

When you reach Sounion, you will be at the edge of the world, or what must have once been thought of as the edge, a springboard for adventure: journeys of ships, either real or mythological. You cannot help but feel the peace and stillness of this place.

You may choose a different road back, the road that takes you up the other side of the peninsula. This will offer a different landscape, a change of color palette. As the sun sets, the putty-colored surroundings will turn purple and after some time, you will discern the twinkling lights of Athens. Refreshed by your foray into nature, you will be ready to dive, once again, into vibrant city life.

LESSON 11

ο Διάλογος:

Daphne and Anna meet in the school library and talk about what they have learned in their art class this year.

Δάφνη: Λοιπόν, Άννα, τι νομίζεις για την τάξη μας; Έμαθες πολλά για την τέχνη;

Άννα: Ω, ναι! Ο κ. Τσούμας είναι ένας εξαιρετικός δάσκαλος! Εξηγήσε τόσο καλά όλες τις ιδέες και μας έδωσε πολλές πληροφορίες για την τέχνη.

Δάφνη: Ποιο μέρος του μαθήματος βρήκες το πιο σπουδαίο;

Άννα: Με ενδιαφέρει πολύ η αρχαία ελληνική ιδέα της ομορφιάς. Πιστεύω ότι αυτή είναι η βάση πολλών άλλων εννοιών της τέχνης, όπως η συμμετρία και η αναλογία του σώματος και των κτιρίων.

Δάφνη: Συμφώνω. Και τώρα μπορείς να καταλάβεις πιο εύκολα την τέχνη του παρελθόντος, δηλαδή, την τέχνη των άλλων αιώνων.

Άννα: Οι συζητήσεις με τους άλλους μαθητές ήταν ενδιαφέρουσες. Μου φαίνεται πως δεν υπάρχει κανένας μαθητής χωρίς την δική του άποψη.

Δάφνη: Ναι, και κανένας στην τάξη μας δεν έχασε την ευκαιρία να εκφράσει την γνώμη του!

Άννα: Θυμάμαι εκείνη την βροχερή μέρα που επισκεπτήκαμε το μουσείο. Ήταν η πρώτη φορά που κοίταξα προσεκτικά τα αγάλματα της αρχαίας εποχής, τον κούρο και την κόρη. Αν και έχουμε τέτοια αγάλματα στο Μητροπολιτικό Μουσείο, ποτέ δεν τα περιεργάστηκα καλά. Αναρωτιέμαι γιατί όχι.

Dialogue:

Daphne: So, Anna, what do you think of our class? Did you learn a lot about art?

Anna: Oh, yes! Mr. Tjoumas is an extraordinary teacher! He explained all the ideas so well and gave us so much information about art.

Daphne: Which part of the course did you find the most important?

Anna: I am very interested in the ancient Greek idea of beauty. I believe that that is the basis of many other concepts in art, such as symmetry and proportion of the body and (of) buildings.

Daphne: I agree. And now you can understand more easily the art of the past, that is, the art of other centuries.

Anna: The discussions with the other students were interesting. It seems to me that there was not one student who did not have his own point of view. (literally: not one student without his own)

Daphne: Yes, and no one in our class missed the chance to express his opinion!

Anna: I remember that rainy day when we visited the museum. It was the first time that I looked carefully at the statues of the Archaic era, the *kouros* and *kore*. Although we have statues like these in the Metropolitan Museum, I never really paid attention to them (literally: I never paid attention to them well). I wonder why not.

Δάφνη: Ίσως εδώ στην Ελλάδα μπορείς να καταλάβεις καλύτερα και περισσότερο καθαρά τον κόσμο από τον οποίον έρχονται τέτοια έργα.

Άννα: Έχεις δίκιο, και όταν γυρίσω στην Νέα Υόρκη, σκεδιάζω να επισκεπτώ, μόνη μου, το μουσείο μας. Δε θέλω να ξεχάσω αυτό που έμαθα εδώ. Από δω και εμπρός, θα κοιτάζω την τέχνη διαφορετικό.

Δάφνη: Ας ελπιίσουμε. Ποιες έννοιες ακριβώς βρήκες τις πιο ενδιαψέρουσες;

Άννα: Νομίζω, ο τρόπος με τον οποίον το κεφάλι του αγάλματος βρίσκεται στο λαιμό και στους ώμους. Αυτό δείχνει την περηφάνια του σώματος. Και πρόσεξα επίσης πως ένα ποδί του κούρου πάντοτε βρίσκεται μπροστά από το άλλο και τα χέρια του κούρου βρίσκονται πάντοτε στις πλευρές. Έτσι, τα χέρια αφήνουν ένα χώρο μεταξύ των βραχιόνων και του κορμιού.

Δάφνη: Πρόσεξες ότι το βλέμμα του κούρου είναι μάλλον σοβαρό, ενώ τα μάτια της κόρης εκφράζουν λίγο μυστήριο; Η κόρη έχει αυτό που λένε το αρχαίο χαμογέλο.

Άννα: Ναι, το παρατηρήσα. Δυστυχώς, μέχρι τώρα, δεν ήξερα τίποτε γι'αυτό.

Δάφνη: Κρίμα!

Άννα: Μια ερώτηση—Δυσκολεύομαι λίγο να καταλάβω γιατί ο κούρος πάντοτε δείχνεται γυμνός αλλά η κόρη δείχνεται νπυμένη.

Δάφνη: Πιθανόν είναι από το σεβασμό για τις γυναίκες.

Άννα: Ναι, πιθανόν.

Daphne: Perhaps here in Greece you can understand better and more clearly the world from which these works come.

Anna: You're right, and when I go back to New York, I plan to go alone to our museum. I don't want to forget what I have learned here. From now on, I will look at art differently.

Daphne: Let's hope so. Exactly which concepts did you find the most interesting?

Anna: I think, the way in which the statue's head is set on the neck and shoulders. This shows the pride of the body. And I also noticed that one of the *kouros'* feet is always in front of the other and that his hands are always at his sides. Because of that, the hands leave a space between the arms and the torso.

Daphne: Did you notice that the *kouros'* look is rather serious, while the *kore's* eyes express a little mystery? The *kore* has what is called the "archaic smile."

Anna: Yes, I observed that. Unfortunately, until now, I did not know anything about this.

Daphne: What a shame!

Anna: One question—I find it a little difficult to understand why the *kouros* is always shown nude but the *kore* is always shown clothed.

Daphne: It's probably out of respect for women.

Anna: Yes, probably.

Δάφνη: Λοιπόν, που πηγαίνεις τώρα;

Άννα: Δεν πηγαίνω πουθενά. Δεν έχω κανένα πρόγραμμα. Γιατί;

Δάφνη: Γιατί η βιβλιοθήκη κλείνει σύντομα. Επειδή έχουμε δροσιά σήμερα, μπορούμε να πάμε στο ζαχαροπλαστείο και να καθήσουμε στο ύπαιθρο στην λιακάδα. Ας συνεχίσουμε την συζήτησή μας εκεί.

Άννα: Γιατί όχι; Ό,τι θέλεις!

Daphne: Well, where are you going now?

Anna: I'm not going anywhere. I have no plans. Why?

Daphne: Because the library is closing soon. Since it is cool today (literally: since we have coolness today), we can go to the café and sit outdoors in the sunshine. Let's continue our discussion there.

Anna: Why not? Whatever you want!

VOCABULARY

η αναλογία	proportion
αναρωτιέμαι	to wonder
η άποψη	point of view
η βάση	basis
το βλέμμα	look, glance
ο βραχίονας	arm
βροχερός	rainy
η γνώμη	opinion
γυμνός	nude, naked
δείχνεται	to show oneself
η δροσιά	coolness
δυσκολεύομαι	to have difficulty
το ζαχαροπλαστείο	café
εκφράζω	to express
ενδιαφέρω	to interest, to be interesting (used only in 3rd persons sing. and pl.)
η έννοια	concept
εξηγώ	to explain
η ερώτηση	question (pl. οι ερωτήσεις)
η εποχή	epoch, era
το έργο	work
εύκολα	easily
θυμάμαι	to remember
καθαρά	clearly
κάθομαι	to sit down
κανένας	no one, not one, none
το κεφάλι	head
κλείνω	to close
η κόρη	*kore* (specifically for the art of Ancient Greece.)
το κορμί	torso
ο κόσμος	world
ο κούρος	*kouros* (specifically for the art of Ancient Greece.)
ο λαιμός	neck
η λιακάδα	sunshine

το μάτι	eye
το μέρος	part
μεταξύ	between (used with genitive case)
το μυστήριο	mystery
ντυμένος	clothed
ξεχνώ	to forget
η ομορφιά	beauty
παρατηρώ	to observe
η περηφάνια	pride
πιθανόν	probably
η πλευρά	side
η πληροφορία	information
το πόδι	foot
πουθενά	nowhere
προσεκτικά	carefully
προσέχω	to notice
ο σεβασμός	respect
σκεδιάζω	to plan
σοβαρός	serious
η συζήτηση	discussion
η συμμετρία	symmetry
συμφωνώ	to agree
το χαμόγελο	smile
το χέρι	hand
ο χώρος	space
φαίνομαι	to seem
ο ώμος	shoulder

SMALL BUT IMPORTANT WORDS FOR SENTENCE BUILDING

ενώ	while, whereas
ό,τι	whatever
όπως	as, such as, like

USEFUL EXPRESSIONS AND COMPOUND WORDS

από δω και εμπρός	from now on
γι'αυτό	about this, about that
Κρίμα!	That's a shame!
μέχρι τώρα	until now, up until now, up to now
μπροστά από	in front of
Ό,τι θέλεις!	Whatever you want!

GRAMMATICAL NOTES AND EXERCISES

Verbs from the Dialogue

Regular Verbs:

PRESENT		FUTURE
κλείνω	κλείνουμε	θα κλείσω
κλείνεις	κλείνετε	
κλείνει	κλείνουν	

PAST	
έκλεισα	κλείσαμε

PRESENT		FUTURE
σχεδιάζω	σχεδιάζουμε	θα σχεδιάσω
σχεδιάζεις	σχεδιάζετε	
σχεδιάζει	σχεδιάζουν	

PAST
σχεδίασα

PRESENT		FUTURE
εκφράζω	εκφράζουμε	θα εκφράσω
εκφράζεις	εκφράζετε	
εκφράζει	εκφράζουν	

PAST
εξέφρασα (slightly irregular)

PRESENT

προσέχω   προσέχουμε

προσέχεις   προσέχετε

προσέχει   προσέχουν

FUTURE

θα προσέξω

PAST

πρόσεξα

Contracted Verbs:

PRESENT

παρατηρώ   παρατηρούμε

παρατηρείς   παρατηρείτε

παρατηρεί   παρατηρούν

FUTURE

θα παρατηρήσω

PAST

παρατήρησα

PRESENT

ξεχνώ   ξεχνούμε

ξεχνάς   ξεχνάτε

ξεχνάει   ξεχνούν

FUTURE

θα ξεχάσω

PAST

ξέχασα

PRESENT

εξηγώ   εξηγούμε

εξηγείς   εξηγείτε

εξηγεί   εξηγούν

FUTURE

θα εξηγήσω

PAST

εξήγησα

PRESENT

συμφωνώ	συμφωνούμε
συμφωνείς	συμφωνείτε
συμφωνεί	συμφωνούν

FUTURE

θα συμφωνήσω

PAST

συμφώνησα

A special case: ενδιαφέρω

This verb is only used in the 3rd persons singular and plural and must be used with a d.o.p:

με ενδιαφέρει	it interests me, it is interesting to me.
σε ενδιαφέρει	it interests you, it is interesting to you.
με ενδιαφέρουν	they interest me, they are interesting to me.
τον ενδιαφέρουν	they interest him, they are interesting to him

You can try this on your own with other d.o.p.

Practice sentences with new verbs:

1. Can you explain the question?
2. She probably forgot what she said.
3. He speaks clearly and explains his ideas well.
4. The information doesn't interest me.
5. Did you notice her smile?
6. Yes, I observed it.

New Reflexive Verbs

In the last chapter, you learned one kind of reflexive verb. Here are some other types, a few of which are in this dialogue:

δυσκολεύομαι	to have difficulty
αναρωτιέμαι	to wonder
θυμάμαι	to remember
κάθομαι	to sit down
φαίνομαι	to seem
δείχνομαι	to show oneself, to be shown (a reflexive form of δείχνω)

Let's look at the conjugations, noticing the endings and learning the patterns:

δυσκολεύομαι — to have difficulty

δυσκολεύομαι	δυσκολευόμαστε
δυσκολεύεσαι	δυσκολευόσαστε
δυσκολεύεται	δυσκολεύονται

Practice this verb by translating these sentences:

1. I always have difficulty understanding these works.
2. Are they having difficulty with their car?
3. She is finding it difficult to explain the ideas.

In the future tense, the endings drop off and are replaced with new ones:

θα δυσκολευθώ	θα δυσκολευθούμε
θα δυσκολευθείς	θα δυσκολευθείτε
θα δυσκολευθεί	θα δυσκολευθούν

Change the above sentences to the future tense.

In the past tense, we attach another set of endings:

δυσκολεύ**θηκα**   δυσκολευ**θήκαμε**
δυσκολεύ**θηκες**   δυσκολευ**θήκατε**
δυσκολεύ**θηκε**   δυσκολεύ**θηκαν**

Write these sentences, using the past tense.

Based on what you have just learned, you can now conjugate this verb:
συμβουλεύομαι — to consult

Try this verb in all three tenses.

Let's try another kind of reflexive verb:

αναρωτιέμαι — to wonder

αναρωτιέμαι   αναρωτιόμαστε
αναρωτιέσαι   αναρωτιόσαστε
αναρωτιέται   αναρωτιούνται

Practice sentences:

1. She is wondering why we don't visit her.
2. I wonder who that boy is.
3. We are wondering if you will be able to travel.

Here are the future endings:

αναρωτη**θώ**   αναρωτη**θούμε**
αναρωτη**θείς**   αναρωτη**θείτε**
αναρωτη**θεί**   αναρωτη**θούν**

Translate the above sentences in the future tense.

Here are the past tense endings:

αναρωτή**θηκα**	αναρωτη**θήκαμε**
αναρωτή**θηκες**	αναρωτη**θήκατε**
αναρωτή**θηκε**	αναρωτή**θηκαν**

Now translate the same sentences, using the past tense.

Based on what you have just learned, you can now conjugate this verb: στενοχωριέμαι — to worry. Try it in all three tenses.

Another type of reflexive verb:

θυμάμαι — to remember

θυμάμαι	**θυμόμαστε**
θυμάσαι	**θυμόσαστε**
θυμάται	**θυμούνται**

Try these sentences:

1. What do you remember about (**για**) the past?
2. We do not remember your address.
3. Does she remember her discussion with the class?

Here is the future tense:

θα θυμηθώ	**θα θυμηθούμε**
θα θυμηθείς	**θα θυμηθείτε**
θα θυμηθεί	**θα θυμηθούν**

Write the above sentences in the future.

The past tense:

θυμήθηκα	θυμηθήκαμε
θυμήθηκες	θυμηθήκατε
θυμήθηκε	θυμήθηκαν

Now write the sentences using the past.

Based on what you have learned, you can now conjugate the verb **κοιμάμαι** — to sleep.

Irregular Reflexive Verbs:

κάθομαι — to sit down

κάθομαι	καθόμαστε
κάθεσαι	καθόσαστε
κάθεται	κάθονται

Translate:

1. We are sitting here because there is sunshine.
2. They are probably sitting with their parents.
3. Where are your parents sitting at the performance?

FUTURE

θα καθήσω	θα καθήσουμε
θα καθήσεις	θα καθήσετε
θα καθήσει	θα καθήσουν

As you can see, the endings of the future tense resemble those of a contracted verb. Write the above sentences in the future.

The past tense endings also resemble those of a contracted verb. You can conjugate this verb yourself!

κάθησα	καθήσ
κάθησ	καθήσ
κάθησ	κάθησ

Now write the sentences in the past.

Another irregular reflexive verb:

φαίνομαι — to seem

φαίνομαι	φαινόμαστε
φαίνεσαι	φαινόσαστε
φαίνεται	φαίνονται

Translate:

1. It seems difficult to travel alone.
2. Does she seem sad to you?
3. They seem to be happy together.

FUTURE

θα φανώ	θα φανούμε
θα φανείς	θα φανείτε
θα φανεί	θα φανούν

Write the sentences, using the future tense.

PAST

φάνηκα	φανήκαμε
φάνηκες	φανήκατε
φάνηκε	φάνηκαν

Now write the sentences in the past tense.

In the next chapter, we will learn some other forms of reflexive verbs. For now, you should add all these verbs to your verb table.

A Useful Word: ό,τι

ό,τι (not to be confused with ότι — that), is similar to αυτό που (that which, what), except that it refers to something <u>not yet named</u>.

You will remember that αυτό που refers back to something that has already been mentioned, as in, "He does not understand <u>what</u> you said." By contrast, ό,τι names something that has not happened yet.

Examples of this are:

... whatever you think: ό,τι νομίζεις
... whatever George wants: ό,τι θέλει ο Γιώργος

The Genitive Case

The genitive case is what we use to express *possession* in phrases such as "my father's house" (which is really the house <u>of my father</u>), "the kitchen door" (which is really the door <u>of the kitchen</u>). We have seen a few examples of this construction in the dialogue:

η αναλογία του σώματος	the proportion of the body
το κεφάλι του αγάλματος	the statue's head

Just like the accusative and dative cases, the genitive has a set of articles and endings to append to the noun.

First we will look at <u>definite articles</u> for all <u>singular</u> nouns:

<u>Masculine</u> nouns ending in ας

Nom.	my father	ο πατέρας μου
Gen.	my father's house	το σπίτι του πάτερα μου

What has changed?

1. The article **ο** has become **του**.
2. The letter **ς** has dropped off the word **πατέρας**.

Here is another example:

| <u>Nom.</u> | her husband | ο άνδρας της |
| <u>Gen.</u> | her husband's office | το γραφείο του άνδρα της |

Using the above models, can you translate these phrases?

1. the century
   the beginning of the century (the beginning — **η αρχή**)

2. the cashier
   the cashier's room

3. the husband
   the husband's car

<u>Masculine</u> nouns ending in **ος**

| <u>Νom.</u> | your garden | ο κήπος σου |
| <u>Gen.</u> | the entrance of your garden | η είσοδος του κήπου σου |

What has changed?

1. The article **ο** has become **του**.
2. The letter **ς** has dropped off the word **κήπος** and has been replaced with the letter **υ**.

Here is another example:

| <u>Νom.</u> | my brother | ο αδελφός μου |
| <u>Gen.</u> | my brother's ideas | οι ιδέες του αδελφού μου |

Can you translate these phrases?

1. his friend
   his friend's family

2. the world
   the nations of the world (nations — τα έθνη)

3. the weather
   January's weather

<u>Masculine</u> nouns ending in **ης**

<u>Nom</u>.	the student	**ο μαθητής**
<u>Gen</u>.	the student's book	**το βιβλίο του μαθητή**

What has changed?

1. The article **ο** has become **του**.
2. The letter **ς** has dropped off the word **μαθητής**.

Here is another example:

<u>Nom</u>.	the customer	**ο πελάτης**
<u>Gen</u>.	the customer's money	**τα λεφτά του πελάτη**

Translate:

1. the congressman   **ο βουλευτής**
   the congressman's ideas

2. the shopkeeper   **ο λιανοπώλης**
   the shopkeeper's wife

3. the supervisor   **ο επιστάτης**
   the supervisor's office

Feminine nouns ending in **α**

<u>Nom.</u>	the student	**η μαθήτρια**
<u>Gen.</u>	the student's book	**το βιβλίο της μαθήτριας**

What has changed?

1. The article **η** has become **της**.
2. The letter **ς** has been added at the end of **μαθήτρια**.

Here is another example:

your aunt	**η θεία σας**
your aunt's neighborhood	**η γειτονιά της θείας σας**

Translate:

1. the week
   the days of the week

2. the sea
   a view of the sea

3. the day
   the beginning of the day

Feminine nouns ending in **η**

<u>Nom.</u>	his daughter	**η κόρη του**
<u>Gen.</u>	his daughter's room	**το δωμάτιο της κόρης του**

What has changed?

1. The article **η** has become **της**.
2. The letter **ς** has been added at the end of **κόρη**.

Here is another example:

Nom.	the district	η περιοχή
Gen.	the homes of the district	τα σπίτια της περιοχής

Translate:

1. the bride
   the bride's car

2. Friday
   Friday's lesson

3. the performance
   the end of the performance

Feminine nouns ending in ος

Nom.	our method	η μέθοδός μας
Gen.	the basis of our method	η βάση της μεθόδου μας

What has changed?

1. The article η has become της.
2. The letter ς has dropped off μέθοδος and has been replaced by the letter υ.
3. The accent has moved one space to the right. Why? Because, as you have learned before, ου is a <u>long</u> sound, and a noun that ends in a long sound cannot be stressed on the <u>third syllable from the end</u>. So the accent moves to the 2nd syllable from the end. (This rule does not apply to *adjectives*, as we will see later on.)

Here is another example:

Nom.	the entrance	η είσοδος
Gen.	the door of the entrance	η πόρτα της εισόδου
		(Again, the accent has moved.)

Translate:

1. the Bible
   the words of the Bible (word — **η λέξη** pl: **οι λέξεις**)

2. the exit (exit — **η έξοδος**)
   the door of this exit

<u>Neuter</u> nouns ending in **o**

| <u>Nom.</u> | the bus | **το λεωφορείο** |
| <u>Gen.</u> | the door of the bus | **η πόρτα του λεωφορείου** |

What has changed?

1. The article **το** has become **του**.
2. The letter **υ** has been added to **λεωφορείο**.

Here is another example:

<u>Nom.</u>	the bedroom	**το υπνοδωμάτιο**
<u>Gen.</u>	the door of the bedroom	**η πόρτα του υπνοδωματίου**
		(the accent has moved.)

Translate:

1. the hotel
   the address of the hotel

2. the school
   his school's teachers

<u>Neuter</u> nouns ending in **ι**

| <u>Nom.</u> | the trip | **το ταξίδι** |
| <u>Gen.</u> | the end of the trip | **ο τέλος του ταξιδιού** |

What has changed?

1. The article **το** has become **του**.
2. The letters **ου** have been added to **ταξίδι**.
3. The accent has moved to the last syllable. <u>New Rule</u>: *In the genitive case, neuter nouns that end in* **ι** *are accented on the* <u>*last*</u> *syllable.*

Here is another example:

| <u>Nom</u>. | the living room | **το σαλόνι** |
| <u>Gen</u>. | the living room windows | **τα παράθυρα του σαλονιού** |

Translate:

1. our house
   the windows of our house

2. this game
   the basis of this game

<u>Neuter</u> nouns ending in **μα**

| <u>Nom</u>. | the drama | **το δράμα** |
| <u>Gen</u>. | the story of the drama | **η ιστορία του δράματος** |

What has changed?

1. The article **το** has become **του**.
2. The letters **τος** have been added to **δράμα**.

Here is another example:

| <u>Nom</u>. | the body | **το σώμα** |
| <u>Gen</u>. | the parts of the body | **τα μέρη του σώματος** |

Translate:

1. the verb
   the meaning of the verb (meaning — **η σημασία**)

2. the letter
   the beginning of the letter

3. the apartment
   the window of the apartment

Neuter nouns ending in **ος**

<u>NOM.</u>	the government	**το κράτος**
<u>GEN.</u>	The problems of the government	**τα προβλήματα του κράτους**

What has changed?

1. The article **το** has become **του**.
2. The ending **ος** has been replaced with **ους**.

Here is another example:

<u>NOM.</u>	the nation	**το έθνος**
<u>GEN.</u>	the laws of the nation	**οι νόμοι του έθνους**

Translate:

1. the place
   the name of the place (name — **το όνομα**)

2. the forest (forest — **το δάσος**)
   the beauty of the forest

Neuter nouns ending in **ον**

| Noм. | the past | το παρελθόν |
| Gen. | the stories of the past | οι ιστορίες του παρελθόντος |

What has changed?

1. The article **το** has become **του**.
2. The letters **τος** have been added at the end of **παρελθόν**.

Here is another example:

| Noм. | the future | το μέλλον |
| Gen. | the car of the future | το αυτοκίνητο του μέλλοντος |

If there are <u>adjectives, articles</u> or <u>demonstrative pronouns</u> (such as *this, that*) modifying the noun, they must also reflect the genitive endings.

<u>Here are some examples</u>: nominative first, then genitive

1. this place
   αυτό το μέρος

   the name of this ugly place
   το όνομα αυ<u>τού</u> <u>του</u> άσ<u>χημου</u> μέρ<u>ους</u>
   (Notice that the accent has remained on the first syllable of **άσχημου**, despite the long **ου** ending—the "long ending" rule does <u>not</u> apply to adjectives.)

2. my own apartment
   το δικό μου διαμέρισμα

   the window of my own apartment
   το παράθυρο <u>του</u> δικ<u>ού</u> μου διαμερίσμα<u>τος</u>

3. that clever student
εκείνος ο έξυπνος μαθητής

that clever student's book
το βιβλίο εκείν<u>ου</u> <u>του</u> έξυπν<u>ου</u> μαθητ<u>ή</u>

4. his good friend
ο καλός φίλος του

his good friend's brand new car
το καινούριο αυτοκίνητο <u>του</u> καλ<u>ού</u> φίλ<u>ου</u> του

5. this district
αυτή η περιοχή

the homes of this picturesque district
τα σπίτια αυτ<u>ής</u> <u>της</u> γραφικ<u>ής</u> περιοχ<u>ής</u>

6. the difficult trip
το δύσκολο ταξίδι

the story of whole difficult trip
η ιστορία όλ<u>ου</u> <u>του</u> δύσκολ<u>ου</u> ταξιδ<u>ιού</u>

Based on the above models, try to translate these:

1. the beautiful, blue sea
   a view of the beautiful, blue sea

2. his clever cousin (masc.)
   his clever cousin's book

3. the statue
   the tall statue's head

4. the performance
   the end of the whole performance

5. your own family
   the story of your own family

Here are the genitive forms of some of the irregular adjectives you have learned:

υγιούς
υγιούς
υγιούς

παχιού
παχιάς
παχιού

πλατιού
πλατιά
πλατιού

To practice these, translate:

1. the healthy boy's house
2. the fat child's mother
3. houses of the wide street
4. the healthy person's food

The genitive case is also used for showing possession with names in such phrases as "John's book" and "Anna's house." Depending upon the spelling of the name, the relevant rules will apply.

For example:

John's book   το βιβλίο του Γιάννη
Nikos' house   το σπίτι του Νίκου

Anna's mother   η μητέρα της 'Αννας
Daphne's apartment   το διαμέρισμα της Δάφνης

Notice that all the names reflect the correct genitive endings for their spellings!

The Plural

In the plural, all nouns and modifiers, <u>regardless of their gender</u>, change in the same way. These are the changes:

1. the plural, genitive article is always των.
2. all nouns and modifiers take the ending ων.

Here are some examples, *nominative* case first, then *genitive*:

NOM.	the boring lesson (boring — ανιαρός)	το ανιαρό μάθημα
GEN.	the end of the boring lessons	το τέλος των ανιαρών μαθημάτων

NOM.	all the little children	όλα τα μικρά παιδιά
GEN.	the names of all of the little children	τα ονόματα όλων των μικρών παιδιών

NOM.	our sisters	οι αδελφές μας
GEN.	our sister's clever friends	οι έξυπνες φίλες των αδελφών μας

NOM.	the beautiful Greek Islands	τα όμορφα ελληνικά νησιά
GEN.	the restaurants of the beautiful Greek islands	τα εστιατόρια των όμορφων ελληνικών νησιών

Here are the plural forms for the irregular adjectives:

υγιών
υγιών
υγιών

παχιών
παχιών
παχιών

πλατιών
πλατιών
πλατιών

Can you translate these phrases?

1. the stores of the beautiful, old streets of New York
2. the faces of the happy people of the small villages of Greece
   (face — το πρόσωπο)
3. the bodies of the weak, old people
4. the beautiful colors of the brand new cars

Now we will look at the genitive case with indefinite articles:

The indefinite article for *masculine* and *neuter* nouns is ενός.

Here are some examples:

a friend's house
το σπίτι ενός φίλου

the smile of a child
το χαμόγελο ενός παιδιού

the sunshine of a morning in (of) spring
η λιακάδα ενός πρωινού της άνοιξης

the accent of a Frenchman (accent — η προφορά)
η προφορά ενός Γάλλου

The indefinite article for *feminine* nouns is **μιας**.

<u>Here are some examples</u>:

the love of a mother (love — **η αγαπή**)
η αγαπή μιας μητέρας

a day's work
η δουλειά μιας μέρας

the home of an elderly woman
το σπίτι μιας ηλικιωμένης γυναίκας

the work of a student (fem.)
η δουλειά μιας μαθήτριας

the difficulty of a European language (European — **Ευρωπαϊκός**)
η δυσκολία μιας Ευρωπαϊκής γλώσσας

How would you say...?

1. a photograph of a country taverna
2. the smile of a curious student
3. the streets of a European city

A New Preposition: μεταξύ — between

This preposition always takes the *genitive* case.

<u>EXAMPLES</u>:

The store is between my house and his house.
Το μαγαζί βρίσκεται μεταξύ του σπιτιού μου και του σπιτιού του.

The store is between the two buildings.
Το μαγαζί βρίσκεται μεταξύ των δύο κτιρίων.

Expressing Age with the Genitive Case

We also use the genitive case to express <u>age</u>.

Q: How old is she?   Πόσων χρονών είναι;
                                 (<u>literally</u>: Of how many years is she?)
A: She is eleven years old.   Είναι ένδεκα χρονών.

Q: How old is he?   Πόσων χρονών είναι;
A: He is fifteen years old.   Είναι δεκαπέντε χρονών.

*Two exceptions: numbers 3 and 4 and their compound numbers (23, 44, etc.) have genitive forms.

He is three years old.   Είναι <u>τριών</u> χρονών.

She is four years old.   Είναι <u>τεσσάρων</u> χρονών.

Relative Pronouns: Which and Whom

You already know the word **ποιος**, which means *which, what* or *who* and you know how to decline it in nominative and the accusative cases.

The word **ποιος** can also express "which" and "whom" to refer to something or someone that has *already been mentioned.* In this case, a special construction is needed.

Let us look some pairs of sentences to learn this grammatical principle:

1. With whom are you going to Paris?
    Με <u>ποιον</u> πηγαίνεις στο Παρίσι;

2. Peter is the man <u>with whom</u> I am going to Paris.
    Ο Πέτρος είναι ο άνθρωπος <u>με τον οποίο(ν)</u> πηγαίνω στο Παρίσι.

In the second sentence, in which *Peter* has already been mentioned, the accusative is also used, but the word ποιος has changed slightly. Notice that it takes the accusative article τον and the accusative ending ιο(ν).

Here are more examples. In the second sentence of each pair, the relative pronoun refers to something already mentioned:

For which performance are they buying the tickets?
Για <u>ποια</u> παράσταση αγοράζουν τα εισιτήρια; (ticket — το εισιτήριο)

That is the performance <u>for which</u> I am buying the tickets.
Εκείνη είναι η παράσταση <u>για την οποία</u> αγοράζουν τα εισιτήρια.

In which car shall we go?
Σε <u>ποιο</u> αυτοκίνητο θα πάμε;

That's the car <u>in which</u> we will go.
Εκείνο είναι το αυτοκίνητο <u>με το οποίο</u> θα πάμε.

In which way did you write the story?
Με ποιον τρόπο έγραψες την ιστορία;

I like the way <u>in which</u> you wrote the story.
Μ'αρέσει ο τρόπος <u>με τον οποίον</u> έγραψες την ιστορία.

Here are some examples using *plural* nouns. Notice the *plural accusative* endings:

Those are the customers <u>about whom</u> we spoke.
Εκείνοι είναι οι πελάτες <u>για τους οποίους</u> μιλήσαμε.

Those are the women <u>with whom</u> they worked.
Εκείνες είναι οι γυναίκες <u>με τις οποίες</u> δούλεψαν.

Those are the children <u>with whom</u> we played.
Εκείνα είναι τα παιδιά <u>με τα οποία</u> παίξαμε.

Using the above models, try translating these:

1. Is that the child for whom you bought the toys?
2. Is she the teacher about whom you spoke?
3. This is the easy way in which I learned Greek.

Whose

To express this idea, we will use this same construction, but in the <u>genitive</u> case. We will look at one example in each gender and one in the plural.

<u>MASC.</u>
He is the teacher <u>whose</u> whole class is going to the museum.
Είναι ο δάσκαλος <u>του οποίου</u> όλη η τάξη πηγαίνει στο μουσείο.

<u>Literally</u>: He is the teacher <u>of whom</u> the class is going to the museum.

<u>FEM.</u>
This is the woman <u>whose</u> beautiful daughter knows my son.
Αυτή είναι η γυναίκα <u>της οποίας</u> η όμορφη κόρη ξέρει το(ν) γιό μου.

<u>Literally</u>: This is the woman <u>of whom</u> the beautiful daughter knows my son.

<u>NEU.</u>
That is the Chinese child <u>whose</u> mother left him here.
Εκείνος είναι το κινέζικο παιδί <u>του οποίου</u> η μητέρα του το άφησε εδώ.

<u>Literally</u>: That is the Chinese child <u>of whom</u> his mother left him here.

<u>PL.</u>
These are the German men <u>whose</u> wives traveled to Italy.
Αυτοί είναι οι Γερμανοί <u>των οποίων</u> οι γυναίκες ταξίδεψαν στην Ιταλία.

Translate:

1. That is the other customer whose wife came here today.
2. She is the Portuguese woman whose son studied in England.
3. These are the Americans whose wonderful children are visiting us.

Negative Expressions

As you can see from these phrases in the dialogue, Greek, unlike English, uses a double negative:

Μου φαίνεται πως <u>δεν</u> υπάρχει <u>κανένας</u> μαθητής ...

... και <u>κανένας</u> στην τάξη μας <u>δεν</u> έχασε ...

Here is a list of "positive" words with their "negative" opposites:

something	κάτι	nothing	τίποτα, τίποτε
everything	τα πάντα		
some, any	κάτι, μερικός	none, not one	κανένας, κανείς (masc.)*
			καμιά (fem.)
			κανένα (neu.)
someone	κάποιος	no one, not one,	κανένας*,
anyone	ο καθένας	nobody	καμιά
			κανένα
everywhere	πάντου	nowhere	πουθενά
somewhere	κάπου		
always	πάντοτε	never	ποτέ, καμιά φορά

---

*accusative for both words: κανένα(ν)

sometimes,	πότε-πότε		ποτέ, καμιά φορά
ever	κάπου-κάπου		ποτέ, καμιά φορά
	κάποτε-κάποτε		ποτέ, καμιά φορά
	μερικές φορές		ποτέ, καμιά φορά

| sometime, at a certain time | κάποτε | | |

| someday | κάποια μέρα | | |

| somehow | κάπως | not at all | καθόλου |

Let's see how these words are used. We will look at a <u>positive</u> statement first, then a <u>negative</u> statement, then a <u>question</u> and its <u>answer</u>. After each sentence is a *rule* for you to learn:

Positive Statement: He <u>sometimes</u> goes to the theatre.
                           Πηγαίνει <u>κάπου-κάπου</u> στο θέατρο.

Use a word from the left-hand column for <u>positive statements</u>.

Negative Statement: He <u>never</u> goes to the theatre.
                           <u>Δεν</u> πηγαίνει <u>ποτέ</u> στο θέατρο.

The <u>double negative</u> used with the <u>negative</u> word from the right-hand column.

Q: Do you <u>ever</u> go to the theatre?
    Πηγαίνεις <u>ποτέ</u> στο θέατρο;

In a question, a <u>negative</u> word used <u>without</u> the word **δεν** means its <u>opposite</u>. (In the above sentence, the word <u>never</u> means <u>ever</u>.)

.

A: No, I <u>never</u> go to the theatre.
     Όχι, <u>δεν</u> πηγαίνω <u>ποτέ</u> στο θέατρο.

This is a negative statement. The <u>double negative</u> is used with the negative word.

Let's look at another set of examples, repeating the rules:

He is going <u>somewhere</u>.
Πηγαίνει <u>κάπου</u>.

Use a word from the left-hand column for <u>positive statements</u>.

I am <u>not</u> going <u>anywhere</u>.
<u>Δεν</u> πηγαίνω <u>πουθενά</u>.

The <u>double negative</u> used with the <u>negative</u> word.

Are you going <u>somewhere</u> (anywhere)?
Πηγαίνεις <u>πουθενά</u>;

In a question, a <u>negative</u> word is used <u>without</u> the word δεν to mean its <u>opposite</u>.

No I am not going anywhere.
Όχι, <u>δεν</u> πηγαίνω <u>πουθενά</u>.

The <u>double negative</u> used with the <u>negative</u> word.

Look at the sets of examples and note how these rules apply:

Someone is coming here today.
Κάποιος έρχεται εδώ σήμερα.

No one is coming here today.
Κανένας δεν έρχεται εδώ σήμερα.

Is someone coming here today?
Έρχεται κανένας εδώ σήμερα;

No, no one is coming here today.
Όχι, κανένας δεν έρχεται εδώ σήμερα.

Someone is in the garden.
Κάποιος είναι στον κήπο.

No one is in the garden.
Κανένας δεν είναι στον κήπο.

Do you see someone in the garden?
Βλέπετε κανένα στον κήπο;

No, I don't see anyone in the garden.
Όχι, δε βλέπω κανένα στον κήπο.

I always shop for groceries before going home.
Πάντοτε ψωνίζω τα τρόφιμα πριν πάω στο σπίτι.

I never shop for groceries.
Ποτέ δεν ψωνίζω τα τρόφιμα.

Do you always shop for groceries before going home?
Ψωνίζεις ποτέ τα τρόφιμα πριν πάς στο σπίτι;

No, I never shop for groceries.
Όχι, ποτέ δεν ψωνίζω τα τρόφιμα.

Try these on your own, applying the rules you have just learned:

I have something for you.
I have nothing for you.
Do you have something for me?
No, I have nothing for you.

I visit her sometimes.
I never visit her.
Does he ever visit her?
No, he never visits her.

She is inviting someone to the theatre.
She is not inviting anyone to the theatre.
Are we inviting someone to the theatre?
No, we are not inviting anyone.

We always travel to Greece in the fall.
We never travel to Greece in the spring.
Do you travel to Greece sometimes?
No, I never travel to Greece.

Numbers: 100 – 1000

100	εκατό
200	διακόσιοι, ες, α
300	τριακόσιοι, ες, α
400	τετρακόσιοι, ες, α
500	πεντακόσιοι, ες, α
600	εξακόσιοι, ες, α
700	επτακόσιοι, ες, α
800	οκτακόσιοι, ες, α
900	εννιακόσιοι, ες, α
1000	χίλιοι, χίλιες, χίλια

To count, we always use the number in the neuter gender. The numbers with endings are used to modify nouns, as in the exercise below:

How would you say…?

243 small children
697 large books
156 important ideas

CULTURAL TIP

An Important Artistic Contribution

One of the most important concepts in realistic art of modern times arose out of an evolutionary step in Greek sculpture: the transition from the portrayal of the human figure as stiff and military, with its weight evenly distributed on both legs, to the figure in counterpoise—an uneven distribution of weight.

One might ask why this shift, both literally and figuratively, was so significant. Its importance lies in its freeing up of the figure from an angular and rigid posture to a relaxed, more human stance in which the character's emotions would be visible and discernible.

Let us look at the *kouros* (youth) and *kore* (maiden), the Greek sculptures of the Archaic period (about 600–500 B.C.). They are often seen in museums and books, as they were abundantly produced during that time period. The *kouros* is a nude male figure who stands straight, with one foot in front of the other. He is tense and rigid, his eyes stare straight ahead, his mouth is fixed in a serious, unrevealing expression. His hair, sculpted in a braided wig, hangs straight down his back and his fists are clenched at his sides. He portrays a bodily ideal of symmetry and perfect proportion.

His counterpart, the *kore*, who is clothed in a soft garment, appears about 100 years later. She also assumes a rigid posture, but there are some changes. Her braided hair is draped down her shoulders in a gentle curve and her face bears a somewhat optimistic expression punctuated by the "archaic smile"—a soupçon of a smile that is barely there and reveals almost nothing.

No one knows whom these figures represented or why so many of them appeared during the Archaic era. Though they are human in form, they are missing something of their humanity. And that "something" makes itself known during the Classical era, around 450 B.C.

It was then that the Greeks discovered the key to imbuing a figure with truly human qualities: the technique of creating a figure standing on one leg while the other leg remains free or mobile, in what is called *counterpoise*.

Counterpoise allows the figure to lunge forward to lance a weapon, to fall on its knees in despair or to simply stand in an easy pose. Counterpoise infuses the figure with more curves and fewer angles, with more qualities of a human and less with those of a deity. With the swiveling of the shoulders, the forward pitch of the spine or the gentle extension of the neck, what has to follow naturally is more emotion through the movement of the body. In counterpoise, we see the blending of movement of the body with the expression of the heart, these both coming forward in more explicit facial expression.

As a result of this technique, we see faces that are closer to life as it is really lived. Most poignantly, we can experience *pathos*—the Greek concept of suffering coupled with dignity. Pathos lifts us one step above sympathy to a place of compassion and admiration for the sufferer. The viewer is moved emotionally, but without revulsion or pain.

And so when we see a piece of Greek sculpture of the Classical era, we are witnessing western civilization's arrival to a place of better understanding of the human spirit. We can appreciate the transition from the Archaic era's rigid embodiment of humankind to portrayals of humans much more like ourselves—humans who are vulnerable and who are affected by the world around them, humans who experience the full range of their emotions.

LESSON 12

ο Διάλογος:

Nikos, Daphne, Anna and Aliki meet at the café to talk about their plans to keep in touch after school is over.

Άννα: Γειά σας! Τι νέα;

Νίκος: Όλα πολύ καλά. Είσαι έτοιμη να φύγεις από την Ελλάδα;

Άννα: Λοιπόν, πρώτα απ'όλα, θα πάω με τους γονείς μου να περάσουμε μια εβδομάδα στην Σαντορίνη μέχρι τις τριάντα του μηνός. Ύστερα, θα γυρίσουμε, και οι τρεις μας, στις Ηνωμένες Πολιτείες. Αφού γυρίσω, θα αρχίσω τις σπουδές μου στο πανεπιστήμιο.

Αλίκη: Κανόνισες όλα με τα εισιτήρια, το διαβατήριό σου, κ.τ.λ.;

Άννα: Ναι, αλλά πρέπει να σας δώσω την διεύθυνσή μου στην Νέα Υόρκη.

Δάφνη: Ναι, την θέλουμε. Και δώσε μας επίσης τον αριθμό τηλεφώνου.

Αλίκη: Θέλουμε να συνεχίσουμε την φιλία μας.

Άννα: Αυτό να λέγεται! Μη(ν) στενοχωριέσαι!

Νίκος: Θα μας λείψεις, Άννα!

Άννα: Θα μου λείψετε και εσείς. Ίσως μπορείτε να με επισκεφθείτε στην Νέα Υόρκη. Θέλω να δείτε την χώρα στην οποία γεννήθηκα.

Δάφνη: Ας ελπίσουμε ότι θα μπορέσουμε! Αλλά στο μεταξύ, θα αλληλογραφούμε. . . . Μπορούμε να σε βοηθήσουμε σχετικά με το ταξίδι σου;

Dialogue:

Anna: Hey, there! What's new?

Nikos: Everything is fine. Are you ready to leave Greece?

Anna: Well, first of all, I am going with my parents to spend a week in Santorini until the 30th of the month. Then, the three of us will go back to the United States. After I return, I will begin my studies at the university.

Aliki: Did you arrange everything with the tickets, your passport, etc.?

Anna: Yes, but I have to give you my address in New York.

Daphne: Yes, we want it. And also give us your telephone number.

Aliki: We want to continue with our friendship.

Anna: That goes without saying! Not to worry!

Nikos: We'll miss you, Anna!

Anna: I will miss you too. Maybe you can visit me in New York. I want you to see the country where I was born.

Daphne: Let's hope that we can (do that). But in the meantime, we'll write to each other. Can we help you with the (things) related to your trip?

Άννα: Όχι, ευχαριστώ. Κανόνισα κιόλας όλες τις λεπτομέρειες. Μόλις φτασαν οι γονείς μου και μου έφεραν όλα αυτά που χρειάζομαι.

Δάφνη: Πώς θα συνεχίσεις να καλυτερεύεις τα ελληνικά σου;

Άννα: Θα πρέπει να διαβάζω κάτι στα ελληνικά κάθε μέρα... ίσως μια εφημερίδα ή ένα περιοδικό.

Αλίκη: Νομίζεις ότι τα Αγγλικά είναι τόσο δύσκολα όσο τα Ελληνικά;

Άννα: Όχι, νομίζω ότι είναι πιο δύσκολα από τα ελληνικά. Τα αγγλικά δεν είναι φωνητικά, σαν τα ελληνικά.

Νίκος: Λοιπόν, ας κάνουμε πρόποση—ας περιμένουμε τη μέρα που θα είμαστε πάλι μαζί.

Δάφνη: Ναι, στο επανιδείν!

Anna: No, thanks. I took care of all the details. My parents just got here and they brought everything that I need.

Daphne: How will you continue improving your Greek?

Anna: I will have to read something in Greek every day ... maybe a newspaper or a magazine.

Aliki: Do you think that English is as hard as Greek?

Anna: No, I think that it is more difficult than Greek. English is not phonetic, like Greek.

Nikos: Well, let's make a toast—let's look forward to (<u>literally</u>: let's wait for) the day when we will be together again.

Daphne: Yes, let's drink to seeing each other again!

VOCABULARY

αλληλογραφώ	to keep in touch, to write to each other
ο αριθμός τηλεφώνου	telephone number
αφού	after (it is followed by future form of verb *without* **θα**)
βοηθώ	to help (takes d.o.p.)
γεννιέμαι	to be born
το διαβατήριο	passport
η διεύθυνση	address
η εφημερίδα	newspaper
καλυτερεύω	to improve
κανονίζω	to arrange, take care of
λείπω	to be missing from
η λεπτομέρεια	detail
περιμένω	to wait for
το περιοδικό	magazine
η πρόποση	toast
οι σπουδές	studies
ύστερα	then
φέρνω	to bring
η φιλία	friendship
φωνητικός	phonetic
η χώρα	country

SMALL BUT IMPORTANT WORDS FOR SENTENCE BUILDING

μην	don't, not
πάλι	again
πιο	more
σαν	like (followed by the acc. case).

USEFUL EXPRESSIONS AND COMPOUND WORDS

Αυτό να λέγεται!	That goes without saying!
Δώσε μας	give us
στο επανιδείν!	Let's drink to when we will be together again!
Μη(ν) στενοχωριεσαι!	Not to worry!
πρώτα απ'όλα	first of all
στο μεταξύ	in the meantime
σχετικά με	relating to
Τι νέα;	What's new?

GRAMMATICAL NOTES AND EXERCISES

New Verbs from the Dialogue

Regular Verbs:

φέρνω

φέρνω	φέρνουμε
φέρνεις	φέρνετε
φέρνει	φέρνουν

FUTURE (you fill in the rest!)

θα φέρω	θα
θα	θα
θα	θα

PAST

έφερα

περιμένω

περιμένω	περιμένουμε
περιμένεις	περιμένετε
περιμένει	περιμένουν

FUTURE

θα περιμένω	θα
θα	θα
θα	θα

περίμενα

καλυτερεύω

καλυτερεύω	καλυτερεύουμε
καλυτερεύεις	καλυτερεύετε
καλυτερεύει	καλυτερεύουν

F_{UTURE}

θα καλυτερέψω	θα
θα	θα
θα	θα

P_{AST}

καλυτέρεψα

κανονίζω

κανονίζω	κανονίζουμε
κανονίζεις	κανονίζετε
κανονίζει	κανονίζουν

F_{UTURE}

θα κανονίσω	θα
θα	θα
θα	θα

P_{AST}

κανόνισα

A Special Case: λείπω — to be missing from

When we want to express the idea that we "miss" someone," we say, literally, that the person is "missing to me." To do this, we use the verb λείπω
preceded by the *indirect object pronoun*. Here are some examples:

I miss you.	**Μου λείπεις.** (You are missing to me.)
We miss him.	**Μας λείπει.** (He is missing to us.)
She misses them.	**Της λείπουν.** (They are missing to her).
We miss them.	**Μας λείπουν.** (They are missing to us.)

The <u>future</u> of λείπω is θα λείψω, etc.

The past is έλειψα.

Contracted Verbs

βοηθώ

βοηθώ	**βοηθούμε**
βοηθείς	**βοηθείτε**
βοηθεί	**βοηθούν**

<u>FUTURE</u>

θα βοηθήσω	**θα βοηθήσουμε**
θα βοηθήσεις	**θα βοηθήσετε**
θα βοηθήσει	**θα βοηθήσουν**

<u>PAST</u> (you fill in the rest!)

βοήθησα

αλληλογραφώ

αλληλογραφώ	αλληλογραφούμε
αλληλογραφείς	αλληλογραφείτε
αλληλογραφεί	αλληλογραφούν

FUTURE

θα αλληλογραφήσω	θα
θα	θα
θα	θα

PAST

αλληλογράφησα

Reflexive Verbs

γεννιέμαι

γεννιέμαι	γεννιόμαστε
γεννιέσαι	γεννιόσαστε
γεννιέται	γεννιούνται

FUTURE

θα γεννηθώ	θα
θα	θα
θα	θα

PAST

γεννήθκα

Translate these sentences, using the verbs you have just learned:

1. What are you going to bring to my house on Sunday?
2. How will you improve your French?

3. I arranged everything related to my studies at the university.
4. She did not help us at all.
5. We will write to each other again.
6. Where were they born?

A useful little word: μην — don't, not

You have seen this word in the dialogue used in this expression:
Να μην στενοχωριεσαι! (Like δεν, this word can drop its final ν before certain consonants and be written as μη.)

Μην functions as a word that injects the idea of "don't" before a verb in the continuous future. When it is placed <u>after</u> the word να, as in να μη στενοχωριέσαι, it acts as a sort of negative command. You are telling the addressee "don't," as in "Not to worry!" You may say it as a *very* simple command, like this:

EXAMPLES: Don't talk like that!   Μην μιλάς έτσι!
          Don't come today.   Μην έρχεσαι σήμερα.

How would you say…?

1. Don't read that book.
2. Don't come into the kitchen.
3. Don't arrive late!

In these sentences, the subject is really <u>you</u>, because the speaker is telling <u>you</u> not to do something. In a sentence where we are talking about someone else, the structure is a little different:

EXAMPLE: She told him <u>not to do</u> it. Του είπε <u>να μην το κάνει</u>.

In this sentence, the subject is <u>she</u>. Look at the word order of the phrase "not to do": The word μην comes <u>between</u> the two pieces of the continuous future.

EXAMPLE: He asked her <u>not to send</u> her the money.
      Ζήτησε απ'αυτήν <u>να μην του στέλνει</u> τα λεφτά.

How would you say...?

1. He told me not to buy that house.
2. They asked us not to study in the library.

You can also use **μην** to negate the commands that you have learned that begin with "Let's." Notice that **μην** comes after the word **Ας**.

Let's do it.	Ας το κάνουμε.
Let's <u>not</u> do it.	Ας μην το κάνουμε.

Let's leave now!	Ας φύγουμε τώρα!
Let's <u>not</u> leave now!	Ας μην φύγουμε τώρα!

At the next level, when you learn commands, the word **μην** will be more useful to you.

Expressing Dates

What is the date?   **Ποια είναι η ημερομηνία;** or
                         Πόσες του μηνός έχουμε σήμερα;

Dates are expressed in cardinal numbers, except for the <u>first</u> day of the month, which uses the <u>ordinal</u>.

Today is (the) 1st of the month.   **Σήμερα είναι πρώτη του μηνός.**

Today is (the) 1st of January.   **Σήμερα είναι πρώτη Ιανουαρίου.**

Today is the 22nd of April.   **Σήμερα είναι είκοσι δύο Απριλίου.**
                                   (Notice that the month is expressed in the <u>genitive</u> case.)

Yesterday was June 14th.   **Χθες ήταν δεκατέσσερεις Ιουνίου.**
(We use the <u>feminine</u> form of the number twenty-four because we are referring to **η μέρα**—the day—which is <u>feminine</u>.)

How would you say…?

the 16th of March
the 23rd of November

Expressing years

I was born in 1954.   Γεννήθηκα το χίλια εννεακόσια πενήντα τέσσερα.
(Here, we use the <u>neuter</u> form of the number four because we are referring
to **το έτος** — the year.)

Answer these questions in Greek:

1. Πότε είναι τα γενέθλιά σου;
2. Ποια είναι η ημερομηνία;

Telling Time

Τι ώρα είναι;   What time is it?

For <u>whole</u> numbers, we say:

Είναι μία <u>η ώρα</u>.   It is one o'clock.
Είναι μία <u>η ώρα το απόγευμα</u>.   It is one o'clock in the afternoon.

Είναι πέντε <u>η ώρα</u>.   It is five o'clock.
Είναι πέντε <u>η ώρα το πρωί</u>.   It is five o'clock in the morning.

For the <u>half</u> hour, we say:

Είναι δέκα <u>και μισή</u>.   It is ten thirty. (It is half past ten.)
Είναι δέκα <u>και μισή τη νύχτα</u>.   It is ten thirty at night.

For the <u>quarter</u> hour, we say:

Είναι <u>τρεις και τέταρτο</u>.	It is a <u>quarter after</u> three.
Είναι <u>τρεις παρά τέταρτο</u>.	It is a <u>quarter to</u> three.

For <u>specific number segments</u>, we say:

Είναι έξι <u>και δέκα</u> το βράδυ.	It is <u>ten after</u> six in the evening.
Είναι έξι <u>παρά δέκα</u> το βράδυ.	It is <u>ten to</u> six in the evening.

Related expressions

Είναι μία η ώρα <u>περίπου</u>.	It is <u>about</u> one o'clock.
Είναι εννέα παρά δέκα <u>ακριβώς</u>.	It is ten to nine <u>sharp</u>.
<u>Πάει</u> δέκα η ώρα.	It is almost ten o'clock.
Είναι μεσημέρι.	It is noon.
Είναι μεσάνυχτα.	It is midnight.

At what time?	Τι ώρα;

<u>Στην</u> μία η ώρα.	<u>At</u> one o'clock.
Στην μία η ώρα <u>περίπου</u>.	At <u>around</u> one o'clock.

<u>Στις</u> εννέα η ώρα.	<u>At</u> nine o'clock.
Στις εννέα παρά δέκα <u>ακριβώς</u>.	At ten to nine <u>sharp</u>. (At <u>exactly</u> ten to nine.)

το μεσημέρι	at noon
τα μεσάνυχτα	at midnight

Expressing seconds and minutes

μία στιγμή	a second
ένα λεπτό	a minute

He left a second ago.	Έφυγε μία στιγμή πριν.
I will be there in 15 minutes.	Θα είμαι εκεί σε δεκαπέντε λεπτά.

For practice, translate these sentences, using the time expressions you have just learned:

1. The performance begins at 8:15 P.M.
2. We arrived home at about 11:05 A.M.
3. It is exactly 10:55 P.M.
4. They have to leave at 4:30 sharp.
5. We will eat at about 6:45 in the evening.

Adverbs

An adverb is a word that describes a verb. In English, words such as *slowly, carefully, quietly, well, quickly*, etc. are adverbs.

EXAMPLES: How does he walk? He walks *slowly*.
          How does she speak Greek? She speaks <u>well</u>.

As you may have figured out by now, a Greek adverb is *usually* formed by replacing an adjective's **ος, η, o**, etc. ending with the letter **α**.

You already know some adverbs:

βέβαια	certainly
γενικά	generally
κανονικά	regularly
προσεκτικά	carefully
εύκολα	easily
καλά	well
καθαρά	clearly
<u>exception</u>: **δυστυχώς**	unfortunately

Can you make adverbs out of these adjectives?

ADJECTIVE	ADVERB	ENGLISH MEANING
απλός		
αδιάφορος		
σωστός		
ήσυχος		
δύσκολος		

Translate:

1. He spoke clearly and correctly.
2. Let's walk carefully and calmly.
3. Does she write easily or with difficulty?
4. She answered me indifferently.
5. I'll explain it simply.

Prepositions

This part of speech refers to words that indicate <u>location</u> and <u>direction</u>. You have learned many prepositions during the lessons in this book. Here are the prepositions you already know:

after	μετά (followed by acc. + noun)
	αφού (followed by future form of verb *without* θα)
behind	πίσω
between	μεταξύ
by, by way of, with	με
for	για
from, of	από
inside of	μέσα σε
in front of	μπροστά από
near	κοντά (+ σε) -
next to, near	δίπλα (can take σε)
on, in, to, at	σε
together	μαζί με
toward	προς

without	χωρίς
up to, up until	μέχρι

With the exception of **μεταξύ**, which is followed by the genitive case, most prepositions are followed by the *accusative* case. Here are some more prepositions to fill in the complete set.

above, over	πάνω από
alongside	δίπλα
against	κατά
around	γύρω από
below, under	κάτω από
down, down by	κάτω σε
far	μακριά
on top of	πάνω σε
outside of	έξω από
up, up by	πάνω σε

Three more important prepositions:

to the left	αριστερά
to the right	δεξιά
straight ahead	κατευθείαν
backwards	προς τα πίσω

A special case: **απέναντι** — across from

In a sentence like this: "She is sitting across from me," the word <u>me</u> is translated as an i.o.p.: **Κάθεται απέναντί μου.**

Rule: The personal pronoun following this preposition is an i.o.p.

EXAMPLE: They are sitting across from us.   **Κάθονται απέναντί μας.**

But in a sentence like this: "You are sitting across from my sister," you add **από** + the accusative case:

Κάθεσαι απέναντί από την αδελφή μου.

To practice using prepositions, translate these sentences:

1. The newspaper is under the table.
2. They are travelling around the world.
3. Is Greece far from Italy?
4. The chair is against the door.
5. In order to arrive at my house, you have to drive straight ahead.
6. Our magazines are on top of your books.
7. He is walking backwards.
8. He lives in a small apartment above a store.

Comparisons

Here is the simplest method to express these:

Comparisons of Equality: as … (adj.) … as

He is <u>as</u> clever <u>as</u> she.   **Είναι <u>τόσο</u> έξυπνος <u>όσο</u> αυτή.**
(Notice that **οσο** is followed by the *nominative* case.)

Comparisons of Inequality: more … (adj.) …   than
                                 πιο   **από**
                  and
                                 less   … (adj.) …   than
                                 λιγότερο   από

He is <u>more</u> clever <u>than</u> she.   **Είναι <u>πιο</u> έξυπνος <u>από</u> αυτήν.**
(Notice that because of **από**, the *accusative* is used.)

He is <u>less</u> clever than <u>she</u>.   **Είναι <u>λιγότερο</u> έξυπνος <u>από</u> αυτήν.**

For comparisons of both equality and inequality, you can also use the word **σαν**, which means <u>like</u>. Here is the example from the dialogue:

Τα αγγλικά δεν είναι φωνητικά, <u>σαν</u> τα ελληνικά.
English is not phonetic, <u>like</u> Greek.

Special cases: better, worse and bigger

ADJECTIVE		COMPARATIVE	
good	καλός	better	καλύτερος
bad	κακός	worse	χειρότερος
big	μεγάλος	bigger	μεγαλύτερος

Remember: the above comparatives are adjectives and have to be declined, depending upon the context.

Using the models above, translate these sentences to read:

a) "as ...   (adj.) ... as"
b) "more ... (adj.) ... than"
c) "less ... (adj.) ... than"

1. The handicrafts in Portugal are <u>as</u> beautiful <u>as</u> the handicrafts in Spain.
    a)
    b)
    c)

2. Your language is as complicated as mine.
    a)
    b)
    c)

3. The English newspapers are as interesting as the American newspapers.
    a)
    b)
    c)

Using the word σαν, which is always followed by the accusative case, how would you say:

1. They are smart, like their brother.
2. She is not pretty, like her mother.

Superlatives: the most ...

The superlative is expressed in almost the same way as the comparative, except that we insert the definite article in front of the comparative. Let's look at the progression from comparative to superlative:

a large house	ένα μεγάλο σπίτι
a larger house	ένα μεγαλύτερο σπίτι
the largest house	το μεγαλύτερο σπίτι
a small child	ένα μικρό παιδί
a smaller child	ένα πιο μικρό παιδί
the smallest child	το πιο μικρό παιδί

How would you say...?

1. This is the most difficult lesson in the book.
2. That restaurant has the best food in Paris.

Expressing either ... or and neither ... nor

We express *either ... or* with the words ή ... ή (literally: "or ... or")

EXAMPLE:

You may have <u>either</u> tea <u>or</u> coffee. **Μπορείς να πιείς ή τσάι ή καφέ.**

How would you say...?

1. I can visit you either on Monday or on Thursday.
2. We are going either to Italy or to Spain.

We express *neither ... nor* with the words **ούτε ... ούτε** and we use the negative.

<u>EXAMPLE</u>:

I have <u>neither</u> tea <u>nor</u> coffee. <u>**Δεν**</u> έχω <u>**ούτε**</u> τσάι <u>**ούτε**</u> καφέ.

How would you say...?

1. She wants neither this book nor that (one).
2. I can come neither on Monday nor on Friday.

CULTURAL TIP

Good Friends Everywhere

Congratulations. If you have come this far, you have come a long way. By now, you have gained enough knowledge of Greek to communicate in a wide range of situations with a fairly broad vocabulary.

And where will you use your Greek? Perhaps you will travel to Greece for a holiday or for work. Or maybe you will just chat with Greek friends in one of the Greek communities around the world. Fortunately, there are many of these. Some are just small pockets of Greek culture tucked into another culture and some are expansive neighborhoods with their own intricate social structures.

But wherever and whenever you have the chance to speak Greek, it will be as though you have a new circle of good friends. Greek people always appreciate your effort to communicate in their language. They will be quite astonished that you have gone to the trouble of learning it and will be amused and delighted that you were interested enough to enter their culture.

Στο επανιδείν!

APPENDICES

The following tables are useful, practical information that has not been covered yet. The vocabulary contained in these tables is not in your glossary.

APPENDIX 1

Ordinal Numbers

These are adjectives and are given in the masculine.

first	πρώτος
second	δεύτερος
third	τρίτος
fourth	τέταρτος
fifth	πέμπτος
sixth	έκτος
seventh	έβδομος
eighth	όγδοος
ninth	ένατος
tenth	δέκατος
eleventh	ενδέκατος
twelfth	δωδέκατος
thirteenth	δεκάτος τρίτος
fourteenth	δεκάτος τέταρτος
fifteenth	δεκάτος πέμπτος
sixteenth	δεκάτος έκτος
seventeenth	δεκάτος έβδομος
eighteenth	δεκατος ογδοος
nineteenth	δεκάτος ένατος
twentieth	εικοστός
twenty-first	εικοστός πρώτος
thirtieth	τριακοστός

fortieth	τεσσαρακοστός
fiftieth	πεντηκοστός
sixtieth	εξηκοστός
seventieth	εβδομηκοστός
eightieth	ογδοηκοστός
ninetieth	ενενηκοστός
one hundredth	εκατοστός
three hundredth	τριακοστός
one thousandth	χιλιοστός

Appendix 2

The Weather

This is always a good topic of discussion. Here is a little chart to help you:

Πώς είναι ο καιρός;   How is the weather?

rain	It is raining.	It is a rainy day.
η βροχή	Βρέχει.	Είναι βροχερή μέρα.
good weather	It is a beautiful day.	The weather is good.
καλός καιρός	Είναι ωραία μέρα.	Ο καιρός είναι καλός.
bad weather	It is a bad day.	The weather is bad.
άσχημος καιρός	Είναι άσχημη μέρα.	Ο καιρός είναι άσχημος.
fog	It is foggy.	
η ομίχλη	Έχει ομίχλη.	
sun	It is sunny.	
ο ήλιος	Έχουμε λιακάδα. or Έχει λιακάδα.	
heat	It is hot.	
η ζέστη	Κάνει ζέστη.	

humidity	It is humid.	
η υγρασία	Είναι υγρασία. or Έχει υγρασία.	

cold	It is cold.	It is cool.
το κρύο	Κάνει κρύο.	Έχουμε δροσιά. or Είναι δροσερός.

wind	It is windy.
ο άνεμος	Έχει αέρα.

snow	It is snowing.
το χιόνι	Χιονίζει.

cloud	It's cloudy.	It's getting cloudy.
το σύννεφο	Έχει συννεφιά.	Συννεφιάζει.

APPENDIX 3

Expressing Directions

NOUN	ADJECTIVE	PREPOSITION/ADVERB
North	Northern	to the north
ο βορράς	βόρειος, α, ο	προς τον βορρά, βόρεια
South	Southern	to the south
ο νότος	νότιος, α, ο	προς τον νότο, νότια
East	Eastern	to the east
η ανατολή	ανατολικός, ή, ό	προς ανατολάς ανατολικά
West	Western	to the west
η δύση	δυτικός, ή, ό	προς την δύση, δυτικά

APPENDIX 4

In the Neighborhood and City

You have already learned many words pertaining to city life. They are in your glossary and are not included here. Here is a supplementary list to fill in the gaps:

airport	το αεροδρόμιο
bakery	το αρτοπωλείο
bar	το μπαρ
barbershop	ο κομμωτής
bus stop	η στάση λεωφορείου
church	η εκκλησία
florist	ο ανθοπώλης
gas station	το πρατήριο βενζίνης
hairdresser	η κομμώτρια
hospital	το νοσοκομείο
jeweler	ο κοσμηματοπώλης
kiosk	το περίπτερο
movie theater	η αίθουσα κινηματογράφου
park	το πάρκο
pharmacy	το φαρμακείο
police	η αστυνομία
police station	ο αστυνομικός σταθμός
post office	το ταχυδρομείο
shoemaker	ο παπουτσής
square, plaza	η πλατεία
taxi	το ταξί
taxi stand	η στάση ταξί

APPENDIX 5

Clothing, Accessories and Colors

Clothing: τα ρούχα

What is your size?   Ποιο είναι το μέγεθός σου;

apron	η ποδιά
belt	η ζώνη
blouse	η μπλούζα
bra	το σουτιέν
coat	το παλτό
dress	το φόρεμα
hat	το καπέλο
jacket	η ζακέτα
nightgown	η νυχτικιά
pajamas	οι πιτζάμες
panties	η κιλότα γυναικεία
petticoat	το μεσοφόρι
raincoat	το αδιάβροχο
robe	η ρόμπα
scarf	το φουλάρι
shirt	το πουκάμισο
shoes	τα παπούτσια
skirt	η φούστα
slippers	η παντόφλα
socks	η κάλτσα
stockings	η κάλτσα κοντή
suit	το κοστούμι

sweater	το πουλόβερ
T-shirt	η φανέλα
trousers	το πανταλόνι
underwear	τα εσώρουχα

Accessories and Sundries:

button	το κουμπί
hairbrush	η βούρτσα των μαλλιών
comb	η χτένα
jewelry	τα κοσμήματα
umbrella	η ομπρέλα
purse	το πορτοφόλι
wallet	το πορτοφόλι
watch	το ρολόι
zipper	το φερμουάρ

Colors: τα χρώματα

These are adjectives and are given here in the masculine, singular form, *except for those with an asterisk* (these are nouns):

red	κόκκινος
blue	γαλάζιος
yellow	κίτρινος
green	πράσινος
orange	πορτοκαλί
purple	πορφυρός
grey	γκρίζος
black	μαύρος
white	άσπρος
pink	ρόδινος
lilac	μοβ χρώμα*
turquoise	γαλάζο-πράσινος
navy blue	βάθυ-μπλε
light green	ανοιχτό πράσινο χρωμα*
dark green	σκούρο πράσινο χρωμα*

APPENDIX 6

Eating and Drinking

Food and Drink:

breakfast	το πρωϊνό
lunch	το γεύμα
dinner	το δείπνο
juice	ο χυμός
toast	η φρυγανιά
eggs	τα αυγά
bread	το ψωμί
butter	το βούτυρο
salad	η σαλάτα
Greek salad	η χωριάτικη σαλάτα
tomato	η ντομάτα
olive	η ελιά
cheese	το τυρί
appetizers	τα ορεκτικά
meat	το κρέας (pl. — τα κρέατα)
fish	το ψάρι
chicken	το κοτόπουλο
vegetables	τα λαχανικά
potatoes	η πατάτα
rice	το ρύζι

fruit	το φρούτο
watermelon	το καρπούζι
apricot	το βερίκοκο
apple	το μήλο
wine	το κρασί
lemonade	η λεμονάδα
oil	το λάδι
vinegar	το ξίδι
salt	το αλάτι
pepper	το πιπέρι
lemon	το λεμόνι
cream	η κρέμα
cinnamon	η κανέλα
honey	το μέλι
dessert	τα επιδόρπια

Tableware: τα επιτραπέζια

bottle	το μπουκάλι
cup	το φλιτζάνι
dish, plate	το πιάτο
fork	το πιρούνι
knife	το μαχαίρι
napkin	η πετσέτα
pitcher	η κανάτα
platter	η πιατέλα
saucer	το πιατάκι
spoon	το κουτάλι
tablecloth	το τραπεζομάντηλο

APPENDIX 7

Titles and Miscellaneous Expressions

Titles:

In the table below, the first line is singular and the next line is plural.

ENGLISH	NOMINATIVE	ACCUSATIVE	GENITIVE	DIRECT SPEECH
Mr., Sir	ο κύριος	τον κύριο	του κυρίου	κύριε
Gentlemen	οι κύριοι	τους κυρίους	των κυρίων	κύριοι
Miss	η δεσποινίς	την δεσποινίδα	της δεσποινίδος	δεσποινίς
Misses	οι δεσποινίδες	τις δεσποινίδες	των δεσποινίδων	δεσποινίδες
Mrs., Madame	η κυρία	την κυρία	της κυρίας	κυρία
Mesdames	οι κυρίες	τις κυρίες	των κυριών	κυρίες
Ladies and Gentleman	κυρίες και κύριοι			

Miscellaneous Expressions:

Attention! Caution!	**Προσοχή!**
Bon appetit!	**Καλή όρεξη!**
Bon voyage!	**Καλό ταξίδι!**
Bravo!	**Εύγε!**
Congratulations.	**Χρόνια πολλά.**

Excuse me	**Με συγχωρείτε.** or **Συγγνώμη.**
Get well soon.	**Περαστικά.**
Good luck!	**Καλή τύχη!**
Hurry up!	**Γρήγορα!**
I am sorry.	**Λυπάμαι.**
I am very sorry.	**Λυπάμαι πολύ.**
It is wrong.	**Είναι λάθος.**
My condolences.	**Συλλυπητήρια.**
So long, good-bye.	**Γειά χαρά.**

KEY TO EXERCISES

The Greek Alphabet

Lower case spelling and approximate pronunciation:

πως (pos)	ρε (ray)
την (teen)	των (ton)
προς (pross)	ως (ohss)
δρυς (drees)	δεν (then)
θα (thah)	ζω (zoh)

Lesson 2

Gender, Definite and Indefinite Articles:

<u>Masculine Nouns</u>:

The **definite article**:

ο άνδρας	the man
ο κήπος	the garden
ο δάσκαλος	the teacher
ο ταμίας	the cashier
ο φίλος	the friend
ο μαθητής	the student
ο πελάτης	the customer
ο καθρέφτης	the mirror

The **indefinite article**:

ένας άνδρας	a man
ένας κήπος	a garden
ένας δάσκαλος	a teacher
ένας ταμίας	a cashier
ένας φίλος	a friend
ένας μαθητής	a student
ένας πελάτης	a customer
ένας καθρέφτης	a mirror

The Plural: write the plurals here of:

ο πατέρας	οι πατέρες
ο ταμίας	οι ταμίες
ο κήπος	οι κήποι
ο φίλος	οι φίλοι
ο πελάτης	οι πελάτες
ο καθρέφτης	οι καθρέφτες

Feminine Nouns:

The **definite article**:

η γυναίκα	the woman
η δασκάλα	the teacher
η ανάγκη	the need
η διακοπή	the interruption
η νύφη	the bride
η μέθοδος	the method
η είσοδος	the entrance
η Βίβλος	the Bible

The **indefinite article**:

μια γυναίκα	a woman
μια δασκάλα	a teacher
μια ανάγκη	a need
μια διακοπή	an interruption
μια νύφη	a bride
μια μέθοδος	a method
μια είσοδος	an entrance
μια Βίβλος	a Bible

The Plural: write the plurals here of:

η μαθήτρια	οι μαθήτριες
η δασκάλα	οι δασκάλες

η ανάγκη	οι ανάγκες
η διακοπή	οι διακοπές
η πόλη	οι πόλεις
η είσοδος	οι είσοδοι

Neuter Nouns:

The **definite article**:

το κτίριο	the building
το σχέδιο	the plan
το σπίτι	the house
το γυαλί	the glass
το ταξίδι	the trip
το δράμα	the drama
το ρήμα	the verb
το σώμα	the body
το έθνος	the nation
το κράτος	the government
το μέρος	the place

The **indefinite article**:

ένα κτίριο	a building
ένα σχέδιο	a plan
ένα σπίτι	a house
ένα γυαλί	a glass
ένα ταξίδι	a trip
ένα δράμα	a drama
ένα ρήμα	a verb
ένα σώμα	a body
ένα έθνος	a nation
ένα κράτος	a government
ένα μέρος	a place

<u>The Plural</u>: write the plurals here of:

το κτίριο	τα κτίρια
το σχέδιο	τα σχέδια
το γυαλί	τα γυαλιά
το ταξίδι	τα ταξίδια
το ρήμα	τα ρήματα
το σώμα	τα σώματα
το κράτος	τα κράτη
το μέρος	τα μέρη

	GENDER	NOUN W/ DEF. ART.	NOUN W/INDEF. ART.	PL. NOUN W/PL. ART.
τρόπος (way, means)	masc.	ο τρόπος	ένας τρόπος	οι τρόποι
παλάμη (palm)	fem.	η παλάμη	μια παλάμη	οι παλάμες
ενθύμιο (souvenir)	neut.	το ενθύμιο	ένα ενθύμιο	τα ενθύμια
ιδιοκτήτης (owner)	masc.	ο ιδιοκτήτης	ένας ιδιοκτήτης	οι ιδιοκτήτες
πτώμα (corpse)	neut.	πτώμα	ένα πτώμα	τα πτώματα
όνειρο (dream)	neut.	το όνειρο	ένα όνειρο	τα όνειρα
τρίχα (small hair)	fem.	η τρίχα	μια τρίχα	οι τρίχες
αξίνα (pickaxe)	fem.	η αξίνα	μια αξίνα	οι αξίνες
σημάδι (sign)	neut.	το σημάδι	ένα σημάδι	τα σημάδια
ταμίας (cashier)	masc.	ο ταμίας	ένας ταμίας	οι ταμίες

Words in which the accents change position in the plural:

Exercises with είμαι:

1. Ο μαθητής είναι από την Νέα Υόρκη.
2. Οι άνθρωποι είναι εδώ.
3. Είμαστε από την Ελλάδα.
4. Σας αρέσει η Νέα Υόρκη;
5. Η γυναίκα είναι δασκάλα.

Translation:

1. Our house is very small.
2. Why are you here?
3. I am learning Greek and I am from New York.
4. Are you studying art and theatrical works?
5. The student (fem.) is from the U. S.
6. Mr. Pavlos and my mother are from Athens.

Lesson 3

Place the word δεν before each verb in the sentences from Lesson 2, thereby making them negative.

1. Το σπίτι μας δεν είναι πολύ μικρό.
2. Δεν μαθαίνω ελληνικά και δεν είμαι από την Νέα Υόρκη.
3. Δεν σπουδάζετε τέχνη και θεατρικά έργα.
4. Η μαθήτρια δεν είναι από τις Ηνωμένες Πολιτείες.
5. Ο κύριος Πάυλος και η μητέρα μου δεν είναι από την Αθήνα.

Translation:

1. Έχεις πορτοκαλάδα; Έχετε πορτοκαλάδα;
2. Όχι, δεν έχω πορτοκαλάδα αλλά έχω τσάι.
3. Θέλουν καφέ με γάλα.
4. Ευχαριστώ, δεν θέλω νερό.
5. Έχει καφέ και τσάι αλλά θέλουμε γάλα.
6. Θέλει ένα ποτό;

Translation: αρέσω:

SINGULAR:

1. Το τσάι μ'αρέσει πολύ.
2. Το βιβλίο σ'αρέσει;
3. Ναι, ο καφές με ζάχαρι μ'αρέσει.
4. Σ'αρέσει η Αθήνα;

PLURAL:

1. Τα φαγητά στις Ηνωμένες Πολιτείες μ'αρέσουν.
2. Τα θεατρικά έργα σ'αρέσουν.
3. Οι δάσκαλοι εδώ μ'αρέσουν.
4. Σ'αρέσουν οι μαθητές;

Negative Sentences:

1. Δεν μ'αρέσει το τσάι με γάλα.
2. Δεν σ'αρέσει η τέχνη;
3. Δεν μ'αρέσουν τα σπίτια εδώ.
4. Σ'αρέσει το δράμα; Όχι δεν μ'αρέσει.

Verbs:

σπουδάζω — to study

SINGULAR:	σπουδάζω	σπουδάζεις	σπουδάζει
PLURAL:	σπουδάζουμε	σπουδάζετε	σπουδάζουν

ξέρω — to know

SINGULAR:	ξέρω	ξέρεις	ξέρει
PLURAL:	ξέρουμε	ξέρετε	ξέρουν

παίρνω — to take, to have

SINGULAR:	παίρνω	παίρνεις	παίρνει
PLURAL:	παίρνουμε	παίρνετε	παίρνουν

καταλαβαίνω — understand

SINGULAR:	καταλαβαίνω	καταλαβαίνεις	καταλαβαίνει
PLURAL:	καταλαβαίνουμε	καταλαβαίνετε	καταλαβαίνουν

νομίζω — to think

SINGULAR:	νομίζω	νομίζεις	νομίζει
PLURAL:	νομίζουμε	νομίζετε	νομίζουν

θέλω — to want

SINGULAR:	θέλω	θέλεις	θέλει
PLURAL:	θέλουμε	θέλετε	θέλετε

έχω — to have

SINGULAR:	έχω	έχεις	έχει
PLURAL:	έχουμε	έχετε	έχετε

Translation:

1. Παίρνει το τσάι με γάλα.
2. Δεν καταλαβαίνει το βιβλίο.
3. Δεν καταλαβαίνω τα αγγλικά.
4. Ο δάσκαλός μας δεν έχει τα βιβλία.
5. Δεν ξέρω το παιδί.
6. Ο Πέτρος και η Άννα δεν ξέρουν θεατρικά έργα.
7. Σπουδάζεις εδώ; Σπουδάζετε εδώ;
8. Έλα μέσα! Δεν σπουδάζουμε.
9. Μαθαίνει καλά.
10. Νομίζεις;

Interrogative Sentences:

1. Πού είναι η Μαρία;
2. Πού διαβάζει ο Νίκος;
3. Γιατί δεν καταλαβαίνετε;
4. Γιατί σπουδάζει η Άννα εδώ;
5. Τι νομίζετε;
6. Τι διαβάζει ο Νίκος;
7. Ποιος είναι η Μαρία;
8. Ποιος είσαι; Ποιος είστε;
9. Πότε σπουδάζουν;
10. Πώς παίρνεις το τσάι;
11. Πώς παίρνουν το τσάι;
12. Ποια γυναίκα είναι η Άννα;
13. Ποιος άνθρωπος είναι;
14. Ποιος μαθητής είναι ο Νίκος;
15. Τίνος μαθητής είναι ο Νίκος;

Lesson 4

Write the correct form of τέτοιος in front of the noun:

τέτοιος κήπος   τέτοιο σχέδιο
τέτοιοι μαθητές   τέτοια βιβλία
τέτοια μαθήτρια   τέτοιοι άνθρωποι

Write the correct form of πολύς in front of the noun.

πολύς θόρυβος   πολλοί δάσκαλοι
πολλή πορτοκαλάδα   πολύ αίμα
πολλά σπίτια   πολλές ανάγκες

The Accusative Case: masculine nouns:

Translation:

1. Αφήνω τον δίσκο εδώ.
2. Αφήνει έναν δίσκο εδώ.
3. Αφήνουμε τους δίσκους εδώ.
4. Δεν ξέρουν τον πατέρα μας.
5. Ξέρετε τους άνδρες;
6. Δεν έχει τους καθρέφτες.
7. Ξέρετε τον πελάτη;
8. Αγοράζεις έναν καθρέφτη;
9. Καταλαβαίνει τους μαθητές;

The Accusative Case: feminine nouns:

Translation:

1. Έχει μια καρέκλα;
2. Αφήνουμε την καρέκλα εδώ.
3. Έχουμε έναν φίλο στην Αθήνα.
4. Δεν ξέρει την γλώσσα.
5. Δεν ξέρουμε την μαθήτρια.
6. Διαβάζουν τις κάρτες.
7. Δεν ξέρει τις γυναίκες.
8. Δεν ξέρεις τις μεθόδους.

The Accusative Case: neuter nouns:

Translation:

1. Ξέρω το έργο.
2. Αγοράζουμε το γάλα.
3. Δεν καταλαβαίνει το παιδί.
4. Θέλει ένα ποτό.
5. Κάνουμε ένα ταξίδι μαζί.
6. Δεν καταλαβαίνουμε τα ελληνικά.
7. Αγοράζουν τα σπίτια.
8. Ξέρετε το ρήμα;

The Accusative Case with Prepositions: Translation:

1. Θέλώ γάλα στο τσάι.
2. Νομίζω ότι είναι ένας φίλος από το σχολείο.
3. Γιατί αγοράζεις τα βιβλία για την μητέρα μου;
4. Απόψε έχουμε ένα γράμμα από τον δάσκαλό μας.
5. Ίσως οι γυναίκες δεν είναι στην κουζίνα.
6. Τίνος παιδιά είναι στην τάξη;
7. Είναι πάρα πολλή ζάχαρη στον καφέ.
8. Πότε πηγαίνει με τους ανθρώπους στο γραφείο;
9. Είναι μια παράσταση στο θέατρο απόψε;

Translate, using the accusative case.

1. Σε ποιον δρόμο είναι το σπίτι;
2. Σε ποιους δρόμους είναι τα μαγαζιά;
3. Με ποιους δασκάλους σπουδάζεις;
4. Για ποια παιδιά είναι τα παιχνίδια;
5. Δεν έχουμε πολλές καρέκλες στον κήπο μας, αλλά έχω μια καρέκλα στο σπίτι.
6. Αγοράζω πολύ γάλα για τα παιδιά.
7. Πόσες καρέκλες έχετε;
8. Νομίζεις ότι θέλει πολλή πορτοκαλάδα;
9. Δεν καταλαβαίνω τέτοια θεατρικά έργα.
10. Δεν αγοράζω τέτοια βιβλία.
11. Ποια βιβλία αγοράζεις για το σχολείο;
12. Ξέρει ότι έχεις πολλές ιδέες.
13. Δεν έχουμε πολλά λεφτα.

Lesson 5

The Future Tense:

ENGLISH	PRESENT	FUTURE
I read	διαβάζω	θα διαβάσω
I buy	αγοράζω	θα αγοράσω

I celebrate	γιορτάζω	θα γιορτάσω
I think	νομίζω	θα νομίσω
I study	σπουδάζω	θα σπουδάσω
I clean	καθαρίζω	θα καθαρίσω
I return	γυρίζω	θα γυρίσω

Practice sentences:

1. **Πού θα σπουδάσουν αύριο;**
2. **Τι θα αγοράσει για την τάξη;**
3. **Ευχαριστώ, αλλά δεν θα γιορτάσω με τα παιδιά απόψε.**

ENGLISH	PRESENT	FUTURE
I look at	κοιτάζω	θα κοιτάξω
I change	αλλάζω	θα αλλάξω
I play	παίζω	θα παίξω
I frighten	τρομάζω	θα τρομάξω
I shake off	τινάζω	θα τινάξω

Practice sentences:

1. **Τα παιδιά θα παίξουν στην γειτονιά;**
2. **Γιατί θα αλλάξετε το πρόγραμμα;**
3. **Δυστυχώς, δεν θα κοιτάξω το βιβλίο απόψε.**

ENGLISH	PRESENT	FUTURE
I travel	ταξιδεύω	θα ταξιδέψω
I cook	μαγειρεύω	θα μαγειρέψω
I believe	πιστεύω	θα πιστέψω
I work	δουλεύω	θα δουλέψω
I accompany	συνοδεύω	θα συνοδέψω

Practice sentences:

1. **Το εστιατόριο θα μαγειρέψει για την οικογένεια;**
2. **Θα δουλέψεις στο καφενείο απόψε;**
3. **Θα πιστέψει τις ιστορίες;**

ENGLISH	PRESENT	FUTURE
I write	γράφω	θα γράψω
I nod	γνέφω	θα γνέψω
I describe	περιγράφω	θα περιγράψω

Practice sentences:

1. Πώς θα περιγράψουν την παράσταση;
2. Θα γράψεις στους φίλους μας στην εξοχή;
3. Θα γνέψει;

ENGLISH	PRESENT	FUTURE
I leave	αφήνω	θα αφήσω
I pay	πληρώνω	θα πληρώσω
I lift	σηκώνω	θα σηκώσω
I finish	τελειώνω	θα τελειώσω

Practice sentences:

1. Θα πληρώσω τον λογαριασμό στο εστιατόριο.
2. Δεν θα σηκώσουν τα βιβλία.
3. Θα αφήσουμε τα ευθύμια εδώ.

ENGLISH	PRESENT	FUTURE
I know	ξέρω	θα ξέρω
I have	έχω	θα έχω
I want	θέλω	θα θέλω
I do	κάνω	θα κάνω
I am	είμαι	θα είμαι
it is pleasing	αρέσει	θα αρέσει

Practice sentences:

1. Τι θα κάνουμε αύριο με την Άννα;
2. Θα θέλουν καφέ.
3. Δεν θα σ'αρέσει τα φαγητά εκεί.

<u>Exercise</u>:

Change the following sentences to the future.

1. Θα μαγειρέψουμε το φαγητό στην κουζίνα.
2. Νίκος δεν θα πιστέψει την ιστορία.
3. Οι φίλοι μας θα πάρουν τον καφέ τους μαζί.
4. Τι θα σπουδάσετε στο σχολείο;
5. Η παράσταση θα μ' αρέσει πολύ.
6. Θα κοιτάξεις το παιχνίδι;
7. Θα τρομάξετε τα παιδιά.
8. Θα μάθουν την μουσική για την παράσταση.
9. Θα καταλάβει την γλώσσα;

<u>Translate</u>:

1. Πού θα πάμε αύριο;
2. Θα πάτε στο θέατρο με την τάξη;
3. Οι μουσικοί θα πάνε στην εξοχή μαζί.

<u>Translate</u>:

1. Πηγαίνει το παιδί στο σχολείο στην γειτονιά.
2. Θα πάει το παιδί στο σχολείο αύριο.
3. Πηγαίνουμε την Άννα στο μαγαζί γιατί θέλει να αγοράσει ευθύμια.
4. Δυστυχώς, δεν θα πάνε την Άννα στο θέατρο.
5. Πηγαίνω την οικογένεια στο σπίτι.
6. Λοιπόν, θα πάω την οικογένεια στο σπίτι.

Write the sentences substituting **άμα** for the other three words.

1. Άμα πάω στο μαγαζί, θα αγοράσω τα τρόφιμα.
2. Άμα δουλέψει αύριο, δεν θα πάει στο θέατρο.
3. Άμα γυρίσουμε, θα γράψουμε το γράμμα.

Translate:

1. Θα αφήνετε τα βιβλία σας εδώ όταν πάτε στην δουλειά.
2. Θα αγοράζει τα δώρα για την οικογένεια.

Helping Verbs: translate:

1. Θέλει να πάει στα μαγαζιά στην γειτονιά μας.
2. Νομίζω ότι θέλει να κάνω καφέ για τους μουσικούς.
3. Θέλει να γιορτάσουμε μαζί την άλλη φορά.
4. Ξέρει ότι θέλουμε να πληρώσουν τον λογαρισμό στο καφενείο.
5. Δεν ξέρω γιατί θέλεις να γυρίσεις αύριο.
6. Θέλουμε να πάμε την Άννα στο θέατρο αλλά δυστυχώς, έχει πολλή δουλειά για το σχολείο.
7. Παρακαλώ έλα μέσα ... θέλουμε να σηκώσεις τις καρέκλες.

To have to (must) — πρέπει: translate:

1. Πρέπει να καθαρίσει το σπίτι.
2. Πρέπει να γυρίσουμε στο Παρίσι.

In the negative: translate:

1. Δεν πρέπει να πληρώσεις τον λογαριασμό.
2. Δεν πρέπει να αλλάξει το σχέδιο.

In the future: translate:

1. Δυστυχώς, θα πρέπει να γράψετε στο σχολείο.
2. Θα πρέπει να αγοράσουμε τα δώρα από το Παρίσι.

In the *negative* in the *future*: translate:

1. Δεν θα πρέπει να περιγράψουμε την παράσταση.
2. Δεν θα πρέπει να σηκώσει τα βιβλία για τις γυναίκες.

Practice sentences using πρέπει:

1. Πρέπει να σπουδάσουμε την Βιβλο μαζί.
2. Θα πρέπει να σπουδάσουμε την Βίβλο μαζί αύριο.
3. Ο Νίκος και η Άννα πρέπει να πάνε στο θέατρο απόψε.
4. Θα πρέπει να πάνε στο θέατρο αύριο.
5. Δεν πρέπει να αγοράσεις τα τρόφιμα.
6. Δεν θα πρέπει να αγοράσεις τα τρόφιμα αύριο.

The verb πρέπει, translated as "should":

1. Ίσως πρέπει να πάει στο μαγαζί με τον φίλο μου.
2. Κάθε άνθρωπος πρέπει να καθαρίσει το σπίτι.
3. Δεν πρέπει να αλλάξουμε το πρόγραμμα.
4. Δεν πρέπει να τρομάξεις τα παιδιά.

Using αρέσει, can you say...?

1. Μ'αρέσει να δουλέυω στο σπίτι γιατί είναι πολύς θόρυβος στο σχολείο.
2. Γιατί δεν σ'αρέσει να παίζεις στον κήπο;
3. Σ'αρέσει να διαβάζετε βιβλία στα ελληνικά;

Lesson 6

Future	Past	English translation
1. θα σπουδάσεις	σπούδασες	you studied
2. θα συνοδέψουμε	συνοδέψαμε	we accompanied
3. θα πιστέψω	πίστεψα	I believed
4. θα παίξετε	παίξατε	you played
5. θα αλλάξουν	άλλάξαν	they changed
6. θα γιορτάσεις	γιόρτασες	you celebrated
7. θα τελειώσω	τελείωσα	I finished
8. θα αφήσουν	άφησαν	they left

How would you say...?

1. Σπουδάσαμε μαζί και μετά συνοδέψαμε τους φίλους μας στην Ακρόπολη;
2. Δυστυχώς, η Ελληνίδα δεν πίστεψε την ιστορία.
3. Πότε άλλαξε τα λεφτά;
4. Γιατί αποφάσισες να πας στην Νέα Υόρκη;
5. Για παράδειγμα, πόσα παιδιά γιόρτασαν μαζί;
6. Τελειώσατε τα χειροτεχνήματα για το σχολείο;
7. Τελειώσαμε την δουλειά και μετά ψωίσαμε στο μαγαζί.
8. Δεν συνοδέψαμε την Άννα στην είσοδο.

PRESENT	FUTURE	PAST
1. μαγειρεύεις	θα μαγειρέψεις	μαγείρεψες
2. κοιτάζουν	θα κοιτάξουν	κοίταξαν
3. σηκώνω	θα σηκώσω	σήκωσα
4. αρχίζετε	θα αρχίσετε	αρχίσατε
5. νομίζει	θα νομίσει	νόμισε
6. αγοράζω	θα αγοράσω	αγόρασα
7. καταλαβαίνουν	θα καταλάβουν	κατάλαβαν
8. περιγράφεις	θα περιγράψεις	περίγραψες

Translate:

1. Κατάλαβε την ιστορία;
2. Αγόρασες έναν καθρέφτη στο μαγαζί;
3. Περίγραψε την θέα πολύ καλά.
4. Μαγειρέψαμε την σούπα για τον άνθρωπο.
5. Ωραία! Αλλά άρεσε στην Ελληνίδα η σούπα;
6. Άρχισε να διαβάζει.
7. Σήκωσα το τραπέζι.
8. Κοιτάξατε την θέα;

The verbs κάνω and θέλω:

PRESENT: κάνω   FUTURE: θα κάνω

<u>PAST</u> (all forms):

έκανα	κάναμε
έκανες	κάνατε
έκανε	έκαναν

<u>PRESENT</u>: θέλω   <u>FUTURE</u>: θα θέλω

<u>PAST</u> (all forms):

ήθελα	θάλαμε
ήθελες	θάλατε
ήθελε	ήθελαν

<u>Translate</u>:

1. Δεν ήθελε να γράψει στην φίλη μου στην εξοχή.
2. Τι έκανες στην Πλάκα;
3. Πόσο μάθατε στο σχολείο;
4. Έγραψε τόσο πολλές κάρτες.
5. Για παράδειγμα, τι έκάναν οι δάσκαλοι με την τάξη;
6. Έγραψαν ένα βιβλίο αλλά δεν μ'άρεσε.
7. Πόση δουλειά έκαναν τα παιδιά στο σπίτι;

Translate these sentences using έπρεπε:

1. Έπρεπε να πάει στην τράπεζα στην γειτονιά μας.
2. Δεν έπρεπε να διαβάσουμε τέτεια βιβλία.
3. Έπρεπε να μαγειρέψετε την σούπα για τα παιδιά;

<u>Translate</u>:

1. Οι μουσικοί δεν ήταν στον δρόμο. Αλήθεια; Πού ήταν;
2. Πήρες καφέ στο καφενείο;
3. Δεν ήμουν στο σπίτι γιατί πήγα τον φίλο μου στο μαγαζί.
4. Πού ήσουν; Πού ήσαστε;
5. Πήγαμε με τους φίλους μας στο θέατρο.

6. Πήγε το παιδί στο σχολείο. Αλήθεια; Πήγατε μαζί;
7. Πήγε τα βιβλία στο γραφείο.
8. Τι πήρες όταν πήγες στο μαγαζί απόψε;

Translate:

Το βιβλίο είναι στο τραπέζι.
Αυτό το βιβλίο είναι στο τραπέζι.

Η ιστορία είναι ενδιαφέρουσα.
Αυτή η ιστορία είναι ενδιαφέρουσα.

Οι μουσικοί είναι στο εστιατόριο.
Αυτοί οι μουσικοί είναι στο εστιατόριο.

Exercise: Translate both sentences in each set; the first uses the nominative case, the second uses the accusative. Make all necessary changes:

1. Αυτό το εστιατόριο μας αρέσει.
   Πηγαίνουμε σε αυτό το εστιατόριο.

2. Ο θέατρο έχει μια παράσταση.
   Πηγαίνουμε σε αυτό το θέατρο.

3. Αυτές οι γυναίκες είναι οι φίλες μου.
   Ξέρω αυτές τις γυναίκες.

4. Αυτοί οι φίλοι θέλουν να ταξιδέψουν.
   Θέλω να ταξιδέψω με αυτούς τους φίλους.

5. Αυτή η γυναίκα είναι η μητέρα μου.
   Ξέρετε αυτήν την γυναίκα;

6. Αυτός ο μαθητής είναι πολύ έξυπνος.
   Σπουδάζω με αυτόν τον μαθητή.

7. Αυτές οι μαθήτριες είναι στο σχολείο.
   Θα γράψουμε σε αυτές τις μαθήτριες.

8. Αυτά τα σχέδια είναι στο τραπέζι.
   Πρέπει να κοιτάξω αυτά τα σχέδια.

9. Αυτοί οι πελάτες ψωνίζουν στο μαγαζί.
   Θα συνοδέψω αυτούς τους πελάτες στην πόρτα.

10. Αυτοί οι παραστάσεις θα τελεώσουν αργά.
    Δεν θα πάμε σε αυτός τις παραστάσεις.

Translate:

1. Μόλις διαβάσει αυτά τα βιβλία, θα ξέρει την αλήθεια.
2. Ποιος θα αρχίσει να σηκώνει εκείνες τις καρέκλες;
3. Αν αγοράσω πολλά τρόφιμα, θα μαγειρέψεις τα φαγητά;
4. Πόσα παιδιά θα παίξουν σε αυτούς τους δρόμους;
5. Πότε θα μάθετε κάθε ρήμα;
6. Δεν σ' αρέσει τέτεια δώρα.
7. Πόσο ζάχαρι ήταν στα ποτά;
8. Δεν ξέρει ότι μερικά παιδιά θέλουν να παίξουν εδώ.
9. Πώς θα πληρώσουμε αυτούς τους λογαριασμούς;
10. Αγοράσαμε αυτά τα παιχνίδια για τα παιδιά.
11. Όλοι οι μαθητές ήθελαν να σπουδάσουν σε αυτό το σχολείο.
12. Δεν πρέπει να αγοράσεις τα τρόφιμα για αυτήν την οικογένεια.
13. Θέλουμε να πάμε στην άλλη παράσταση.
14. Νομίζετε ότι αυτό το καφενείο είναι καλό;
15. Αυτός ο άνθρωπος δεν είναι ο πατέρας μου.

Lesson 7

to give — δίνω

FUTURE	PAST
θα δώσω	έδωσα
θα δώσεις	έδωσες
θα δώσει	έδωσε
θα δώσουμε	δωσαμε
θα δώσετε	δωσατε
θα δώσουν	έδωσαν

to live, stay — **μένω**

FUTURE	PAST
θα μείνω	**έμεινα**
θα μείνεις	**έμεινες**
θα μείνει	**έμεινε**
θα μείνουμε	**μείναμε**
θα μείνετε	**μείνατε**
θα μείνουν	**έμειναν**

Translate:

1. **Ο ήλιος δεν μπαίνει στα παράθυρα σε αυτό το διαμέρισμα.**
2. **Πριν από δύο χρόνια είδαμε εκείνη την γραφική περιοχή.**
3. **Πότε έφτασαν στο Παρίσι;**
4. **Έδωσαν σε κάθε παιδί το δικό σου βιβλίο αυτό το πρωί;**
5. **Θα φτάσουμε εκεί το πρωί.**
6. **Φέτος, δεν θα δώσει δώρα στις φίλες τις.**
7. **Δεν θα μπει στο εστιατόριο με εκείνους τους ανθρώπους.**
8. **Θα νοικιάσετε ένα σπίτι κοντά στην θάλασσα;**
9. **Τι θέλουν να δουν όταν πάνε στην Νέα Υόρκη;**
10. **Είδες τα βιβλία που άφησα εδώ αυτό το απόγευμα;**

Sentences using **που**: translate:

1. **Σ'αρέσουν οι καρέκλες που αγόρασαν;**
2. **Αυτό είναι το βιβλίο που διάβασα.**
3. **Εκείνη είναι η γυναίκα που ξέρουμε.**
4. **Εκείνη είναι η δασκάλα που ήρθε στο σχολείο.**
5. **Εκείνοι είναι οι φίλοι που πηαίνουν σε αυτό το σχολείο.**

Possessive adjectives:

your house	**το σπίτι σου**
his house	**το σπίτι του**
her house	**το σπίτι της**
our house	**το σπίτι μας**

| your house (pl.) | το σπίτι σας |
| their house | το σπίτι τους |

Add the possessives to these nouns and make the appropriate change in the accent:

his apartment	το διαμέρισμά του
their statue	το άγαλμά τους
our statues	τα αγάλματά μας
her room	το δωμάτιό της
my family	η οικογένειά μου

Translate these nouns, using the possessive adjective:

my books	τα βιβλία μου
your (fam.) sister	η αδελφή της
your sisters	οι αδελφές της
his brother	ο αδελφός του
our children	τα παιδιά μας
your (pl). cards	οι κάρτες σας
their students	οι μαθητές τους

Translate these using the right form of δικός:

her own doctor	ο δικός της γιατρός
our own language	η δική μας γλώσσα
your (fam.) own customers	οι δικοί σου πελάτες
their own families	οι δικές τους οικογένιες

Τίνος παιδιά είναι αυτά; Είναι τα δικά τους.
Τίνος σούπα είναι αυτή; Είναι η δική της.

Construct the question and the answer in Greek:

1. Τίνος λεφτά είναι αυτά; Δεν είναι τα δικά μου.
2. Τίνος καρέκλες είναι αυτές; Νομίζω ότι είναι οι δικές σου.
3. Τίνος δώρα είναι αυτά; Είναι τα δικά της.

Change the examples given in the nominative to the accusative, making any necessary modifications:

in my own room	στο δικό μου δωμάτιο
with his own cars	με τα δικά του αυτοκίνητα
in our own neighborhood	στην δική μας γειτονιά
with your own parents	με τους δικούς σας γονείς

Using the time words and expressions that you know, try translating these sentences.

1. Πέρσι, ανακαλύψαμε ένα ξενοχείο σε μια παλιά περιοχή.
2. Δύο χρόνια πριν, είδε τους γονείς σου στην Νέα Υόρκη.
3. Σήμερα, θα δούμε τα γραφικά χωριά στην εξοχή.
4. Φέτος, θα νοικιάσουμε το διαμέρισμα του κοντά στην θάλασσα.
5. Την άλλη φορά, θέλουμε να νοικιάσουμε το παλιό σπίτι στο χωριό.
6. Σήμερα αρίζω το πανεπιστήμιο.
7. Μ'αρέσει αυτό το διαμέρισμα γιατί το απόγευμα ο ήλιος μπαίνει στα παράθυρα.
8. Την περασμένη νύχτα πολλοί τουρίστες έφτασαν στο χωριό μας.
9. Το σπίτι σας είναι από αυτόν τον αιώνα ή τον περασμένο αιώνα;
10. Είσαι αργά — το πρόγραμμα κιόλας άρχισε μία ώρα πριν.
11. Στην γειτονιά μας είναι συχνά πολύς θόρυβος. Γ'αυτό δεν μας αρέσει.
12. Την άλλη εβδομάδα θα αλλάξουμε το πρόγραμμα.
13. Την περασμένη εβδομάδα αποφασίσαμε να μείνουμε με τους δικούς μας φίλους.

Months of the Year — Οι Μήνες

in January	τον Ιανουάριο
in February	τον Φεβρουάριο
in March	τον Μάρτιο
in April	τον Απρίλιο
in May	τον Μάιο
in June	τον Ιούνιο

in July	τον Ιούλιο
in August	τον Αύγουστο
in September	τον Σεπτέμβριο
in October	τον Οκτώβριο
in November	τον Νοέμβριο
in December	τον Δεκέμβριο

Translate:

1. Σε ποια μήνα είναι τα γενέθλιά σου;
2. Τα γενέθλιά μου είναι τον Απρίλιο.
3. Θα ταξιδέψουμε στην Νέα Υόρκη τον Οκτώβριο.
4. Πρέπει να αρχίσει να σπουδάζει τον Φεβρουάριο.
5. Το Λονδίνο μ' αρέσει τον Μάϊο.

Lesson 8

Substitution drill:

1. Βλέπεις τους ανθρώπους; Όχι, δεν τους βλέπω καθόλου.
2. Μιλάς τα ελληνικά; Ναι, τα μιλώ λίγο.
3. Κάνατε τις διακοπές σας στο εξωτερικό; Όχι. Τις κάναμε στην Ελλάδα.
4. Ο δάσκαλος με κοιτάζει; Ναι, σε κοιτάζει.
5. Η Μαρία μας προσκαλάει στο σπίτι της; Ναι, μας προσκαλάει στο σπίτι της.
6. Προσκαλούμε την Μαρία στο σπίτι μας; Μάλιστα, την προσκαλούμε!

Translate these questions and answers, using direct object pronouns:

1. Γνωρίζετε τα ελλινικά νησιά; Ναι, τα γνωρίζω καλά.
2. Αγόρασες το παιχνίδι για το παιδί; Ναι, το αγόρασα.
3. Η Μαρία είδε τους τουρίστες στην γειτονιά; Ναι, τους είδε.
4. Κοιτάζει τον Νίκο; Όχι, δεν τον κοιτάζει.
5. Βλέπει τις παραλίες; Ναι, τις βλέπει.

6. Ποιον κοιτάζεις; Σε κοιτάζω. Σας κοιτάζω.
7. Σας βλέπει; Ναι, με βλέπει.

Two sets of sentences in the present and future:

Βλέπεις τους ανθρώπους;   Όχι, δεν τους βλέπω καθόλου.
Θα δεις τους ανθρώπους;   Όχι, δεν θα τους δω καθόλου.

Ο δάσκαλος με κοιτάζει;   Ναι, σε κοιτάζει.
Ο δάσκαλος θα με κοιτάξει;   Ναι, θα σε κοιτάξει.

FUTURE:

Translate:

1. Θα έχετε τα λεφτά αύριο; Όχι, δεν θα τα έχω.
2. Θα αγοράσει το γάλα για τους ξένους; Ναι, θα το αγοράσει.
3. Πήρες το γυαλί από την κουζίνα; Όχι, αλλά θα το πάρω τώρα.
4. Πότε θα τελειώσει την δουλειά του; Θα την τελειώσει το Σαββατοκύριακο.
5. Πότε θα καθαρίσουμε το αυτοκίνητο; Θα το καθαρίσουμε τώρα.

How would you say…?

1. Ζητάει ένα δωμάτιο που βλέπει στην θάλασσα.
2. Ζητάει από τον πατέρα του αν μπορεί να έχει ένα παιχνίδι.
3. Ζητούμε το πανεπιστύμιο.
4. Τι ζήτασες από την οικογένειά σου;

Translate:

1. Θα ζητήσει ένα δωμάτιο που βλέπει στην θάλασσα.
2. Θα ζητήσει από τον πατέρα του αν μπορεί να έχει ένα παιχνίδι.
3. Θα ζητήσουμε το πανεπιστύμιο.

Write out the rest of the future forms of **ρωτώ** here:

ρωτώ — future tense

θα ρωτήσω	**θα ρωτήσουμε**
θα ρωτήσεις	**θα ρωτήσετε**
θα ρωτήσει	**θα ρωτήσουν**

Translate:

Τον ρωτάει απόψε.
Θα τον ρωτήσει αυτόν τον χρόνο.

Μας ρωτούν τώρα.
Θα μας ρωτήσουν την άλλη εβδομάδα.

Τους ρωτώ.
Θα τους ρωτήσω αύριο.

Με ρωτάς;
Θα με ρωτήσεις τον Μάρτιο;

Νομίζω ότι τον ρωτάει.
Νομίζω ότι θα τον ρωτήσει σύντομα.

προτιμώ — to prefer

PRESENT	FUTURE
προτιμώ	**θα προτιμήσω**
προτιμάς	**θα προτιμήσεις**
προτιμάει	**θα προτιμήσει**
προτιμούμε	**θα προτιμήσουμε**
προτιμάτε	**θα προτιμήσετε**
προτιμούν	**θα προτιμήσουν**

μιλώ — to speak

PRESENT	FUTURE
μιλώ (also μιλάω)	θα μιλήσω
μιλάς	θα μιλήσεις
μιλάει	θα μιλήσει
μιλούμε	θα μιλήσουμε
μιλάτε	θα μιλήσετε
μιλούν	θα μιλήσουν

Sentences using **προτιμώ, οδηγώ, μιλώ** and **προσκαλώ**:

1. **Μερικές φορές προτιμούμε να μείνουμε σ'ένα ξενοδοχείο κοντά στην θάλασσα.**
2. **Θα τους προσκαλείτε;**
3. **Ξέρεις να οδηγήσεις;**
4. **Μιλάει ελληνικά πολύ καλά.**
5. **Προτιμώ να προσκαλέσω τους αδελφούς μου σ'ένα εστιατόριο.**
6. **Πότε θα μιλήσουν στον γιατρό;**
7. **Πού θα οδηγήσουμε την άλλη εβδομάδα;**
8. **Νομίζω ότι θα προτιμήσουν να μείνουν στο δωμάτιο κοντά στο λουτροδωμάτιο.**
9. **Σύντομα θα οδηγήσουμε στην Γαλλία μαζί.**
10. **Δεν θα μας προσκαλέσουν αύριο.**
11. **Μιλούμε στην τάξη τώρα.**
12. **Δεν προσκαλούν την αδελφή μου αυτήν την φορά.**
13. **Προτιμάτε να ταξιδέψετε την άνοιξη ή τον χειμώνα;**
14. **Δεν νομίζω ότι θα με προσκαλέσει.**
15. **Δεν της αρέσει να μιλάει ισπανικά.**

Translate these sentences, using the verb **περνώ**:

1. **Πού περνούν τις διακοπές τους;**
2. **Πού θα περάσουν το Σαββατοκύριακο;**
3. **Φέτος, περνούμε τον χειμώνα στην Αθήνα.**
4. **Πέρσι, περάσαμε τον χειμώνα στην Νέα Υόρκη.**
5. **Γενικά, περνώ τα Σαββατοκύριακο στο σπίτι.**
6. **Θα περάσω το άλλο Σαββατοκύριακο στην εξοχή.**

Translate, using the verb **μπορώ**:

1. **Δεν μπορώ να δώ καλά την νύχτα.**
2. **Πότε μπορούμε να αρχίσουμε;**
3. **Μπορείτε να μιλήσετε με τον γιατρό αύριο;**

Fill in the past tense for the rest of the persons for the past tense of:

μιλώ:

μίλησα	**μιλήσαμε**
μίλησες	**μιλήσατε**
μίλησε	**μίλησαν**

μπορώ:

μπόρεσα	**μπορέσαμε**
μπόρεσες	**μπορέσατε**
μπόρεσε	**μπόρεσαν**

οδηγώ:

οδήγησα	**οδηγήσαμε**
οδήγησες	**οδηγήσατε**
οδήγησε	**οδήγησαν**

περνώ:

πέρασα	**περάσαμε**
πέρασες	**περάσατε**
πέρασε	**πέρασαν**

προσκαλώ:

προσκάλεσα	**προσκαλέσαμε**
προσκάλεσες	**προσκαλέσατε**
προσκάλεσε	**προσκάλεσαν**

προτιμώ:

προτίμησα	προτιμήσαμε
προτίμησες	προτιμήσατε
προτίμησε	προτίμησαν

ρωτώ:

ρώτησα	ρωτήσαμε
ρώτησες	ρωτήσατε
ρώτησε	ρώτησαν

Sentences to translate using contracted verbs in the past tense:

1. Δύο χρόνια πριν, προσκάλεσαν τους γονείς μου στο σπίτι τους στα ελληνικά νησιά.
2. Την περασμένη άνοιξη, οδηγήσαμε στην Γαλλία και μείναμε εκεί για δεκαπέντε μέρες.
3. Δυστυχώς, δεν περάσαμε το απόγευμα στην παραλία.
4. Τον περασμένο Ιούλιο, ζητήσαμε ένα διαμέρισμα στην Μύκονο, αλλά δεν θέλαμε να το νοικιάσουμε.
5. Ίσως προτίμησε να μείνει στο ξενοδοχείο.
6. Κιόλας μίλησε με τους ξένους και τους ρώτησε αν αγόρασαν πολλά ευθύμια.
7. Τρεις μήνες πριν, πέρασα μια εβδομάδα στην Ισπανία.
8. Πήγε στο σχολείο στην Νέα Υόρκη και μετά, πέρασε το καλοκαίρι εκεί.
9. Μόλις μίλησα με τον μουσικό, ήξερε ότι ήθελα να ζητήσω ένα τραγούδι.
10. Δεν μπόρεσαν να μπουν στο σπίτι.
11. Πέρσι, μπορέσαμε να ταξιδέψουμε στο εξωτερικό.
12. Το πρωί, μερικοί φίλοι στην γειτονιά μας προσκάλεσαν στο σπίτι τους.
13. Την περασμένη φορά που οδήγησα εκεί, πέρασα καλά.
14. Τον περασμένο Μάιο, ζήτησα από τον πατέρα μου να πληρώσει τον λογαριασμό μου, αλλά τότε, δεν είχε τα λεφτά.
15. Πού πέρασαν το περασμένο καλοκαίρι;
16. Με προσκάλεσε να δώ το σπίτι του, αλλά προτίμησα να ψωνίσω στα μαγαζιά.

Using your <u>direct object pronouns</u>, how would you say…?

1. Πώς τους λένε;
2. Πώς τις λένε;

And how would you answer:

1. Τον λένε Πέτρο.
2. Την λένε Μαρία.
3. Με λένε ᾽Αννα.
4. Τις λένε Δάφνη και Αλίκη.
5. Τους λένε Γιάννη και Πέτρο.

Translate, using the verb λέω:

1. Τι λέει;
2. Τι θα πει;
3. Τι είπε;

4. Λέει την ιστορία;
5. Θα πει την ιστορία;
6. Είπε την ιστορία;

7. Λέμε την αλήθεια;
8. Θα πούμε την αλήθεια;
9. Είπαμε την αλήθεια;

10. Τι λές στο παιδί; Τι λέτε στο παιδί;
11. Τι θα πεις στο παιδί; Τι θα πείτε στο παιδί;
12. Τι είπες στο παιδί; Τι είπατε στο παιδί;

13. Λένε κάτι;
14. Θα πουν κάτι;
15. Είπαν κάτι;

16. Δεν λέω την αλήθεια.
17. Δεν θα πω την αλήθεια.
18. Δεν είπα την αλήθεια.

Translate, using time-related expressions:

1. Το μέλλον, θα πρέπει να τελειώσεις την δουλειά σου στην ώρα.
2. Πού πήγες με τους φίλους σου χθες;
3. Πηαίνετε συχνά στο Παρίσι;
4. Συνήθως μένει σ'ένα μάλλον παλιό ξενοδοχείο όταν ταξιδεύει στο Λονδίνο.
5. Πρέπει να μείνω σ'εκείνο το δωμάτιο σήμερα; Για την ώρα, ναι.
6. Στο παρελθόν, μείναμε στο δικό μας σπίτι κοντά στο πανεπστύμιο.
7. Την άλλη φορά, θέλω να φτάσεις στην ώρα ή νωρίς.
8. Στην γειτονιά μας, είναι συχνά πολύς θόρυβος.
9. Μερικές φορές μας αρέσει να ταξδεύουμε στο εξωτερικό, αλλά για την ώρα, θα περάσουμε τις διακοπές μας στην Αθήνα.
10. Θέλω να σας ρωτήσω κάτι αργότερα.
11. Πριν πάει στο σχολείο πάντοτε τρώει.
12. Είμαστε πάντοτε στο σπίτι το βράδυ.

Days of the Week

on Sunday	την Κυριακή
on Monday	τη(ν) Δευτέρα
on Tuesday	την Τρίτη
on Wednesday	την Τετάρτη
on Thursday	την Πέμπτη
on Friday	την Παρασκευή
on Saturday	το Σάββατο

Translate:

1. Έχετε ένα πρόγραμμα για το Σάββατο;
2. Πηαίνω στο θέατρο την Τρίτη.
3. Την Παρασκευή, οι φίλοι μας θα φτάσουν στην Αθήνα.
4. Πρέπει να δουλέψω τη(ν) Δευτέρα.
5. Πού θα πάτε το Σαββατοκύριακο;

Lesson 9

How would you say…?

1. Δεν της αρέσει να ταξιδεύει.
2. Τις αρέσουν τα φαγητά στην Ελλάδα.
3. Δεν μας αρέσει η μουσική.
4. Τους αρέσουν τα βιβλία.

Translate these sentences using indirect object pronouns:

1. Τι σου είπε; Τι σας είπε;
2. Της αγοράζει ένα αμάξι.
3. Τους διαβάζουμε.
4. Πότε μας έγραψε;

απαντώ Present		Future	
απαντώ	απαντούμε	θα απαντήσω	θα απαντήσουμε
απαντας	απαντάτε	θα απαντήσεις	θα απαντήσετε
απαντά(ει)	απαντούν	θα απαντήσει	θα απαντήσουν

Past	
απάντησα	απαντήσαμε
απάντησες	απαντήσατε
απάντησε	απάντησαν

στέλνω: to send — regular in the present

Future		(Past)	
θα στείλω	θα στείλουμε	έστειλα	στείλαμε
θα στείλεις	θα στείλετε	έστειλες	στείλατε
θα στείλει	θα στείλουν	έστειλε	έστειλαν

τηλεφωνώ — regular in the present

<u>FUTURE</u>

θα τηλεφωνήσω   θα τηλεφωνήσουμε
θα τηλεφωνήσεις   θα τηλεφωνήσετε
θα τηλεφωνήσει   θα τηλεφωνήσουν

<u>PAST</u>

τηλεφώνησα   τηλεφωνήσαμε
τηλεφώνησες   τηλεφωνήσατε
τηλεφώνησε   τηλεφώνησαν

<u>Translate these</u>:

1. Θέλουμε να του στείλουμε τα βιβλία.
2. Πρέπει να τις διαβάσουν.
3. Ήθελε να μου μιλήσει χθες.
4. Δεν μπορεί να τους απαντήσει.
5. Πρέπει να της στείλεις τα λεφτά;
6. Δεν πρέπει να του τηλεφωνήσετε.
7. Θέλεις να μου αγοράζεις μερικά τρόφιμα;
8. Μπορεί να σου δώσει καφέ αργότερα.

<u>Substitution drill</u>:

Στέλει τα γράμματα στην μητέρα του.
Της στέλει τα γράμματα.
Της τα στέλει.

Αγοράζουν στην αδελφή σου ένα αμάξι.
Της αγοράζουν ένα αμάξι.
Της το αγοράζουν.

Έστειλε μερικά δώρα στον πατέρα της.
Του έστειλε μερικά δώρα.
Του τα έστειλε.

Διάβασε μια ιστορία στα παιδιά;
Τους διάβασε μια ιστορία;
Τους την διάβασε;

Translate:

1. Κατάλαβε αυτό που ήθελε;
2. Αυτό το φαγητό δεν είναι αυτό που ζήτησα.
3. Έλαβαν αυτά που ζήτησαν;

Translate:

1. Συνηθίζεις να γράφεις στους γονείς σου κανονικά;
2. Συνηθίζουμε να αγοράζουμε τα τρόφιμα πριν πάμε στο σπίτι.
3. Δεν συνηθίζουν να τηλεφωνούν στους γονείς τους την νύχτα.

λαβαίνω — to receive — regular in the present

FUTURE		PAST	
θα λάβω	θα λάβουμε	έλαβα	λάβαμε
θα λάβεις	θα λάβετε	έλαβες	λάβατε
θα λάβει	θα λάβουν	έλαβε	έλαβαν

φεύγω — to go out, to leave — regular in the present

FUTURE		PAST	
θα φύγω	θα φύγουμε	έφυγα	φύγαμε
θα φύγεις	θα φύγετε	έφυγες	φύγατε
θα φύγει	θα φύγουν	έφυγε	έφυγαν

Translate:

1. Από τότε που σπουδάζετε τα γαλλικά, πήγατε στην Γαλλία;
2. Από τότε που τους γνωρίζει, τους μίλησε για την οικογένειά του;
3. Από τότε που άρχισε τα μαθήματά της, έμαθε πολύ;

Translate:

τέσσερεις άνθρωποι
τέσσερεις γυναίκες
τέσσερα παιδιά

Translate:

1. Έχουμε τέσσερεις φίλους που σπουδάζουν στο εξωτερικό.
2. Ταξίδεψα στην Βραζιλία τέσσερεις ή πέντε φορές.
3. Έχουμε μόνο ένα λουτοδωμάτιο στο διαμέρισμά μας.
4. Πηγαίνουν δεκαπέντε παιδιά στην παράσταση.

Review: Days of the Week and Months of the Year

1. Έχω μάθημα....
2. Έχω τις διακοπές ...
3. Ψωνίζω τα τρόφιμα ...
4. Σήμερα είναι ...
5. Χθες ήταν....
6. Τα γενέθλιά μου είναι ...
7. Πρέπει να δουλέψω ...
8. Η άνοιξη αρχίζει ...

Translate these sentences about the seasons:

1. Θα αρχίσετε να σπουδάζετε στο πανεπιστύμιο το καλοκαίρι ή το φθινόπωρο;
2. Δεν μ'αρέσει ο χειμώνας στην Νέα Υόρκη και γ'αυτό, ταξιδεύω στην Ισπανία.
3. Προτιμώ να περάσω την άνοιξη στο Παρίσι.
4. Τι θα κάνες αυτό το καλοκαίρι;

Review: Words About the Home

1. Μένω σ'ένα ...
2. Το υπνοδωμάτιό μου είναι ...
3. Μαγειρεύω το φαγητό....
4. Στο σπίτι μου, είναι _____ λουτροδωμάτιο(α).
5. (Ναι ή Όχι), το σαλόνι (δεν) είναι ...
6. (Ναι ή Όχι), ο ήλιος (δεν) ...
7. Το σαλόνι βλέπει στο(ν) ...
8. (Ναι ή Όχι), (δεν) είναι παλιό το σπίτι μου.

Adjectives:

γεμάτος (+ **από**) — full (of)		**γεμάτοι**
γεμάτη		**γεμάτες**
γεμάτο		**γεμάτα**
γραφικός — picturesque		**γραφικοί**
γραφική		**γραφικές**
γραφικό		**γραφικά**
διαθέσιμος — available		**διαθέσιμοι**
διαθέσιμη		**διαθέσιμες**
διαθέσιμο		**διαθέσιμα**
δύσκολος — difficult		**δύσκολοι**
δύσκολη		**δύσκολες**
δύσκολο		**δύσκολα**
ελληνικός — Greek		**ελληνικοί**
ελληνική		**ελληνικές**
ελληνικό		**ελληνικά**
έξυπνος — clever		**έξυπνοι**
έξυπνη		**έξυπνες**
έξυπνο		**έξυπνα**
εύκολος — easy		**εύκολοι**
εύκολη		**εύκολες**
εύκολο		**εύκολα**
ήσυχος — calm, quiet		**ήσυχοι**
ήσυχη		**ήσυχες**
ήσυχο		**ήσυχα**
θεατρικός — theatrical		**θεατρικοί**
θεατρική		**θεατρικές**
θεατρικό		**θεατρικά**

καλός — good	καλοί
καλή	καλές
καλό	καλά
κουρασμένος — tired	κουρασμένοι
κουρασμένη	κουρασμένες
κουρασμένο	κουρασμένα
μεγάλος — big	μεγάλοι
μεγάλη	μεγάλες
μεγάλο	μεγάλα
μικρός — small	μικροί
μικρή	μικρές
μικρό	μικρά
όμορφος — beautiful	όμορφοι
όμορφη	όμορφες
όμορφο	όμορφα
περασμένος — previous	περασμένοι
περασμένη	περασμένες
περασμένο	περασμένα
προσωπικός — personal	προσωπικοί
προσωπική	προσωπικές
προσωπικό	προσωπικά
χρήσιμος — useful	χρήσιμοι
χρήσιμη	χρήσιμες
χρήσιμο	χρήσιμα

Adjectives that follow a different rule:

παλιός — old	παλιοί
παλιά	παλιές
παλιό	παλιά

ίδιος — the same ίδιοι
ίδια ίδιες
ίδιο ίδια

θαυμάσιος — wonderful θαυμάσιοι
θαυμάσια θαυμάσιες
θαυμάσιο θαυμάσια

Translate:

1. Είναι δύσκολο να καταλάβω γιατί φεύγουν.
2. Δεν είναι καλό να πηγαίνεις στο σπίτι πάρα πολύ αργά.

Translate using the word "alone":

1. Σας αρέσετε να ψωνίζετε μόνες σας;
2. Το μικρό παιδί είναι μόνο του στον κήπο.
3. Μας αρέσει να είμαστε μόνες μας.
4. Συνηθίζουν να είναι μόνοι τους.

Translate:

1. Αυτό το βιβλίο δεν είναι ενδιαφέρον.
2. Η ιστορία της ήταν πολύ ενδιαφέρουσα.
3. Τα μαθήματα στο σχολείο είναι πολύ ενδιαφέροντα.

Translate, using adjectives:

1. Η θάλασσα είναι γαλάζια και ήσυχη.
2. Μας αρέσει να κοιτάζουμε την γαλάζια, ήσυχη θάλασσα.
3. Γνωρίζω μια έξυπνη, νέα μαθήτρια.
4. Έχουμε πολλούς καλούς φίλους.
5. Κοιτάζουν τις όμορφες, νέες γυναίκες.
6. Οδηγεί ένα παλιό, άσπρο αμάξι.
7. Θέλουμε να δούμε τις γραφικές παραλίες στην Ισπανία.
8. Ζητούμε μερικούς διαθέσιμοι μαθητές.
9. Είδες πολλές θεατρικές παραστάσεις;

Translate:

1. Στις Ηνωμένες Πολιτείες, πολλοί άνθρωποι μιλούν ισπανικά.
2. Σπουδάζει γαλλική λογοτεχνία στο πανεπιστύμιο στο Παρίσι.
3. Όλοι οι Ελβετοί μιλούν μερικές γλώσσες;
4. Σπούδασες ιαπωνική τέχνη;
5. Ναι, και ταξίδεψα μερικές φορές στην Ιαπωνία.
6. Γιατί μιλούν οι Βραζιλιάνοι τα πορτογαλικά;

Lesson 10

Translate these sentences, using prepositional pronouns:

1. Θέλεις να πας με μας στα ελληνικά νησιά αυτό το καλοκαίρι;
2. Αποφάσισε να πάει στη παράσταση χωρίς εμένα.
3. Έκανε την δουλειά γ'αυτούς αυτό το απόγευμα;
4. Πότε θα λάβω ένα γράμμα από σας;
5. Οι μαθήτριες δεν είναι εδώ και δε μπορώ να συνεχίσω το μάθημα χωρίς αυτές.
6. Πού είναι τα παιδιά; Έχω κάτι γ'αυτά.

Practice the verb "to visit":

1. Επισκεπτόσαστε τους εξάδελφούς σας στην Αγγλία;
2. Επισκεπτόμαστε την αδελφή σου για να γιορτάσουμε τα γενέθλιά της.
3. Επισκέπτονται τους γονείς σου τα ελληνικά νησιά;

Now change the sentences above to the future tense:

1. Αυτήν την άνοιξη, θα επισκεπτείτε τους εξάδελφούς σας στην Αγγλία;
2. Αύριο, θα επισκεπτούμε την αδελφή σου για να γιορτάσουμε τα γενέθλιά της.
3. Τον άλλο χρόνον, θα επισκεπτούν τους γονείς σου τα ελληνικά νησιά;

Write these sentences, using the past tense:

1. Χθες, επισκεπτήκατε τους εξάδελφούς σας στην Αγγλία;
2. Το περασμένο φθινόπωρο, επισκεπτήκαμε την αδελφή σου για να γιορτάσουμε τα γενέθλιά της.
3. Πέρσι, επισκέπτηκαν τους γονείς σου τα ελληνικά νησιά;

Now translate these sentences, paying close attention to the tense being used:

1. Συχνά ετοιμάζομαι νωρίς.
2. Θα ετοιμαστεί στις δέκα η ώρα περίπου.
3. Δεν ετοιμαστήκαμε χθες.

Conjugate εξαφανίζομαι — to disappear:

PRESENT

εξαφανίζομαι	εξαφανιζόμαστε
εξαφανίζεσαι	εξαφανιζόσαστε
εξαφανίζεται	εξαφανίζονται

Translate:

1. Τα λεφτά μου εξαφανίζονται.
2. Η μέρα εξαφανίζεται αργά.
3. Καμιά φορά, ένα πρόβλημα εξαφανίζεται εύκολα.

FUTURE

θα εξαφανιστώ	θα εξαφανιστούμε
θα εξαφανιστείς	θα εξαφανιστείτε
θα εξαφανιστεί	θα εξαφανιστούν

Change the above sentences to the future tense.

1. Τα λεφτά μου θα εξαφανιστούν.
2. Η μέρα θα εξαφανιστεί αργά.
3. Καμιά φορά, ένα πρόβλημα θα εξαφανιστεί εύκολα.

<u>PAST</u>

εξαφανίστηκα	εξαφανιστήκαμε
εξαφανίστηκες	εξαφανιστήκατε
εξαφανίστηκε	εξαφανίστηκαν

Change the sentences to the past tense.

1. Τα λεφτά μου εξαφανίστηκαν.
2. Η μέρα εξαφανίστηκε αργά.
3. Καμιά φορά, ένα πρόβλημα εξαφανίστηκε εύκολα.

Practice sentences using **βρίσκομαι**:

1. Το τρένο βρίσκεται στο σταθμό.
2. Πού βρίσκεσαι σήμερα;
3. Πού βρισκόσαστε σήμερα;

Write the above sentences in the future tense.

1. Το τρένο θα βρεθεί στο σταθμό.
2. Πού θα βρεθείς σήμερα;
3. Πού θα βρεθείτε σήμερα;

Write the sentences in the past tense.

1. Το τρένο βρέθηκε στο σταθμό.
2. Πού βρέθηκες ήμερα;
3. Πού βρεθήκατε σήμερα;

Write these sentences, using the verb **έρχομαι**:

1. Έρχεται συχνά στο σπίτι μου.
2. Ερχόμαστε να επισκεπτούμε τους φίλους μας στην Αθήνα.
3. Δεν έρχονται εδώ για το καλοκαίρι.

Write the above sentences in the future:

1. Σήμερα θά' ρθει στο σπίτι μου.
2. Αυτό το απόγευμα, θά' ρθουμε να επισκεπτούμε τους φίλους μας στην Αθήνα.
3. Σύντομα θά' ρθουν εδώ για το καλοκαίρι.

Write these above sentences in the past:

1. Προχθές ήρθε συχνά στο σπίτι μου.
2. Τον περασμένο μήνα ήρθαμε να επισκεπτούμε τους φίλους μας στην Αθήνα.
3. Πέρσι, ήρθαν εδώ για το καλοκαίρι.

Regular Verbs: Fill in the missing parts.

PRESENT		FUTURE	
χάνω	χάνουμε	θα χάσω	θα χάσουμε
χάνεις	χάνετε	θα χάσεις	θα χάσετε
χάνει	χάνουν	θα χάσει	θα χάσουν

PAST	
έχασα	χάσαμε
έχασες	χάσατε
έχασε	έχασαν

Translate:

1. Δυστυχώς, έχασε τα γενέθλιά μου.
2. Αν δεν πάμε μ'αυτούς στην εξοχή, θα χάσουμε μια σπουδαία ευκαιρία.
3. Έχασες κάτι;
4. Χάνετε λεφτά σ'αυτήν την κατάσταση.

ελπίζω — to hope

PRESENT		FUTURE		PAST	
ελπίζω	ελπίζουμε	θα ελπίσω	θα ελπίσουμε	έλπισα	ελπίσαμε
ελπίζεις	ελπίζετε	θα ελπίσεις	θα ελπίσετε	έλπισες	ελπίσατε
ελπίζει	ελπίζουν	θα ελπίσει	θα ελπίσουν	έλπισε	έλπισαν

Translate:

1. Ελπίζουμε ότι θά' ρθεις επίσης.
2. Ελπίζω ότι η διαδροπή θα είναι γραφική.
3. Ελπίζει ότι ο θείος του και η θεία του θα τον επισκεπτούν τον άλλο χρόνον.
4. Ελπίζω να μείνω μ'αυτούς τουλάχιστο γιά την ώρα.

PRESENT		FUTURE		PAST	
δείχνω	δείχνουμε	θα δείξω	θα δείξουμε	έδειξα	δείξαμε
δείχνεις	δείχνετε	θα δείξεις	θα δείξετε	έδειξες	δείξατε
δείχνει	δείχνουν	θα δείξει	θα δείξουν	έδειξε	έδειξαν

PRESENT		FUTURE		PAST	
βγάζω	βγάζουμε	θα βγάλω	θα βγάλουμε	έβγαλα	βγάλαμε
βγάζεις	βγάζετε	θα βγάλεις	θα βγάλετε	έβγαλες	βγάλατε
βγάζει	βγάζουν	θα βγάλει	θα βγάλουν	έβγαλε	έβγαλαν

PRESENT		FUTURE		PAST	
βρίσκω	βρίσκουμε	θα βρώ	θα βρούμε	βρήκα	βρήκαμε
βρίσκεις	βρίσκετε	θα βρεις	θα βρείτε	βρήκες	βρήκατε
βρίσκει	βρίσκουν	θα βρει	θα βρούν	βρήκε	βρήκαν

Translate:

1. Αν είσαι έτοιμος, θέλω να σου δείξω μια όμοφη θέση που βρίσκει ένας ερειπωμένος ναός.
2. Βγάζετε φωτογραφίες καλά;
3. Κάνω μια προσπάθεια να βρώ το γιό της γ'αυτήν.
4. Πίνουμε ένα εξαιρετικό ποτό.

5. Δε θέλει να χάσει την ευκαιρία να μας δείξει αυτήν την χωριάτικη ταβέρνα.
6. Αν ο καιρός είναι καλός, θα βρούμε τους αδελφούς μας.

Translate:

1. Πόσοι αρχαίοι ναοί υπάρχουν στη Ρώμη;
2. Υπάρχει ένα καλό ξενοδοχείο που μπορείτε να μείνετε με την οικογένειά σας.
3. Υπάρχουν πολλά λεωφορεία στην Αθήνα.
4. Γιατί υπάρχουν τόσο πολλά καλά εστιατόρια σε αυτήν την περιοχή;

Translate:

1. Πάντοτε πεινώ το πρωί.
2. Μας αρέσει να περπατούμε στη δική μας πόλη.
3. Νομίζεις ότι τα παιδά θα διψάσουν αργότερα;
4. Θα τραβήξει όλες τις φωτογραφίες για σας.
5. Θα φτάσουμε νωρίς και νομίζω ότι θα πεινάσουμε.
6. Δε δίψασαν καθόλου.

Translate, using the verb σταματώ:

1. Γιατί σταματήσατε να τραβείτε φωτογραφίες;
2. Άξαφνα σταμάτησε να μιλάει.
3. Κάθε μέρα σταματούν να σπουδάζουν στις δύο η ώρα.
4. Πότε θα σταματήσουμε να ταξιδεύουμε;

Translate:

1. Τι έφαγες σήμερα με την συντροφιά;
2. Τι τους αρέσει να τρώνε;
3. Τρώνε τέτεια φαγητά;
4. Βέβαια, θα φάμε κάτι όταν φτάσουμε εκεί.
5. Δεν τρώω το πρωί.
6. Δε συνηθίζει να τρώει πριν τις δέκα η ώρα.

Translate:

1. Ας τραβήξουμε φωτογραφίες όταν πάμε στην Ισπανία.
2. Ας επισκεπτούμε τις Ηνωμένες Πολιτείες.
3. Ας μιλήσουμε στη Γαλλίδα για το ταξίδι της .
4. Ας πάμε με το ίδιο αμάξι.

Numbers:

τριαντατρείς
σαρανταεπτά
εκατο ενενηνταέξι
ογδονταοκτώ
εβδομηνταοκτώ
πενηνταένα
εκατο δεκαεννέα

Lesson 11

FUTURE		PAST	
θα κλείσω	θα κλείσουμε	έκλεισα	κλείσαμε
θα κλείσεις	θα κλείσετε	έκλεισες	κλείσατε
θα κλείσει	θα κλείσουν	έκλεισε	έκλεισαν

FUTURE		PAST	
θα σχεδιάσω	θα σχεδιάσουμε	σχεδίασα	σχεδιάσαμε
θα σχεδιάσεις	θα σχεδιάσετε	σχεδίασες	σχεδιάσατε
θα σχεδιάσει	θα σχεδιάσουν	σχεδίασε	σχεδίασαν

FUTURE		PAST	
θα εκφράσω	θα εκφράσουμε	εξέφρασα	εξεφράσαμε
θα εκφράσεις	θα εκφράσετε	εξέφρασες	εξεφράσατε
θα εκφράσει	θα εκφράσουν	εξέφρασε	εξέφρασαν

FUTURE		PAST	
θα προσέξω	θα προσέξουμε	πρόσεξα	προσέξαμε
θα προσέξεις	θα προσέξετε	πρόσεξες	προσέξατε
θα προσέξει	θα προσέξουν	πρόσεξε	πρόσεξαν

Contracted Verbs:

FUTURE		PAST	
θα παρατηρήσω	θα παρατηρήσουμε	παρατήρησα	παρατηρήσαμε
θα παρατηρήσεις	θα παρατηρήσετε	παρατήρησες	παρατηρήσατε
θα παρατηρήσει	θα παρατηρήσουν	παρατήρησε	παρατήρησαν

FUTURE		PAST	
θα ξεχάσω	θα ξεχάσουμε	ξέχασα	ξεχάσαμε
θα ξεχάσεις	θα ξεχάσετε	ξέχασες	ξεχάσατε
θα ξεχάσει	θα ξεχάσουν	ξέχασε	ξέχασαν

FUTURE		PAST	
θα εξηγήσω	θα εξηγήσουμε	εξήγησα	εξηγήσαμε
θα εξηγήσεις	θα εξηγήσετε	εξήγησες	εξηγήσατε
θα εξηγήσει	θα εξηγήσουν	εξήγησε	εξήγησαν

FUTURE		PAST	
θα συμφωνήσω	θα συμφωνήσουμε	συμφώνησα	συμφηνήσαμε
θα συμφωνήσεις	θα συμφωνήσετε	συμφώνησες	συμφηνήσατε
θα συμφωνήσει	θα συμφωνήσουν	συμφώνησε	συμφηνήσαν

Practice sentences:

1. Μπορείς να εξηγήσεις την ερωτήση;
2. Πιθανόν ξέχασε αυτό που είπατε.
3. Μιλάει καθαρά και εξηγεί τις ιδέες του καλά.
4. Δε με ενδιαφέρουν οι πληροφορίες.
5. Πρόσεξες το χαμόγελό της;
6. Ναι, το παρατήρησα.

Reflexive Verbs:

Translate, using the verb **δυσκολεύομαι**:

1. Πάντοτε δυσκολεύομαι να καταλάβω αυτά τα έργα.
2. Δυσκολεύονται με το αυτοκίνητό τους;
3. Δυσκολεύεται να εξηγήσει τις ιδέες.

Change the above sentences to the future tense.

1. Πάντοτε **θα δυσκολευθώ** να καταλάβω αυτά τα έργα.
2. **Θα δυσκολευθούν** με το αυτοκίνητό τους.
3. **Θα δυσκολευθεί** να εξηγήσει τις ιδέες.

Write these sentences, using the past tense.

1. Πάντοτε **δυσκολεύθηκα** να καταλάβω αυτά τα έργα.
2. **Δυσκολευθήκαμε** το αυτοκίνητό τους.
3. **Δυσκολεύθηκε** να εξηγήσει τις ιδέες.

συμβουλεύομαι — to consult

PRESENT

συμβουλεύομαι	συμβουλευόμαστε
συμβουλεύεσαι	συμβουλευόσαστε
συμβουλεύεται	συμβουλεύονται

FUTURE

θα συμβουλευθώ	θα συμβουλευθούμε
θα συμβουλευθείς	θα συμβουλευθείτε
θα συμβουλευθεί	θα συμβουλευθούν

PAST

συμβουλεύθηκα	συμβουλευθήκαμε
συμβουλεύθηκες	συμβουλευθήκατε
συμβουλεύθηκε	συμβουλευθήκαν

Practice sentences using the verb **αναρωτιέμαι**:

1. **Αναρωτιέται γιατί δεν την επισκεπτόμαστε.**
2. **Αναρωτιέμαι ποιος είναι εκείνος ο κούρος.**
3. **Αναρωτιόμαστε αν θα μπορέσεις να ταξιδέψεις.**

Translate the above sentences in the future tense.

1. **Θα αναρωτηθεί γιατί δεν την επισκεπτόμαστε.**
2. **Θα αναρωτηθώ ποιος είναι εκείνος ο κούρος.**
3. **Θα αναρωτηθούμε αν θα μπορέσεις να ταξιδέψεις.**

Now translate the same sentences, using the past tense.

1. **Αναρωτήθηκε γιατί δεν την επισκεπτόμαστε.**
2. **Αναρωτήθηκα ποιος είναι εκείνος ο κούρος.**
3. **Αναρωτηθήκαμε αν θα μπορέσεις να ταξιδέψεις.**

στενοχωριέμαι — to worry

PRESENT

στενοχωριέμαι	στενοχωριόμαστε
στενοχωριέσαι	στενοχωριόσαστε
στενοχωριέται	στενοχωριούνται

FUTURE

θα στενοχωρηθώ	θα στενοχωρηθούμε
θα στενοχωρηθείς	θα στενοχωρηθείτε
θα στενοχωρηθεί	θα στενοχωρηθούν

PAST

στενοχωρήθηκα	στενοχωρηθήκαμε
στενοχωρήθηκες	στενοχωρηθήκατε
στενοχωρήθηκε	στενοχωρήθηκαν

Try these sentences, using the verb **θυμάμαι**:

1. **Τι θυμόσαστε για το παρελθόν;**
2. **Δε θυμόμαστε την διεύθυνσή σου.**
3. **Θυμάται την συζήτησή της με την τάξι;**

Write the above sentences in the future.

1. **Τι θα θυμηθείτε για το παρελθόν;**
2. **Δε θα θυμηθούμε την διεύθυνσή σου.**
3. **Θα θυμηθείς την συζήτησή της με την τάξι;**

Now write the sentences using the past.

1. **Τι θυμηθήκατε για το παρελθόν;**
2. **Δε θυμηθήκαμε την διεύθυνσή σου.**
3. **Θυμήθηκε την συζήτησή της με την τάξι;**

κοιμάμαι — to sleep

PRESENT		FUTURE	
κοιμάμαι	**κοιμόμαστε**	**θα κοιμηθώ**	**θα κοιμθούμε**
κοιμάσαι	**κοιμόσαστε**	**θα κοιμηθείς**	**θα κοιμηθείτε**
κοιμάται	**κοιμούνται**	**θα κοιμηθεί**	**θα κοιμηθούν**

PAST	
κοιμήθηκα	**κοιμθήκαμε**
κοιμήθηκες	**κοιμθήκατε**
κοιμήθηκε	**κοιμήθηκαν**

Translate:

1. **Καθόμαστε εδώ γιατί έχουμε λιακάδα.**
2. **Πιθανόν κάθονται με τους γονείς τους.**
3. **Πού κάθονται οι γονείς σου στην παράσταση;**

Write these sentences in the future:

1. **Θα καθήσουμε εδώ γιατί έχουμε λιακάδα.**
2. **Πιθανόν θα καθήσουν με τους γονείς τους.**
3. **Πού θα καθήσουν οι γονείς σου στην παράσταση;**

Conjugate this verb in the past:

κάθησα	**καθήσαμε**
κάθησες	**καθήσατε**
κάθησε	**κάθησαν**

Now write the sentences in the past.

1. **Καθήσαμε εδώ γιατί έχουμε λιακάδα.**
2. **Πιθανόν κάθησαν με τους γονείς τους.**
3. **Πού κάθησαν οι γονείς σου στην παράσταση;**

Translate:

1. **Φαίνεται δύσκολο να ταξιδεύεις μόνος σου.**
2. **Σου φαίνεται λυπημένη;**
3. **Φαίνονται χαρούμενοι μαζί.**

FUTURE

θα φανώ	**θα φανούμε**
θα φανείς	**θα φανείτε**
θα φανεί	**θα φανούν**

Write the sentences, using the future tense.

1. **Θα φανεί διαφορετικό να ταξιδέψει μόνος του.**
2. **Θα σου φανεί λυπημένη;**
3. **Θα φανούν χαρούμενοι μαζί.**

Now write the sentences in the past tense.

1. **Φάνηκε δύσκολο να ταξιδεύεις μόνος σου.**
2. **Σου φάνηκε λυπημένη;**
3. **Φάνηκαν χαρούμενοι μαζί.**

<u>Genitive Case</u>:

Masculine nouns ending in **ας**

1. **ο αιώνας**
   η αρχή του αιώνα

2. **ο ταμίας**
   το δωμάτιο του ταμία

3. **ο άνδρας**
   το αμάξι του άνδρα

Masculine nouns ending in **ος**

1. **ο φίλος του**
   η οικογένεια του φίλου του

2. **ο κόσμος**
   τα έθνη του κοσμού

3. **ο καιρός**
   ο καιρός του Ιανουαρίου

Masculine nouns ending in **ης**

1. **ο βουλευτής**
   οι ιδέες του βουλευτή

2. **ο λιανοπώλης**
   η γυναίκα του λιανοπώλη

3. ο επιστάτης
   το γραφείο του επιστάτη

Nouns ending in **α**

1. η εβδομάδα
   οι μέρες της εβδομάδας

2. η θάλασσα
   μια θέα της θάλασσας

3. η μέρα
   η αρχή της μέρας

Nouns ending in **η**

1. η νύφη
   το αμάξι της νύφης

2. η Παρασκευή
   το μάθημα της Παρασκευής

3. η παράσταση
   ο τέλος της παραστάσης

Feminine nouns ending in **ος**

1. η Βίβλος
   οι λέξεις της Βίβλου

2. η έξοδος
   η πόρτα αυτής της εξόδου

Neuter nouns ending in **ο**

1. το ξενοδοχείο
   η διεύθυνση του ξενοδοχείου

2. το σκολείο του
   οι δάσκαλοι του σκολείου του

Neuter nouns ending in ι

1. το σπίτι μας
   τα παράθυρα του σπιτιού μας

2. το παιχνίδι
   η βάση αυτού του παιχνιδιού

3. το νήσι
   τα ξενοδοχεία του νησιού

Neuter nouns ending in μα

1. το ρήμα
   η σημασία του ρήματος

2. το γράμμα
   η αρχή του γράμματος

3. το διαμέρισμα
   το παράθυρο του διαμερίσματος

Neuter nouns ending in ος

1. το μέρος
   το όνομα του μέρους

2. το δάσος
   η ομρφιά του δάσους

The Genitive Case with Adjectives, articles or demonstrative pronouns:

1. η όμρφη γαλάζια θάλασσα
   μια θέα της όμορφης γαλάζιας θάλασσας

2. ο έξυπνος εξάδελφός του
   το Βιβλίο του έξυπνου εξάδελφού του

3. το άγαλμα
   το κεφάλι του ψιλού αγάλματος

4. η παράσταση
   ο τέλος όλης της παράστασης

5. η δική σας οικογένεια
   η ιστορία της δικής σας οικογένειας

Genitive forms of some irregular adjectives:

1. το σπίτι του υγιούς κούρου
2. η μητέρα του παχιού παιδιού
3. το σπίτι του πλατιού δρόμου
4. το φαγητό του υγιούς ανθρόπου

Genitive Case with plurals:

1. τα μαγαζιά των όμορφων, παλιών δρόμων της Νέα Υόρκης
2. τα πρόσωπα των χαρούμενων ανθρώπων των μικρών χωριών της
   Ελλάδας
3. τα σώματα των αδύνατων, παλιών ανθρώπων
4. τα όμορφα χρώματα των καινούριων αμαξιών

Genitive Case with indefinite articles:

1. μια φωτογφαφία μιας χωριάτικης ταβέρνας
2. το χαμόγελο ενός περίεργου μαθητή
3. οι δρόμοι μιας Ευρωπαϊκής πόλης

Translate using Relative Pronouns:

1. **Εκείνο είναι το παιδί για το οποίο αγοράσατε τα παιχνίδια;**
2. **Αυτή η δασκάλα για την οποία μήλησες;**
3. **Αυτή είναι η εύκολη μέθοδος με την οποία έμαθα τα ελληνικά.**

Translate:

1. Εκείνος είναι ο άλλος πελάτης του οποίου η γυναίκα ήρθε εδώ σήμερα.
2. Αυτή είναι η Πορτογαλίδα της οποίας ο γιός σπούδασε στην Αγγλία.
3. Αυτοί είναι οι Αμερικανοί των οποίων τα θαυμάσια παιδιά μας επισκέπτονται.

Negative Words:

Έχω κάτι για σένα.
Δεν έχω τίποτε για σένα.
Έχεις τίποτε για μένα;
Όχι, δεν έχω τίποτε για σένα.

Την επισκέπτομαι κάπου-κάπου.
Δεν την επισκέπτομαι ποτέ.
Την επισκέπτεται ποτέ;
Όχι, δεν την επισκέπτεται ποτέ.

Προσκαλάει κάποιο στο θέατρο.
Δεν προσκαλάει κανένα στο θέατρο.
Προσκαλούμε κανένα στο θέατρο;
Όχι, δεν προσκαλούμε κανένα.

Πάντοτε ταξιδεύουμε στην Ελλάδα το φθινόπωρο.
Ποτέ δεν ταξιδεύουμε στην Ελλάδα την άνοιξη.
Ταξιδεύετε ποτέ στην Ελλάδα;
Όχι, δεν ταξδεύω ποτέ στην Ελλάδα.

Numbers:

διακόσια σαραντατρία μικρά παιδιά
εξακόσια ενενηνταεπτά βιβλία
εκατό πενηταέξι σπουδαίες ιδέες

Lesson 12

Regular Verbs:

φέρνω

FUTURE		PAST	
θα φέρω	θα φέρουμε	έφερα	φέραμε
θα φέρεις	θα φέρετε	έφερες	φέρατε
θα φέρει	θα φέρουν	έφερε	έφεραν

περιμένω

FUTURE		PAST	
θα περιμένω	θα περιμένουμε	περίμενα	περιμέναμε
θα περιμένεις	θα περιμένετε	περίμενες	περιμένατε
θα περιμένει	θα περιμένουν	περίμενε	περίμεναν

καλυτερεύω

FUTURE		PAST	
θα καλυτερέψω	θα καλυτερέψουμε	καλυτέρεψα	καλυτερέψαμε
θα καλυτερέψεις	θα καλυτερέψετε	καλυτέρεψες	καλυτερέψατε
θα καλυτερέψει	θα καλυτερέψουν	καλυτέρεψε	καλυτέρεψαν

κανονίζω

FUTURE		PAST	
θα κανονίσω	θα κανονίσουμε	κανόνισα	κανονίσαμε
θα κανονίσεις	θα κανονίσετε	κανόνισες	κανονίσατε
θα κανονίσει	θα κανονίσουν	κανόνισε	κανόνισαν

Contracted Verbs:

βοηθώ

PAST

βοήθησα	βοηθήσαμε
βοήθησες	βοηθήσατε
βοήθησε	βοήθησαν

αλληλογραφώ

FUTURE

θα αλληλογραφήσω	θα αλληλογραφήσουμε
θα αλληλογραφήσεις	θα αλληλογραφήσετε
θα αλληλογραφήσει	θα αλληλογραφήσουν

PAST

αλληλογράφησα	αλληλογραφήσαμε
αλληλογράφησες	αλληλογραφήσατε
αλληλογράφησε	αλληλογράφησαν

Reflexive Verbs:

γεννιέμαι

FUTURE		PAST	
θα γεννηθώ	θα γεννηθούμε	γεννήθηκα	γεννηθήκαμε
θα γεννηθείς	θα γεννηθείτε	γεννήθηκες	γεννηθήκατε
θα γεννηθεί	θα γεννηθούν	γεννήθηκε	γεννήθηκαν

Translate:

1. Τι θα φέρεις στο σπίτι μου την Κυριακή;
2. Πώς θα καλυτερέψετε τα γαλλικά σας;
3. Κανόνισα τα πάντα σχετικά με τις σπουδές μου στο πανεπιστύμιο.
4. Δε μας βοήθησε καθόλου.

5. Θα μας αλληλογραφήσουμε πάλι.
6. Πού γεννήθηκαν;

Translate:

1. Μην διαβάζεις εκείνο το βιβλίο.
2. Μην μπαίνετε στην κουζίνα.
3. Μην φτάνετε αργά.

Translate:

1. Μου είπε να μην αγοράζω εκείνο το σπίτι.
2. Μας ζήτησαν να μην σπουδάζουμε στη βιβλιοθήκη.

Expressing Dates:

δεκαέξι Μαρτίου
είκοσι τρία Νοεμβρίου

Answer in Greek:

1. Τα γενέθλιά μου είναι....
2. Η ημερομηνία είναι ...

Translate these sentences, using time expressions:

1. Η παράσταση αρχίζει στις οκτώ και τέταρτο το βράδυ.
2. Φτάσαμε στις ένδεκα και πέντε το πρωί περίπου.
3. Είναι ένδεκα παρά πέντε ακριβώς.
4. Πρέπει να φύγουν στις τέσσερα και μισή ακριβώς.
5. Θα φάμε στις επτά παρά τέταρτο το βράδυ.

ADJECTIVE	ADVERB	ENGLISH MEANING
απλός	απλά	simply
αδιάφορος	αδιάφορα	indifferently
σωστός	σωστά	correctly
ήσυχος	ήσυχα	calmly
δύσκολος	δύσκολα	with difficulty

Translate:

1. Μίλησε καθαρά και σωστά.
2. Ας περπατήσουμε προσεκτικά και ήσυχα.
3. Γγάφει εύκολα ή δύσκολα;
4. Μου απάντησε αδιάφορα.
5. Θα το εξηγήσω απλά.

Translate, using prepositions:

1. Η εφημερίδα είναι κάτω από το τραπέζι.
2. Ταξιδεύουν γύρω από τον κόσμο.
3. Η Ελλάδα είναι μακριά από την Ιταλία;
4. Η καρέκλα είναι κατά την πόρτα.
5. Για να φτάσεις στο σπίτι μου, πρέπει να οδηγήσείς κατευθείαν.
6. Τα περιοδικά μας είναι πάνω στα βιβλία σου.
7. Περπατάει προς τα πίσω.
8. Μένει σ'ένα μικρό διαμέρισμα πάνω από ένα μαγαζί.

Comparatives:

1.
a) Τα χειροτεχνήματα στην Πορτογαλία είναι τόσο όμοφα όσο τα χειροτεχνήματα στην Ιταλία.
b) Τα χειροτεχνήματα στην Πορτογαλία είναι πιο όμοφα από τα χειροτεχνήματα στην Ιταλία.
c) Τα χειροτεχνήματα στην Πορτογαλία είναι λιγότερο όμοφα από τα χειροτεχνήματα στην Ιταλία.

2.
a) Η γλώσσα σου είναι τόσο περίπλοκη όσο η δική μου.
b) Η γλώσσα σου είναι πιο περίπλοκη από τη δική μου.
c) Η γλώσσα σου είναι λιγότερο περίπλοκη από τη δική μου.

3.
a) Οι αγγλικές εφημερίδες είναι τόσο ενδιαφέρουσες όσο οι αμερικανικές εφημερίδες.

b) Οι αγγλικές εφημερίδες είναι πιο ενδιαφέρουσες από τις αμερικανικές εφημερίδες.

c) Οι αγγλικές εφημερίδες είναι λιγότερο ενδιαφέρουσες από τις αμερικανικές εφημερίδες.

Translate, using the word **σαν**:

1. Είναι έξυπνοι, σαν τον αδελφό τους.
2. Δεν είναι όμορφη, σαν την μητέρα της.

Superlatives:

1. **Αυτό είναι το πιο δύσκολο μάθημα στο βιβλίο.**
2. **Εκείνο το εστιατόριο έχει το πιο καλό φαγητό στο Παρίσι.**

either ... or:

1. **Μπορώ να σου επισκεπτώ ή τη Δευτέρα ή την Πέμπτη.**
2. **Πηγαίνουμε ή στην Ιταλία ή στην Ισπανία.**

neither ... nor:

1. **Δε θέλει ούτε αυτό το βιβλίο ούτε εκείνο.**
2. **Δε μπορώ να έρθω ούτε τη Δευτέρα ούτε την Παρασκευή.**

GREEK–ENGLISH GLOSSARY

Notes: 1. All adjectives and demonstrative pronouns are listed in mascu-
          line, singular form.
          2. This list does not include personal pronouns, direct object
          pronouns, indirect object pronouns or numbers. For these, the
          student should consult the corresponding chapter.

αβέβαιος	uncertain
το άγαλμα	statue
η αγάπη	love
η Αγγλία	England
η Αγγλίδα	Englishwoman
τα αγγλικά	English (language)
η αγγλική	English (language)
αγγλικός	English (adj.)
ο ᾽Αγγλος	Englishman
αγοράζω	to buy
η αδελφή	sister
ο αδελφός	brother
αδιάφορος	indifferent
αδύνατος	weak
το αεροπλάνο	airplane
η Αθήνα	Athens
το αίμα	blood
ο αιώνας	century
ακόμη	yet, still
η Ακρόπολη	the Acropolis
η αλήθεια	truth
αλλά	but
αλλάζω	to change
αλληλογραφώ	to keep in touch, to write to each other
άλλος	other, next
το αμάξι	car
η αμερικανική γλωσσα	English (language)
η Αμερικανίδα	American (woman)
αμερικανικός	American (adj.)
ο Αμερικανός	American (man)
η Αμερική	America, U.S.

αν	if
αν και	although
η ανάγκη	need
η αναλογία	proportion
αναρωτιέμαι	to wonder
ανακαλύπτω	to discover
ο άνδρας	man, husband
άνετος	cozy, comfortable
ανιαρός	boring
η άνοιξη	the spring
άξαφνα	all of a sudden, suddenly
απαντώ	to answer
απασχολημένος	busy
απέναντι	across from
απίστευτος	unbelievable
απλός	simple
από	from, of
το απόγευμα	afternoon
αποφασίζω	to decide
απόψε	tonight
η άποψη	point of view
ο Απρίλιος	April
αργά	late, slowly
αργότερα	later
αρέσω	to please, to be pleasing
αριστερά	to the left
άρρωστος	sick
αρχαίος	ancient
η αρχή	the beginning
αρχίζω	to begin, to start
άσπρος	white
άσχημος	ugly
ο Αύγουστος	August
αύριο	tomorrow
αυτό που	what (in the sense of "that which")
το αυτοκίνητο	automobile, car
αυτός	this (one)
αφήνω	to leave (trans.)

αφού	after (followed by acc. + noun)
η βάση	basis
βέβαια	certainly
βέβαιος	certain
η βίβλος	Bible
το βιβλίο	book
βλάκας	stupid
το βλέμμα	look, glance
βλέπω	to look, to see
βοηθώ	to help
ο βουλευτής	congressman
το βράδυ	the evening
η Βραζιλία	Brazil
βραζιλιάνκος	Brazilian (adj.)
ο Βραζιλιάνος	Brazilian (man)
ο βραχίονας	arm
βρίσκομαι	to be, to be located
βρίσκω	to find
βροχερός	rainy
βρώμικος	dirty
το γάλα	milk
γαλάζιος	blue
η Γαλλία	France
η Γαλλίδα	French (woman)
τα γαλλικά	French (language)
γαλλικός	French (adj.)
ο Γάλλος	Frenchman
η γειτονιά	neighborhood
γεμάτος (+ από)	full (of)
τα γενέθλια	birthday
γενικά	generally
γεννιέμαι	to be born
η Γερμανία	Germany
η Γερμανίδα	German (woman)
τα γερμανικά	German (language)
γερμανικός	German (adj.)
ο Γερμανός	German (man)
γερός	strong

για	for
γιατί	why, because
ο γιατρός	doctor
γιορτάζω	to celebrate
ο γιός	son
η γλώσσα	language
γνέφω	to nod
η γνωμή	opinion
οι γονείς	parents
το γράμμα	letter
το γραφείο	office
γραφικός	picturesque
γράφω	to write
γρήγορος	fast, rapid
το γυαλί	glass
γυμνός	nude, naked
η γυναίκα	woman, wife
γυρίζω	to return
γύρω από	around
ο δάσκαλος, η δασκάλα	teacher
το δάσος	forest
δείχνεται	to show oneself
δείχνω	to show
ο Δεκέμβριος	December
δεν	not
η Δευτέρα	Monday
δεξιά	to the right
δηλαδή	that is to say
το διαβατήριο	passport
η διαδρομή	ride, route
διαθέσιμος	available
οι διακοπές	vacation
η διακοπή	interruption
το διαμέρισμα	apartment
διαφορετικός	different
η διεύθυνση	address
ο δικός	own (followed by possessive adjective)

δίνω	to give
δίπλα	next to, near (+ σε, απο), alongside
ο δίσκος	tray
διψώ	to be thirsty
η δουλειά	work
δουλεύω	to work
το δράμα	drama
ο δρόμος	street
η δροσιά	coolness
δυσκολεύομαι	to have difficulty
δύσκολος	difficult
δυστυχώς	unfortunately
το δωμάτιο	room
το δώρο	gift
η εβδομάδα	week
εδώ	here
το έθνος	nation
είμαι	to be
το εισιτήριο	ticket
η είσοδος	entrance
εκεί	there
εκείνος	that (one)
εκτός αν	unless
εκφράζω	to express
η Ελβετία	Switzerland
ελβετικός	Swiss (adj.)
ο Ελβετός	Swiss (man)
η Ελλάδα	Greece
η Ελλάς	Greece
ο Έλληνας	Greek man
η Ελληνίδα	Greek woman
τα ελληνικά	Greek (language)
τα ελληνικά νησιά	the Greek islands
ελληνικός	Greek (adj.)
ελπίζω	to hope
ενδιαφέρω	to interest, to be interesting (used only in 3rd persons sing. and pl.)
ενδιαφέρων	interesting

το ενθύμιο	souvenir
ενθουσιάζομαι	to become enthusiastic
η έννοια	concept
εντάξει	O.K.
εντυπωσιάζομαι	to be impressed
ενώ	while, whereas
ο εξάδελφος, η εξαδέλφη	cousin
εξαιρετικός	extraordinary
εξαφανίζομαι	to disappear
εξηγώ	to explain
η έξοδος	exit
η εξοχή	the country(side)
έξυπνος	clever
έξω από	outside of
ερειπομένος	ruined
η ερώτηση	question (pl. οι ερωτήσεις)
επειδή	since, because
επίσης	also, too
επισκέπτομαι	to visit
ο επιστάτης	supervisor
ετοιμάζομαι	to get ready
η εποχή	season, era
το έργο	work
έρχομαι	to come
το εστιατόριο	restaurant
εσφαλμένος	incorrect
έτοιμος	ready
το έτος	year
έτσι	thus, that way
η ευκαιρία	opportunity, chance
εύκολα	easily
εύκολος	easy
Ευρωπαϊκός	European
η εφημερίδα	newspaper
το ζαχαροπλαστείο	café
η ζάχαρη	sugar
ζηλεύω	to be jealous
ζητώ	to request, to ask, to ask for, to look for

ή	or
ηλικιωμένος	old, elderly
ο ήλιος	sun
οι Ηνωμένες Πολιτείες	United States
ήσυχος	calm, quiet
θα	[particle used with a verb to create the future and other tenses]
η θάλασσα	sea
θαυμάσιος	wonderful
η θέα	view
θεατρικός	theatrical
το θέατρο	theatre
η θεία	aunt
ο θείος	uncle
θέλω	to want
η θέση	spot, place
ο θόρυβος	noise
θυμάμαι	to remember
ο Ιανουάριος	January
ο Ιάπωνας	Japanese (man)
η Ιαπωνέζα	Japanese (woman)
τα ιαπωνέζικα	Japanese (language)
η Ιαπωνία	Japan
τα ιαπωνικά	Japanese (language)
ιαπωνικός	Japanese (adj.)
η ιδέα	idea
ιδιαίτερα	especially
ο ίδιος	the same
ο Ιούλιος	July
ο Ιούνιος	June
η Ιρλανδή	Irish (woman)
η Ιρλανδία	Ireland
ιρλανδικός	Irish (adj.)
ο Ιρλανδός	Irishman
η Ισπανία	Spain
η Ισπανίδα	Spanish (language)
ισπανίκός	Spanish (adj.)
ο Ισπανός	Spaniard (male)
η ιστορία	story, history

ίσως	maybe, perhaps
η Ιταλία	Italy
η Ιταλίδα	Italian (woman)
τα ιταλικά	Italian (language)
ιταλικός	Italian (adj.)
ο Ιταλός	Italian (man)
καθαρά	clearly
καθαρίζω	to clean
καθαρός	clean, clear
κάθε	each
ο καθένας	anyone
καθοδόν	on the way
καθόλου	not at all
κάθομαι	to sit down
ο καθρέφτης	mirror
και	and
καινούριος	new
ο καιρός	weather, time
κακός	bad
καλά	well
το καλοκαίρι	summer
καλός	good
καλυτερεύω	to improve
το καλύτερο	the best
καμιά	none, not one
καμιά φορά	sometimes, ever, never
κανείς	no one (acc. case)
κανένας	no one, not one, nobody, none
κανονίζω	to arrange, take care of, regulate
κανονικά	regularly
κάποια μέρα	someday
κάποιος	someone
κάποτε	sometime, at a certain time
κάποτε-κάποτε	sometimes
κάπου	somewhere
κάπου-κάπου	sometimes
κάπως	somehow
η καρέκλα	chair

η κάρτα	card
καταλαβαίνω	to understand
η κατάσταση	situation
κατευθείαν	straight ahead
κάτι	something, any
κάτω από	below, under
κάτω σε	down, down by
το καφενείο	cafe
ο καφές	coffee
το κεφάλι	head
ο κήπος	garden
η Κίνα	China
η Κινέζα	Chinese (woman)
τα κινέζικα	Chinese (language)
κινεζικός	Chinese (adj.)
ο Κινέζος	Chinese (man)
η κίνηση	traffic
κιόλας	already
κλείνω	to close
κοιμάμαι	to sleep
κοιτάζω	to look at
το κομπιούτερ	computer
κοντά (+ σε)	near
κοντός	short
η κόρη	daughter, girl, *kore*
το κορμί	torso
ο κόσμος	world
η κουζίνα	kitchen
κουράζομαι	to get tired
κουρασμένος	tired
ο κούρος	boy, youth, *kouros*
το κράτος	government
το κτίριο	building
η Κυριακή	Sunday
ο κύριος, κύριος, κ.	gentleman, Sir, Mr.
λαβαίνω	to receive, to get
ο λαιμός	neck
λείπω	to miss, to be missing from

η λέξη	word (pl: οι λέξεις)
η λεπτομέρεια	detail
λεπτός	thin
τα λεφτά	money
λέω	to say, call
το λεωφορείο	bus
η λιακάδα	sunshine
ο λιανοπώλης	shopkeeper
λίγο	a little
λίγος	a few
ο λογαριασμός	bill
η λογοτεχνία	literature
λοιπόν	well, then
το Λονδίνο	London
το λουτροδωμάτιο	bathroom
λυπημένος	sad
το μαγαζί	store
μαγειρεύω	to cook
μαζί	together
μαθαίνω	to learn
ο μαθητής, η μαθήτρια	student (male, female)
ο Μάϊος	May
μακριά	far
μάλλον	rather, somewhat
ο Μάρτιος	March
μας	our
το μάτι	eye
με	with, by means of, via
μεγάλος	big
το μέγεθος	size
η μέθοδος	method
το μέλλον	the future
η μέρα	day
μερικές φορές	sometimes
μερικός	some, a few
το μέρος	bathroom (slang), part
μέσα	inside (followed by σε)
μετά	then, afterwards, after

μεταξύ	between (used with genitive case)
ο μήνας	month
το μήνυμα	message
η μισή	half
μικρός	small
μιλώ	to speak
μόλις	as soon as
μόνο	only
μόνος (+ i.o.p.)	alone
μου	my
η μουσική	music
ο μουσικός	musician
μπαίνω	to come in, to enter
μπορώ	to be able
η Μύκονος	Mykonos
το μυστήριο	mystery
να	[particle used with a verb to create the infinitive and other tenses]
ναι	yes
ο ναός	temple
η Νέα Υόρκη	New York
νέος	young, new
το νερό	water
το νησί	island
ο Νοέμβριος	November
νοικιάζω	to rent
νομίζω	to think
ντυμένος	clothed
η νύφη	bride
η νύχτα	night
νωρίς	early
το όνομα	the name
το ξενοδοχείο	hotel
ο ξένος	foreigner, stranger, guest
ξέρω	to know
ξεχνώ	to forget
οδηγώ	to drive
η οικογένεια	family

ο Οκτώβριος	October
η Ολλανδή	Dutch (woman)
η Ολλανδία	Holland, the Netherlands
τα ολλανδικά	Dutch (language)
ολλανδικός	Dutch (adj.)
ο Ολλανδός	Dutchman
όλος	all
η ομορφιά	beauty
όμορφος	beautiful
όταν	when
ό,τι	whatever
ότι	that
όχι	no
το παιδί	child
παίζω	to play
παίρνω	to take, to get
το παιχνίδι	game, toy
πάλι	again
παλιός	old
το πανεπιστήμιο	university
τα πάντα	everything
πάντοτε	always
παντού	everywhere
πάνω από	above, over
πάνω σε	up, up by
το παράθυρο	window
η παραλία	beach, coastline
παραλιακός	coastal
η Παρασκευή	Friday
η παράσταση	performance
παρατηρώ	to observe
το παρελθόν	the past
ο πατέρας	father
παχύς	fat
πεινώ	to be hungry
ο πελάτης	customer, client
η Πέμπτη	Thursday
περασμένος	previous, last

περιγράφω	to describe
περίεργος	curious
περιμένω	to wait for
το περιοδικό	magazine
η περιοχή	district
περίπλοκος	complicated
περίπου	about, more or less
περιεργάζομαι	to watch, to be attentive
περισσότερο (+ adj.)	more
η περηφάνια	pride
περνώ	to spend, to pass (time)
πέρσι	last year
περπατώ	to walk around
πηγαίνω	to go
πιθανόν	probably
πίνω	to drink
πιο	more
πιστεύω	to believe
πίσω	behind, in back of
πλατύς	wide
η πλευρά	side
πληκτικός	boring
η πληροφορία	information
πληρώνω	to pay
το πόδι	foot
ποιος	that, which, who
ποιον	whom
πολλοί	many
η πόλη	city
πολύ	very, very much
πολύς	a lot
η πόρτα	door
η Πορτογαλία	Portugal
η Πορτογαλίδα	Portuguese (woman)
τα πορτογαλικά	Portuguese (language)
πορτογαλικός	Portuguese (adj.)
ο Πορτογάλος	Portuguese (man)
η πορτοκαλάδα	orange juice

πόσο	how much
πόσος	how much, how many
πότε	when
ποτέ	never
πότε πότε	sometimes
το ποτό	drink
που	where, that, who
πουθενά	nowhere
το πράγμα	thing
πρέπει (+ να)	to have to, must
πριν	before, ago
το πρόγραμμα	program
η πρόποση	toast (verbal)
προς	toward
προς τα πίσω	backwards
προσεκτικά	carefully
προσέχω	to notice
προσκαλώ	to invite
προσωπικός	personal
το πρόσωπο	face
η πρόταση	sentence
προτιμώ	to prefer
η προφορά	accent
προχθές	the day before yesterday
το πρωί	morning, in the morning
πως	how, that
το ρήμα	verb
η Ρώμη	Rome
ρωτώ	to ask
το Σάββατο	Saturday
το Σαββατοκύριακο	weekend
το σαλόνι	living room
σαν	like
σας	your (pol.)
σε	in, at, to, on
ο σεβασμός	respect
ο Σεπτέμβριος	September
σηκωνώ	to lift

η σημασία	meaning
σήμερα	today
σκεδιάζω	to plan
σκοτεινός	dark
σοβαρός	serious
σου	your (fam.)
η σούπα	soup
σπάνια	seldom
το σπίτι	house
σπουδάζω	to study
σπουδαίος	important
οι σπουδές	studies
ο σταθμός	station
σταματώ	to stop
στεγνός	dry
στέλνω	to send
στενός	narrow
στενοχωριέμαι	to worry
στο εξωτερικό	abroad
η συζήτηση	discussion
συμβουλεύομαι	to consult
η συμμετρία	symmetry
συμφωνώ	to agree
συνεχίζω	to continue
συνηθίζω (+ να)	to be in the habit of
συνήθως	usually
συνοδεύω	to accompany
σύντομα	soon
η συντροφιά	company
συχνά	often
το σχέδιο	plan
σχεδόν	almost
το σχολείο	school
το σώμα	body
σωστός	correct
η ταβέρνα	tavern (casual restaurant)
ο ταμίας	cashier
η τάξη	class

ταξιδεύω	to travel
το ταξίδι	trip
τελειώνω	to finish
το τέλος	the end
η Τετάρτη	Wednesday
τέταρτο	quarter
τέτοιος	such
η τέχνη	art
τηλεφωνώ	to telephone, to call
της	her
τινάζω	to shake off
τίνος	whose
τόσο	so
τόσος	so much, so many
τότε	then, at that time
του	his, its
τουλάχιστο	at least
τους	their
ο τουρίστα, η τουρίστρια	tourist
η Τουρκάλα	Turkish (woman)
η Τουρκία	Turkey
τα τουρκικά	Turkish (language)
η Τουρκική γλώσσα	Turkish (language)
τουρκικός	Turkish (adj.)
ο Τούρκος	Turk (male)
το τραγούδι	song
η τράπεζα	bank
το τραπέζι	table
το τρένο	train
η Τρίτη	Tuesday
τρομάζω	to frighten
ο τρόπος	way, method, means, manner
τρώω	to eat
τα τρόφιμα	groceries
το τσάι	tea
τώρα	now
υγιής	healthy
υγρός	wet

ύστερα	then
το φαγητό	food
φαίνομαι	to seem
φαντάζομαι	to imagine
ο Φεβρουάριος	February
φέρνω	to bring
φέτος	this year
φεύγω	to go out, to leave (intrans.)
το φθινόπωρο	autumn, fall
η φιλία	friendship
ο φίλος, η φίλη	friend
η Φλορεντία	Florence
η φορά	time (as in "this time")
φτάνω	to arrive
φωνητικός	phonetic
φωτεινός	light
η φωτογραφία	photograph
χάνω	to lose, to miss
το χαμόγελο	smile
χαρούμενος	happy
ο χειμώνας	winter
τα χειροτεχνήματα	handicrafts
το χέρι	hand
η χερσόνησος	peninsula
χθες	yesterday
ο χορός	dance
χρειάζομαι	to need
χρήσιμος	useful
ο χρόνος	year (plural: τα χρόνια)
η χώρα	country
χωριάτικος	rural, countrystyle
το χωριό	village
χωρίς	without
ο χώρος	space
ψηλός	tall
ψωνίζω	to shop
ο ώμος	shoulder
η ώρα	hour, time

ENGLISH–GREEK
GLOSSARY

a lot	πολύς
(to be) able	μπορώ
about	περίπου
above	πάνω από
abroad	στο εξωτερικό
accent	η προφορά
(to) accompany	συνοδεύω
Acropolis	η Ακρόπολη
address	η διεύθυνση
after	αφού (followed by acc. + noun), μετά
afternoon	το απόγευμα
afterwards	μετά
again	πάλι
ago	πριν
(to) agree	συμφωνώ
airplane	το αεροπλάνο
all	όλος
all of a sudden	άξαφνα
almost	σχεδόν
alone	μόνος (+ i.o.p.)
alongside	δίπλα
already	κιόλας
also	επίσης
although	αν και
always	πάντοτε
America	η Αμερική, οι Ηνωμένες Πολιτείες
American (adj.)	αμερικανικός
American (man)	ο Αμερικανός
American (woman)	η Αμερικανίδα
ancient	αρχαίος
and	και
(to) answer	απαντώ
any	κάτι
anyone	ο καθένας
apartment	το διαμέρισμα
April	ο Απρίλιος
arm	ο βραχίονας
around	γύρω από

(to) arrange	κανονίζω
(to) arrive	φτάνω
art	η τέχνη
as soon as	μόλις
(to) ask	ρωτώ, ζητώ
(to) ask for	ζητώ
at	σε
at a certain time	κάποτε
at least	τουλάχιστο
at night	τη νύχτα
at that time	τότε
Athens	η Αθήνα
(to be) attentive	περιεργάζομαι
August	ο Αύγουστος
aunt	η θεία
automobile	το αυτοκίνητο
autumn	το φθινόπωρο
available	διαθέσιμος
backwards	προς τα πίσω
bank	η τράπεζα
basis	η βάση
bathroom	το λουτροδωμάτιο, το μέρος (slang)
(to) be	είμαι, υπάρχω, βρίσκομαι
beach	η παραλία
beautiful	όμορφος
beauty	η ομορφιά
because	γιατί, επειδή
(to) become enthusiastic	ενθουσιάζομαι
bedroom	το υπνοδωμάτιο
before	πριν
(to) begin	αρχίζω
beginning	η αρχή
behind	πίσω
(to) believe	πιστεύω
below	κάτω από
the best	το καλυτέρο
between	μεταξύ (used with genitive case)
Bible	η βίβλος

big	μεγάλος
bill	ο λογαριασμός
birthday	τα γενέθλια
blood	το αίμα
blue	γαλάζιος
body	το σώμα
book	το βιβλίο
boring	πληκτικός, ανιαρός
(to be) born	γεννιέμαι
boy	ο κούρος
Brazil	η Βραζιλία
Brazilian (adj.)	βραζιλιανικός
Brazilian (man)	ο Βραζιλιάνος
bride	η νύφη
(to) bring	φέρνω
brother	ο αδελφός
building	το κτίριο
bus	το λεωφορείο
busy	απασχολημένος
but	αλλά
(to) buy	αγοράζω
by means of	με
café	το καφενείο, το ζαχαροπλαστείο
(to) call	λέω, τηλεφωνώ
calm	ήσυχος
car	το αμάξι, το αυτοκίνητο
card	η κάρτα
carefully	προσεκτικά
cashier	ο ταμίας
(to) celebrate	γιορτάζω
century	ο αίωνας
certain	βέβαιος
certainly	βέβαια
chair	η καρέκλα
chance	η ευκαιρία
(to) change	αλλάζω
child	το παιδί
China	η Κίνα

Chinese (adj.)	κινεζικός
Chinese (language)	τα κινεζικά
Chinese (man)	ο Κινέζος
Chinese (woman)	η Κινέζα
city	η πόλη
class	η τάξη
clean	καθαρός
(to) clean	καθαρίζω
clear	καθαρός
clearly	καθαρά
clever	έξυπνος
client	ο πελάτης
(to) close	κλείνω
clothed	ντυμένος
coastal	παραλιακός
coastline	η παραλία
coffee	ο καφές
(to) come	έρχομαι
(to) come in	μπαίνω
comfortable	άνετος
company	η συντροφιά
complicated	περίπλοκος
computer	το κομπιούτερ
concept	η έννοια
congressman	ο βουλευτής
(to) consult	συμβουλεύομαι
(to) continue	συνεχίζω
(to) cook	μαγειρεύω
coolness	η δροσιά
correct	σωστός
country	η χώρα
cozy	άνετος
country(side)	η εξοχή
country style	χωριάτικος
cousin	ο εξάδελφος, η εξαδέλφη
curious	περίεργος
customer	ο πελάτης
dance	ο χορός

dark	σκοτεινός
daughter	η κόρη
day	η μέρα
day before yesterday	προχθές
December	Δεκέμβριος
decide	αποφασίζω
(to) describe	περιγράφω
detail	η λεπτομέρεια
different	διαφορετικός
difficult	δύσκολος
(to have) difficulty	δυσκολεύομαι
dirty	βρώμικος
disappear	εξαφανίζομαι
(to) discover	ανακαλύπτω
discussion	η συζήτηση
district	η περιοχή
doctor	ο γιατρός
door	η πόρτα
down, down by	κάτω σε
drama	το δράμα
(to) drink	πίνω
drink	το ποτό
(to) drive	οδηγώ
dry	στεγνός
Dutch (adj).	ολλανδικός
Dutch (language)	τα ολλανδικαά
Dutchman	ο Ολλανδός
Dutch (woman)	η Ολλανδή
each	κάθε
early	νωρίς
easily	εύκολα
easy	εύκολος
(to) eat	τρώω
elderly	ηλικιωμένος
end	ο τέλος
England	η Αγγλία
English (adj.)	αγγλικός

English (language)	τα αγγλικά, η αμερικανική γλώσσα, η αγγλική γλώσσα
Englishman	ο Άγγλος
Englishwoman	η Αγγλίδα
(to) enter	μπαίνω
entrance	η είσοδος
epoch	η εποχή
era	η εποχή
especially	ιδιαίτερα
European	Ευρωπαϊκός
evening	το βράδυ
ever	καμιά φορά
everything	τα πάντα
everywhere	παντού
(to) exist	υπάρχω
exit	η έξοδος
(to) explain	εξηγώ
(to) express	εκφράζω
extraordinary	εξαιρετικός
eye	το μάτι
face	το πρόσωπο
fall (the season)	το φθινόπωρο
family	η οικογένεια
far	μακριά
fast	γρήγορος
fat	παχύς
father	ο πατέρας
February	ο Φεβρουάριος
few	μερικός
(to) find	βρίσκω
finish	τελειώνω
Florence	η Φλορεντία
food	το φαγητό
foot	το πόδι
foreigner	ο ξένος
forest	το δάσος
(to) forget	ξεχνώ
France	η Γαλλία

French (adj.)	γαλλικός
French (language)	τα γαλλικά
Frenchman	ο Γάλλος
French (woman)	η Γαλλίδα
Friday	η Παρασκευή
friend	ο φίλος, η φίλη
friendship	η φιλία
(to) frighten	τρομάζω
from	από
full (of)	γεμάτος (+ από)
future	το μέλλον
game	το παιχνίδι
garden	ο κήπος
generally	γενικά
gentleman	ο κύριος
German (adj.)	γερμανικός
German (language)	τα γερμανικά
German (man)	ο Γερμανός
German (woman)	η Γερμανίδα
Germany	η Γερμανία
(to) get	παίρνω, λαβαίνω
(to) get ready	ετοιμάζομαι
(to) get tired	κουράζομαι
gift	το δώρο
girl	η κόρη
(to) give	δίνω
glance	το βλέμμα
glass	το γυαλί
(to) go	πηγαίνω
(to) go out	φεύγω (intrans.)
good	καλός
government	το κράτος
Greece	η Ελλάδα, η Ελλάς
Greek (adj.)	ελληνικός
Greek islands	τα ελληνικά νησιά
Greek (language)	τα ελληνικά
Greek (man)	ο Έλληνας
Greek (woman)	η Ελληνίδα

groceries	τα τρόφιμα
guest	ο ξένος
(to) be in the <u>habit</u> of	συνηθίζω (+ να)
half	η μισή
hand	το χέρι
handicrafts	τα χειροτεχνήματα
happy	χαρούμενος
(to) have	έχω
(to) have to	πρέπει (+ να)
head	το κεφάλι
healthy	υγιής
(to) help	βοηθώ
her	της
here	εδώ
his	του
history	η ιστορία
Holland	η Ολλανδία
(to) hope	ελπίζω
hotel	το ξενοδοχείο
hour	η ώρα
house	το σπίτι
how	πως
how much, how many	πόσος (quantitative)
how much	πόσο
(to be) hungry	πεινώ
husband	ο άνδρας
idea	η ιδέα
if	αν
(to) imagine	φαντάζομαι
important	σπουδαίος
(to be) impressed	εντυπωσιάζομαι
(to) improve	καλυτερεύω
in	σε
in back of	πίσω
in the afternoon	το απόγευμα
in the morning	το πρωί
incorrect	εσφαλμένος
indifferent	αδιάφορος

information	η πληροφορία
inside	μέσα (σε)
(to) interest	ενδιαφέρω (used only in 3ʳᵈ per. sing. and pl.)
(to be) interesting	ενδιαφέρω (used only in 3ʳᵈ per. sing. and pl.)
interesting	ενδιαφέρων
interruption	η διακοπή
invite	προσκαλώ
Ireland	η Ιρλανδία
Irish (adj.)	ιρλανδικός
Irishman	ο Ιρλανδός
Irish (woman)	η Ιρλανδή
island	το νησί
Italian (adj.)	ιταλικός
Italian (language)	τα ιταλικά
Italian (man)	ο Ιταλός
Italian (woman)	η Ιταλίδα
Italy	η Ιταλία
its	του
January	ο Ιανουάριος
Japan	η Ιαπωνία
Japanese (adj.)	ιαπωνικός
Japanese (language)	τα ιαπωνέζικα, τα ιαπωνικά
Japanese (man)	ο Ιάπωνας
Japanese (woman)	η Ιαπωνέζα
(to be) jealous	ζηλεύω
July	Ιούλιος
June	ο Ιούνιος
(to) keep in touch	αλληλογραφώ
kitchen	η κουζίνα
(to) know	ξέρω
kore	η κόρη
kouros	ο κούρος
language	η γλώσσα
last	περασμένος
last year	πέρσι
late	αργά

later	αργότερα
(to) learn	μαθαίνω
(to) leave	αφήνω (trans.), φεύγω (intrans.)
letter	το γράμμα
(to) lift	σηκώνω
light	φωτεινός
like	σαν
literature	η λογοτεχνία
(a) little	λίγο, λίγος
(to) live	μένω
living room	το σαλόνι
(to be) located	βρίσκομαι
London	το Λονδίνο
look	το βλέμμα
(to) look	βλέπω
(to) look at	κοιτάζω
(to) look for	ζητώ
(to) lose	χάνω
love	η αγάπη
magazine	το περιοδικό
man	ο άνδρας, ο άνθρωπος
manner	ο τρόπος
many	πολλοί
March	ο Μάρτιος
May	ο Μάιος
maybe	ίσως
meaning	η σημασία
means	ο τρόπος
message	το μήνυμα
method	η μέθοδος, ο τρόπος
milk	το γάλα
mirror	ο καθρέφτης
(to) miss	χάνω, λείπω (to be missing from)
Monday	η Δευτέρα
money	τα λεφτά
month	ο μήνας
more	πιο, περισσότερο
more or less	περίπου

morning	το πρωί
Mr.	ο κύριος, κ.
much	πολύς
music	η μουσική
musician	ο μουσικός
must	πρέπει (+ να)
my	μου
Mykonos	η Μύκονος
mystery	το μυστήριο
naked	γυμνός
name	το όνομα
narrow	στενός
nation	το έθνος
near	κοντά (+ σε), δίπλα
neck	ο λαιμός
need	η ανάγκη
(to) need	χρειάζομαι
neighborhood	η γειτονιά
(the) Netherlands	η Ολλανδία
never	ποτέ, καμιά φορά
new	νέος, καινούριος
newspaper	η εφημερίδα
New York	η Νέα Υόρκη
next	άλλος
next to	δίπλα (+ σε, από)
night	η νύχτα
no	όχι
no one, nobody, not one	κανένας (masc.), καμιά (fem.), κανένα (neu.)
(to) nod	γνέφω
noise	ο θόρυβος
none	καμιά, κανένας
not	δεν
not at all	καθόλου
(to) notice	προσέχω
November	ο Νοέμβριος
now	τώρα

nowhere	πουθενά
nude	γυμνός
(to) observe	παρατηρώ
October	ο Οκτώβριος
of	από
office	το γραφείο
often	συχνά
O.K.	εντάξει
old	παλιός, ηλικιωμένος
on	σε
on the way	καθοδόν
only	μόνος
opinion	η γνωμή
opportunity	η ευκαιρία
or	ή
orange juice	η πορτοκαλάδα
other	άλλος
our	μας
outside of	έξω από
over	πάνω από
own	ο δικός
parents	οι γονείς
part	το μέρος
(to) pass (time)	περνώ
passport	το διαβατήριο
past	το παρελθόν
(to) pay	πληρώνω
peninsula	η χερσόνησος
performance	η παράσταση
perhaps	ίσως
personal	προσωπικός
phonetic	φωνητικός
photograph	η φωτογραφία
picturesque	γραφικός
place	το μέρος, η θέση
plan	το σχέδιο
(to) plan	σκεδιάζω
(to) play	παίζω

(to) please, be pleasing	αρέσω
point of view	η άποψη
Portugal	η Πορτογαλία
Portuguese (adj.)	πορτογαλικός
Portuguese (language)	τα πορτογαλικά
Portuguese (man)	ο Πορτογάλος
Portuguese (woman)	Πορτογαλίδα
(to) prefer	προτιμώ
previous	περασμένος
pride	η περηφάνια
probably	πιθανόν
program	το πρόγραμμα
proportion	η αναλογία
quarter	τέταρτο
question	η ερώτηση (pl.: οι ερωτήσεις)
quiet	ήσυχος
rainy	βροχερός
rapid	γρήγορος
rather	μάλλον
ready	έτοιμος
(to) receive	λαβαίνω
regularly	κανονικά
(to) regulate	κανονίζω
(to) remember	θυμάμαι
(to) rent	νοικιάζω
(to) request	ζητώ
respect	ο σεβασμός
restaurant	το εστιατόριο
(to) return	γυρίζω
ride	η διαδρομή
Rome	η Ρώμη
room	το δωμάτιο
route	η διαδρομή
ruined	ερειπομένος
rural	χωριατικός
sad	λυπημένος
same	ο ίδιος
Saturday	το Σάββατο

(to) say	λέω
school	το σχολείο
sea	η θάλασσα
season	η εποχή
(to) see	βλέπω
(to) seem	φαίνομαι
seldom	σπάνια
(to) send	στέλνω
sentence	η πρόταση
September	ο Σεπτέμβριος
serious	σοβαρός
(to) shake off	τινάζω
(to) shop	ψωνίζω
shopkeeper	ο λιανοπώλης
short	κοντός
shoulder	ο ώμος
(to) show	δείχνω
(to) show oneself	δείχνεται
sick	άρρωστος
side	η πλευρά
simple	απλός
since	επειδή
Sir	ο κύριος, κ.
sister	η αδελφή
(to) sit down	κάθομαι
situation	η κατάσταση
size	το μέγεθος
(to) sleep	κοιμάμαι
slowly	αργά
small	μικρός
smile	το χαμόγελο
so	τόσο
so much, so many	τόσος
some	μερικός
someday	κάποια μέρα
somehow	κάπως
someone	κάποιος
something	κάτι

sometime	κάποτε
sometimes	μερικές φορές, κάπουκάπου, καμιά φορά, πότε πότε, κάποτε κάποτε
somewhat	μάλλον
somewhere	κάπου
son	ο γιός
song	το τραγούδι
soon	σύντομα
soup	η σούπα
souvenir	το ενθύμιο
space	ο χώρος
Spain	η Ισπανία
Spaniard (female)	η Ισπανίδα
Spaniard (male)	ο Ισπανός
Spanish (adj.)	ισπανικός
Spanish (language)	τα ισπανικά
(to) speak	μιλώ
(to) spend (time)	περνώ
spot	η θέση
spring	η άνοιξη
(to) start	αρχίζω
station	ο σταθμός
statue	το άγαλμα
(to) stay	μένω
still	ακόμη
(to) stop	σταματώ
store	το μαγαζί
story	η ιστορία
straight ahead	κατευθείαν
stranger	ο ξένος
street	ο δρόμος
strong	γερός
student (male, female)	ο μαθητής, η μαθήτρια
studies	οι σπουδές
(to) study	σπουδάζω
stupid	βλάκας
such	τέτειος
suddenly	άξαφνα

sugar	η ζάχαρη
summer	το καλοκαίρι
sun	ο ήλιος
Sunday	η Κυριακή
sunshine	η λιακάδα
supervisor	ο επιστάτης
Swiss (adj.)	ελβετικός
Swiss (man)	ο Ελβετός
Swiss (woman)	η Ελβετή
Switzerland	η Ελβετία
symmetry	η συμμετρία
table	το τραπέζι
(to) take	παίρνω
(to) take care of	κανονίζω
tall	ψηλός
tavern	η ταβέρνα
tea	το τσάι
teacher	ο δάσκαλος, η δασκάλα
(to) telephone	τηλεφωνώ
temple	ο ναός
that	πως, ότι, που
that (one)	εκείνος
that way	έτσι
theatre	το θέατρο
theatrical	θεατρικός
their	τους
then	μετά, ύστερα
then, at that time	τότε
there	εκεί
thin	λεπτός
thing	το πράγμα
(to) think	νομίζω
(to be) thirsty	διψώ
this (one)	αυτός
this year	φέτος
Thursday	η Πέμπτη
thus	έτσι
ticket	το εισιτήριο

time	η ώρα, ο καιρός
time (as in "*this* time")	η φορά
tired	κουρασμένος
to	σε
to the left	αριστερά
to the right	δεξιά
toast (verbal)	η πρόποση
today	σήμερα
together	μαζί
tomorrow	αύριο
tonight	απόψε
too	επίσης
torso	το κορμί
tourist	ο τουρίστας, η τουρίστρια
toward	προς
toy	το παιχνίδι
traffic	η κίνηση
train	το τρένο
(to) travel	ταξιδεύω
tray	ο δίσκος
trip	το ταξίδι
truth	η αλήθεια
Tuesday	η Τρίτη
Turk (female)	η Τουρκάλα
Turk (male)	ο Τούρκος
Turkey	η Τουρκία
Turkish (adj.)	τουρκικός
Turkish (language)	η τουρκική γλώσσα
ugly	άσχημος
unbelievable	απίστευτος
uncertain	αβέβαιος
uncle	ο θείος
under	κάτω από
(to) understand	καταλαβαίνω
unfortunately	δυστυχώς
United States	οι Ηνωμένες Πολιτείες, η Αμερική
university	το πανεπιστήμιο
unless	εκτός αν
up, up by	πάνω σε

useful	χρήσιμος
usually	συνήθως
vacation	οι διακοπές
verb	το ρήμα
very	πολύ
view	η θέα
village	το χωριό
(to) visit	επισκέπτομαι
(to) wait for	περιμένω
(to) walk around	περπατώ
to want	θέλω
to watch	περιεργάζομαι
water	το νερό
way	ο τρόπος
weak	αδύνατος
Wednesday	η Τετάρτη
week	η εβδομάδα
weekend	το Σαββατοκύριακο
well	καλά
well, then	λοιπόν
wet	υγρός
what, which	ποιος
what ("that which")	αυτό που
whatever	ό,τι
when	πότε, όταν
where	που
whereas	ενώ
while	ενώ
white	άσπρος
who	ποιος, που
whom	ποιον
whose	τίνος
why	γιατί
wide	πλατύς
wife	η γυναίκα
window	το παράθυρο
winter	ο χειμώνας
with	με

without	χωρίς
woman	η γυναίκα
(to) wonder	αναρωτιέμαι
wonderful	θαυμάσιος
word	η λέξη (pl: οι λέξεις)
work	το έργο, η δουλειά
(to) work	δουλεύω
world	ο κόσμος
(to) worry	στενοχωριέμαι
(to) write	γράφω
(to) write to each other	αλληλογραφώ
year	ο χρόνος (pl: τα χρόνια), το έτος
yes	ναι
yesterday	χθες
yet	ακόμη
young	νέος
your	σου, σας

GLOSSARY OF COMPOUNDS WORDS AND EXPRESSIONS: GREEK–ENGLISH

Αλήθεια;	Really?
Αλήθεια ...	By the way ...
από δω και εμπρός	from now on
από τότε που	since the time that ... (+verb)
ο αριθμός τηλεφώνου	telephone number
Ας πάμε!	Let's go!
αυτή τη φορά	this time
Αυτό να λέγεται!	That goes without saying!
βγάζω φωτογραφίες	to take pictures
βλέπω (+ σε)	to look out onto
Γειά σας! or Γειά σου!	Hello!
για να (+ verb in future)	in order to
για παραδείγμα	for example
γι'αυτό	that's why (literally: "for that"), about this, about that
για την ώρα	for now
δεν νομίζω	I don't think so
δύο χρόνια πριν	two years ago
είμαι καλά	I am fine
στο επανιδείν!	Let's drink to when we will be together again!
έλα μέσα	come in
Εμπρός!	Hello! (for the telephone)
Επίσης	You too
έτσι κι'έτσι	so so
Έχεις δίκιο	You're right
Ευχαριστώ	Thank you
και οι δύο	both
Καλημέρα	Good morning
Καληνύχτα	Good night
Καλησπέρα	Good evening
Καλώς τον, Καλώς την, Καλώς το	Welcome
κάνει κρύο	it's cold
κάνω μια βόλτα	to take a walk
κάνω μια προσπάθεια	to make an attempt

κι'άλλα	others, the rest
Κρίμα!	That's a shame!
κ.τ.λ. = και τα λοιπά	and the rest, etc.
μαζί τους	with them
Μάλιστα!	Of course! Certainly!
με λένε ...	my name is ...
μέχρι τώρα	until now, up until now, up to now
μπροστά από	in front of
Μη στενοχωριέσαι!	Not to worry!
Να περάσεις καλά	Have a good time
νότια της Αθήνας	south of Athens
Ό,τι θέλεις!	Whatever you want!
οι δυό μας	the two of us
οι τρεις μας	the three of us
πάνω σε	on top of
πάρα πολύ (+ adj.)	very, very (+ adj.), too
Παρακαλώ	Please, You're welcome
περνώ καλά	to have a good time
ποιος άλλος	who else
πρώτα απ'όλα	first of all
Πώς σας λένε; or Πώς σε λένε;	What is your name?
σιγά σιγά	little by little; slowly
στην ώρα	on time
στις δεκά η ώρα	at ten o'clock
Στο καλό	good-bye
στο μεταξύ	in the meantime
τα μεσάνυχτα	at midnight
το μεσημέρι	at noon
στο τέλος	at the end
στο ύπαιθρο	outdoors
την άλλη φορά	next time
την άνοιξη	in the spring
τι κάνεις; τι κάνετε;	how are you? (literally: what are you doing?)
Τι νέα;	What's new?
το βράδυ	in the evening

το καλύτερο	the best
το ξέρω	I know
το χειμώνα	in winter
Τι ώρα είναι;	What time is it?
τραβώ φωτογραφίες	to take pictures
ψωνίζω τα τρόφιμα	to go grocery shopping
Ω!	Oh!
Ωραία!	Great!

GLOSSARY OF COMPOUNDS WORDS AND EXPRESSIONS: ENGLISH–GREEK

about this, about that	γι'αυτό
across from	απέναντι
and the rest	κ.τ.λ. = και τα λοιπά
at midnight	τα μεσάνυχτα
at noon	το μεσημέρι
at ten o'clock	στις δέκα η ώρα
at the end	στο τέλος
both	και οι δύο
By the way ...	Αλήθεια ...
Certainly!	Μάλιστα!
come in	έλα μέσα
etc.	κ.τ.λ. = και τα λοιπά
first of all	πρώτα απ'όλα
for example	για παράδειγμα
for now	για την ώρα
for that	γι'αυτό
from now on	από δω και εμπρός
Good-bye	Στο καλό
Good evening	Καλησπέρα
Good morning	Καλημέρα
Good night	Καληνύχτα
Great!	Ωραία!
(to go) grocery shopping	ψωνίζω τα τρόφιμα
(to) have a good time	περνώ καλά
Have a good time	Να περάσεις καλά
Hello!	Γειά σας! Γειά σου!
Hello (for the telephone)	Εμπρός!
how are you?	τι κάνεις; τι κάνετε;
I am fine	είμαι καλά
I don't think so	δεν νομίζω
I know	το ξέρω
in front of	μπροστά από
in order to	για να (+ verb in future)
in the evening	το βράδυ
in the meantime	στο μεταξύ
in the spring	την άνοιξη
in winter	το χειμώνα
it's cold	κάνει κρύο

Let's go!	Ας πάμε!
Let's drink to when we will be together again!	στο επανιδείν!
little by little	σιγά σιγά
(to) look out onto	βλέπω (+ σε)
my name is ...	με λένε ...
next time	την άλλη φορά
Not to worry!	Μη στενοχωριέσαι!
Of course!	Μάλιστα!
Oh!	Ω!
on time	στην ώρα
on top of	πάνω σε
others, the rest	κι'άλλα
outdoors	στο ύπαιθρο
Really?	Αλήθεια;
relating to	σχετικά με
since the time that ...	από τότε που (+ verb)
slowly	σιγά σιγά
so so	έτσι κι'έτσι
south of Athens	νότια της Αθήνας
telephone number	ο αριθμός τηλεφώνου
Thank you	Ευχαριστώ
That goes without saying!	Αυτό να λέγεται!
that is to say	δηλαδή
that's why	γι'αυτό
That's a shame!	Κρίμα!
the three of us	οι τρεις μας
the two of us	οι δυό μας
this time	αυτή τη φορά
(to) make an attempt	κάνω μια προσπάθεια
(to) take a walk	κάνω μια βόλτα
(to) take pictures	βγάζω φωτογραφίες, τραβώω φωτογραφίες
too	πάρα πολύ (+ adj.)
two years ago	δύο χρόνια πριν
until now, up until now, up to now	μέχρι τώρα
very, very (+ adj.)	πάρα πολύ (+ adj.)
Welcome	Καλώς τον, Καλώς την, Καλώς το

What is your name?	Πώς σας λένε; or Πώς σε λένε;
What time is it?	Τι ώρα είναι;
Whatever you want!	Ό,τι θέλεις!
What's new?	Τι νέα;
who else	ποιος άλλος
with them	μαζί τους
You too	Επίσης
You're right	Έχεις δίκιο
You're welcome	Παρακαλώ

From Hippocrene's Greek Library

Greek-English/English-Greek Concise Dictionary
Michael Kambas

This dictionary lists over 8,000 headwords on each side, totaling about 16,000 words. Because the series concentrates on the needs of travelers, *Greek Concise* includes vocabulary of practical use to people traveling, staying, or living outside their native land. The author focused on tourists, emigrants, and businesspeople when compiling this list, but kept the worker for government and international organizations in mind as well. As a phonetic aid to the reader, pronunciation is facilitated using a simple transliteration system for both languages. Both the feminine and the neuter endings are listed in addition to the masculine ones.

Born and raised in Greece, Michael Kambas has been a Greek/English instructor, translator and interpreter since 1982. After he moved to the United States, he became an official translator/interpreter for the Greek Consulate, the Judicial Council of California, and the U.S. Department of State. His published works include *VocabuLearn, Levels I & II*, an English/Greek self-instructive course (Penton Overseas, 1992); the *Court Interpreter's English/Greek Glossary* (GTS Press, 1999); and several specialty online glossaries.

16,000 entries • 400 pages • 4 x 6 • $14.95 paperback • 0-7818-1002-7 • W • (182)

Greek-English/English-Greek Dictionary & Phrasebook
Tom Stone

This dictionary and phrasebook aims to assist the student or traveler in expanding his or her knowledge of the language and culture of Greece. The dictionary emphasizes the proper tools for communication by including pronunciation phonics, perfect grammar, and useful tips and phrases for understanding Modern Greek culture.

- 1500 dictionary entries
- Complete phonetic guide
- Up-to-date phrases and cultural information
- Easy-to-use travel size

260 pages • 3¾ x 5½ • $14.95 paperback • 0-7818-0635-6 • W • (715)

The Essential Greek Handbook
Tom Stone

This book covers everything a traveler to Greece would want to know. It features an English-Greek dictionary and phrasebook, common Greek expressions, and a calendar of Greek festive and religious occasions. All entries include phonetic pronunciation. An appendix of geographical names and maps as well as weights, measures, and numbers complement the volume.

270 pages • 4½ x 7 • $14.95 paperback • 0-7818-0668-2 • W • (714)

Greece: An Illustrated History
Tom Stone

From the Cenozoic upheavals that formed the Greek archipelago to the political movements in the twentieth century that overturned both a military junta and the monarchy, this informative and entertaining survey covers the political, artistic, and religious evolution of one of the world's most significant and fascinating civilizations.

Tom Stone traveled to Greece in 1970 to write a novel and stayed twenty-two years, pursuing a career as a writer, teacher, and theatrical lighting designer and director. He has written numerous books and articles about Greece.

181 pages • 5 x 7 • $14.95 hardcover • 0-7818-0755-7 • W • (557)

The Best of Greek Cuisine: Cooking With Georgia
Expanded Edition
Georgia Sarianides

> *"All of the recipes are uncomplicated, delicious, and satisfying . . .*
> *I highly recommend this cookbook as a wonderful source of traditional*
> *Greek recipes . . ."*
> —Bella Online

> *"Let Chef Georgia Sarianides introduce you to the world of authentic*
> *Greek cuisine, with its emphasis on fresh produce, fragrant olive oil, and*
> *liberal use of herbs and spices, all served with classic Mediterranean*
> *warmth and gusto."*
> —The International Cookbook Revue

From traditional favorites like *spanakopita* and *baklava* to delectable lamb and seafood specialties, Chef Georgia Sarianides outlines over 100 easy-to-follow, health-conscious recipes. Now expanded with a new chapter on *Mezedes* (appetizers) and other select favorites, *The Best of Greek Cuisine* continues to be the comprehensive resource on Greek cooking!

Chef Georgia Sarianides of the Boston area hosts her own top-rated Greek cooking television program, runs a successful catering business, and has just begun to produce her own brand of Greek olive oil. She was born in Amaliada in Peloponnese, Greece.

208 pages • 5½ x 8½ • $12.95 paperback • 0-7818-0883-9 • W • (33)

CPSIA information can be obtained at www.ICGtesting.com
Printed in the USA
BVOW11s1406270514

354613BV00011B/87/P